Health Security Intelligence

Health Security Intelligence introduces readers to the world of health security, to threats like COVID-19, and to the many other incarnations of global health security threats and their implications for intelligence and national security.

Disease outbreaks like COVID-19 have not historically been considered a national security matter. While disease outbreaks among troops have always been a concern, it was the potential that arose in the first half of the twentieth century to systematically design biological weapons and to develop these at an industrial scale, which initially drew the attention of security, defence and intelligence communities to biology and medical science. This book charts the evolution of public health and biosecurity threats from those early days, tracing how perceptions of these threats have expanded from deliberately introduced disease outbreaks to also incorporate natural disease outbreaks, the unintended consequences of research, laboratory accidents, and the convergence of emerging technologies. This spectrum of threats has led to an expansion of the stakeholders, tools and sources involved in intelligence gathering and threat assessments.

This edited volume is a landmark in efforts to develop a multidisciplinary, empirically informed, and policy-relevant approach to intelligence-academia engagement in global health security that serves both the intelligence community and scholars from a broad range of disciplines.

The chapters in this book were originally published as a special issue of the journal, *Intelligence and National Security.*

Michael S. Goodman is Professor of Intelligence and International Affairs and Head of the Department of War Studies at King's College London.

James M. Wilson is Practicing Paediatrician specializing in operational health security intelligence, and the CEO of M2 Medical Intelligence, Inc.

Filippa Lentzos is Senior Lecturer in Science & International Security at the Department of War Studies, and Co-Director of the Centre for Science and Security Studies (CSSS) at King's College London.

Health Security Intelligence

Edited by
Michael S. Goodman, James M. Wilson and
Filippa Lentzos

Routledge
Taylor & Francis Group
LONDON AND NEW YORK

First published 2022
by Routledge
2 Park Square, Milton Park, Abingdon, Oxon OX14 4RN

and by Routledge
605 Third Avenue, New York, NY 10158

Routledge is an imprint of the Taylor & Francis Group, an informa business

British Library Cataloguing in Publication Data
A catalogue record for this book is available from the British Library

ISBN: 978-1-032-15738-2 (hbk)
ISBN: 978-1-032-15739-9 (pbk)
ISBN: 978-1-003-24548-3 (ebk)

DOI: 10.4324/9781003245483

Typeset in Myriad Pro
by Newgen Publishing UK

Publisher's Note
The publisher accepts responsibility for any inconsistencies that may have arisen during the conversion of this book from journal articles to book chapters, namely the inclusion of journal terminology.

Contents

Citation Information

The following chapters were originally published in the journal, *Intelligence and National Security*, volume 35, issue 4 (2020). When citing this material, please use the original page numbering for each article, as follows:

Introduction

Health Security Intelligence: engaging across disciplines and sectors
Filippa Lentzos, Michael S. Goodman and James M. Wilson
Intelligence and National Security, volume 35, issue 4 (2020), pp. 465–476

Chapter 1

The West Africa Ebola outbreak (2014-2016): a Health Intelligence failure?
Robert L. Ostergard, Jr.
Intelligence and National Security, volume 35, issue 4 (2020), pp. 477–492

Chapter 2

The use of HUMINT in epidemics: a practical assessment
Rose Bernard and Richard Sullivan
Intelligence and National Security, volume 35, issue 4 (2020), pp. 493–501

Chapter 3

Influenza pandemic warning signals: Philadelphia in 1918 and 1977-1978
James M. Wilson, Garrett M. Scalaro and Jodie A. Powell
Intelligence and National Security, volume 35, issue 4 (2020), pp. 502–518

Chapter 4

The 1999 West Nile virus warning signal revisited
James M. Wilson and Tracey McNamara
Intelligence and National Security, volume 35, issue 4 (2020), pp. 519–526

Chapter 5

Rapid validation of disease outbreak intelligence by small independent verification teams
Steven J. Hatfill
Intelligence and National Security, volume 35, issue 4 (2020), pp. 527–538

Chapter 6

Threat potential of pharmaceutical based agents
D. J. Heslop and P. G. Blain
Intelligence and National Security, volume 35, issue 4 (2020), pp. 539–555

Chapter 7

Towards understanding cybersecurity capability in Australian healthcare organisations: a systematic review of recent trends, threats and mitigation
K. L. Offner, E. Sitnikova, K. Joiner and C. R. MacIntyre
Intelligence and National Security, volume 35, issue 4 (2020), pp. 556–585

Chapter 8

Improving 'Five Eyes' Health Security Intelligence capabilities: leadership and governance challenges
Patrick F. Walsh
Intelligence and National Security, volume 35, issue 4 (2020), pp. 586–602

Notes on Contributors

Rose Bernard is currently a doctoral student at Kings College London examining intelligence sharing in epidemics and pandemics. She works in intelligence, specialising in the mapping of crime groups and cybercrime; prior to this she focused on counter-narcotics. Her most recent work has examined the integration of intelligence into PHEICs, and the impact of the internet on global health security.

P. G. Blain is Director of the Medical Toxicology Centre at Newcastle University UK. He is clinical professor and hospital physician with over 30 years' experience in the application of medical knowledge to intelligence, security and operational issues, including high value asset protection for UK Government. He is a recognized international expert in clinical medicine and medical research, and provides high-level expert advice in CBRN medicine, related sciences, and emergency response medicine to both UK and US Governments and major international bodies.

Michael S. Goodman is Professor of Intelligence and International Affairs, Head of the Department of War Studies and Dean of Research Impact, King's College London. He is also a Visiting Professor at the Norwegian Defence Intelligence School and at Sciences Po in Paris. Goodman has recently finished a secondment to the Cabinet Office where he has been the *Official Historian of The Joint Intelligence Committee: Volume II* which will be published in 2020.

Steven J. Hatfill is specialist physician and virologist with 16 years of medical experience in Africa including Zaire, Rhodesia, South Africa. His Fellowships include the National Institutes of Health, Oxford University, and the NRC. In 2018, he was awarded Honorary U.S. Army Parachute Wings with Bronze Star by the U.S. Army 1st Special Warfare Training Group (Airborne). He is adjunct assistant professor in two departments at the George Washington University Medical Center and School.

D. J. Heslop is Director of Health Management at the School of Public Health and Community Medicine, at UNSW Sydney and is practising General Practitioner and Occupational and Environmental Physician. He has senior advisory responsibilities in CBRNE and Occupational Medicine in Army Headquarters, Australian Defence Force. He has published in the areas of epidemic modeling, disaster management, CBRNE medicine, and military health systems.

K. Joiner is Group Captain (Ret'd), and Senior Lecturer Test, Evaluation & Aircraft Systems. He is an Educationally Focussed Academic at The UNSW Canberra Cyber at the Australian Defence Force Academy.

Filippa Lentzos is Senior Lecturer in Science & International Security and Co-Director of the Centre for Science and Security Studies at King's College London. She is also an Associate Senior Researcher at the Stockholm International Peace Research Institute (SIPRI), and a Non-Resident Scholar at the James Martin Center for Nonproliferation Studies (CNS).

C. R. MacIntyre is Professor of Global Biosecurity and NHMRC Principal Research Fellow at the Kirby Institute, UNSW Australia, and an adjunct professor at Arizona State University. She is a specialist physician with a masters and PhD in epidemiology. She leads a research program in control and prevention of infectious diseases, spanning epidemiology, risk analysis, vaccinology, bioterrorism, mathematical modelling, public health and clinical trials.

Tracey McNamara is Veterinary Pathologist and a Professor of Pathology at Western University of Health Sciences College of Veterinary Medicine in Pomona, CA. Dr. McNamara specializes in the recognition and understanding of the diseases of captive and free-ranging wildlife and is best known for her work on West Nile virus. She is actively involved in the One Health movement and advocates for a species neutral approach to the detection of pandemic threats.

K. L. Offner is Clinical Nurse Educator, currently studying a Master of Public Health and Health Management.

Robert L. Ostergard, Jr. is Associate Professor of Political Science at the University of Nevada. His general areas of research are in national and international security issues, with a specific focus on sub-Saharan Africa. His current research projects include projects on the security implications of the HIV/AIDS and Ebola epidemics and state security responses to global health crises.

Jodie A. Powell was research analysts with the Nevada Medical Intelligence Center in the School of Community Health Sciences, University of Nevada-Reno.

Garrett M. Scalaro was research analysts with the Nevada Medical Intelligence Center in the School of Community Health Sciences, University of Nevada-Reno.

E. Sitnikova is award-winning academic and researcher at UNSW Canberra and Adjunct Professor at University of Alabama in Huntsville. She is a global leader in cutting-edge research in Critical Infrastructure protection, focusing on intrusion detection for Supervisory Control and Data Acquisition (SCADA) systems cyber security, cyber-physical systems and Industrial Internet of Things (IIoT). Her contribution in the field is demonstrated through the recent Spitfire Memorial Defence Fellowship Award. She is one of the first Australians to be certified in CSSLP - Certified Secure Software Lifecycle Professional.

Richard Sullivan is Professor of Cancer & Global Health at Kings College London, Director, Institute of Cancer Policy and Co-Director of King's Conflict & Health Research Group. Richard is past UK Director of the Council for Emerging National Security Affairs (CENSA) a national security think-tank where he specialised in bioweapons counter-proliferation. Richard qualified in medicine and trained in surgery (urology) gaining his PhD from University College London.

Patrick F. Walsh is former intelligence analyst and has worked in Australia's national security and law enforcement environments. He is associate professor in Intelligence and Security Studies, Charles Sturt University, Australia. He is also a consultant to government agencies on intelligence reform and capability issues. His research grants and publications focus on a range of areas related to intelligence capability; including but not limited to: governance, leadership, intelligence and ethics, biosecurity and cyber.

James M. Wilson is the CEO of M2 Medical Intelligence, Inc. He is a board-certified, practicing pediatrician who specializes in operational health security intelligence, with a focus on the anticipation, detection, and warning of infectious disease crises. Wilson led the private intelligence teams that provided tracking of H5N1 avian influenza as it spread from Asia to Europe and Africa, detection of vaccine drifted H3N2 influenza in 2007, warning of the 2009 H1N1 influenza pandemic, discovery of the United Nations as the source of the 2010 cholera disaster in Haiti, and several investigations of alleged and confirmed laboratory accidents and biological weapon deployments.

Preface

"It all started with a beer..." In March 2019, Jim Wilson and Mike Goodman met over drinks during the International Studies Association annual meeting in Toronto. Jim had just led a panel discussion on health security intelligence, having provided a review of warning intelligence failures for influenza pandemics and coronaviruses such as Severe Acute Respiratory Syndrome (SARS) and Middle East Respiratory Syndrome (MERS). There were less than five people in the audience, but it wasn't the volume of people that was important – it was who they were. One of them was Mike. Another was Steve Marrin, the *Editor* for the journal *Intelligence and National Security*. There was purpose in the panel and purpose in those beers, which was to raise the concern that the world was repeating history and missing critical warning indicators of health security crises. The debate that night was whether we were over-hyping the risk or simply lucky after seeing the rise of HIV/AIDS, the introduction of West Nile and Zika viruses to the Western Hemisphere, the 2009 H1N1 influenza pandemic, and the multiple rounds of Ebola, Marburg, and Nipah viruses. The discussion focused on health security intelligence as its own discipline, however an orphan among our nations.

This chance encounter led Jim and Mike to approach Filippa Lentzos to edit a Special Issue on 'Health Security Intelligence' in *Intelligence and National Security*. This triumvirate was a great meeting of minds: Jim is a medical doctor in the US who has worked on the prediction and responses of natural outbreaks of disease; Mike is a Professor of Intelligence and International Affairs at King's College London, who has worked at the interface of the academic and practitioner worlds of intelligence and has a particular interest in scientific intelligence; whereas Filippa, a senior lecturer at King's and co-director of the Centre for Science and Security, is an international expert on biological threats who has regularly briefed the UN and other august bodies. Each offered a different perspective to the project and focused on their own areas of expertise to bring what we thought at that time, in the autumn/Fall of 2019, to be a novel and prescient idea.

About two weeks after the manuscripts were submitted, an unusual outbreak of respiratory disease was reported in Wuhan, China – the beginning of the COVID pandemic. The Special Issue appeared shortly thereafter, and suddenly we looked like fortune tellers. This book is a re-publication of that Special Issue. Despite the dramatic changes the world has faced in the last 18 months, we decided to preserve the chapters in their original presentation and not ask authors to update them in the light of what we now know. The majority have nothing to do with what has happened, but they do reflect broader issues around health security intelligence.

Many of those who have worked in this area were not surprised by the COVID outbreak, but it has served to highlight how governments need to move beyond traditional conceptions of threat and risk to consider a broader array of topics, particularly those that might arise naturally. At the time of this writing, there is no indication of a COVID Commission in the midst of questions about whether the virus' abrupt appearance was the result of an undisclosed laboratory accident. There is no indication the world will finally invest in a health security warning intelligence system. The future is uncertain and portends a repeat of the outcomes should we again fail to heed the lessons of the past.

Filippa, Jim and Mike
July 2021

Introduction: Health Security Intelligence: engaging across disciplines and sectors

Filippa Lentzos, Michael S. Goodman and James M. Wilson

ABSTRACT

This article introduces the Special Issue on Global Health Security. It provides an overview of the health security threat spectrum, tracing how perceptions of biological and health security threats have evolved in broad terms over the last century from deliberately introduced disease outbreaks to also incorporate natural disease outbreaks, unintended consequences of research, laboratory accidents, lack of awareness, negligence, and convergence of emerging technologies. This spectrum of threats has led to an expansion of the stakeholders and tools involved in intelligence gathering and threat assessments. The article argues that to strengthen global health security and health intelligence, the traditional state-based intelligence community must actively engage with non-security stakeholders and incorporate space for new sources of intelligence. The aim of the Special Issue is to contribute to the larger effort of developing a multidisciplinary, empirically informed and policy-relevant approach to intelligence-academia engagement in global health security that serves both the intelligence community and scholars from a broad range of disciplines.

As we write, coronavirus disease (COVID-19) is rapidly spreading around the globe, with more new cases of infection now being detected outside China than in it. There are significant concerns not only about the pandemic's health impacts, but about its socio-economic impacts. Stock markets are tumbling, borders are closing, supply chains are interrupted, international meetings and sports events are cancelled, and there is talk of more severe social distancing measures.

This Special Issue of *Intelligence & National Security* introduces readers to the world of health security, to threats like COVID-19, but also to the many other incarnations of global health security threats and their implications for intelligence and national security. The Special Issue was conceived and written before COVID-19 emerged and hit our headlines in early 2020. Yet while the individual articles do not engage with the outbreak explicitly, the points they make form valuable reading in these unsettling times. The over-arching message is that to strengthen global health security and health intelligence, we need to engage across disciplines and sectors. This Special Issue is an effort to nurture that debate. By way of introduction, we provide readers with an overview of the health security threat spectrum, and how perceptions of biological and health security threats, as well as the political responses to them, have evolved over the last century. We also provide a brief sketch of intelligence and biological threat assessments, today and in the past. The authors in the Special Issue are briefly introduced along the way; more extensive biographies accompany their individual articles.

Deliberate disease outbreaks

Disease outbreaks like COVID-19 have not historically been considered a national security matter. While disease outbreaks among troops have always been a concern, it was the potential that arose in the twentieth century to systematically design biological weapons (i.e. combine dangerous bacteria or viruses with a delivery mechanism to inflict harm) and then develop these weapons at an industrial scale, that initially drew the attention of security, defence and intelligence communities to biology and medical science.[1] Still reeling from the horrors of gas warfare in World War I, and from the 'Spanish flu' that killed over 50 million people towards the end of the war, the 'civilised world,' represented by the League of Nations, prohibited the use of asphyxiating, poisonous or other gases in war as well as 'bacteriological methods of warfare' under the 1925 Geneva Protocol. Essentially a no-first-use agreement, the Geneva Protocol was not designed to stop the development of biological weapons, and significant programmes to build biowarfare capacities soon ensued in several states. Yet, despite intensive development and testing, which eventually demonstrated that biological weapons could form as great a threat to large populations as nuclear weapons, biological weapons were not assimilated into military thinking and planning, and there has been no known use since 1945.[2] In a political move that caught American bioweaponeers off-guard, the newly-elected President Richard Nixon unilaterally renounced biological weapons in 1969, paving the way for the multilateral Biological Weapons Convention comprehensively prohibiting biological weapons to be negotiated and agreed at the United Nations in the early 1970s.

Bioterrorism first emerged as a political concept during the early 1990s in the United States.[3] As the Cold War faded, the threat of terrorists armed with biological weapons and other 'weapons of mass destruction' began to replace the Soviet threat. Different assessments of the importance, urgency and scale of the threat were present in the early political debates on bioterrorism.[4] 'Alarmists,' who included prominent scientific and technical advisers, tended to emphasise the possibility of 'apocalyptic' attacks with natural pathogens and genetically engineered hybrids, and the vulnerability of the civilian population. They were less focused on the identities of 'bioterrorists' and in their interests in pursuing such attacks or in their capacities to do so. 'Sceptics,' on the other hand, tended to have background and training in the history, politics and culture of terrorism, and for them, questions of identity, interests and details of past attackers were the primary questions to ask. Although little credible evidence existed at the time that such states or terrorists would, or even could, resort to biological weapons, alarmism ultimately overcame scepticism, and federal funds poured into new US preparedness and civilian biodefense programmes of considerable institutional proportions.[5]

The 'Amerithrax' attacks – as the FBI code-named the series of anonymous letters containing anthrax sent to media outlets and the US Senate within weeks of the '9/11' terrorist attacks on New York and Washington on September 11th, 2001 – revealed serious shortcomings in US biosecurity. They also raised fears about the growing potential for bioterrorism on American soil. The threat of bioterrorism became one of the Bush administration's key security concerns during its two terms in office, and initiated a series of new regulations, policies and programmes to further strengthen US preparedness and defence against a bioweapon attack.

Concern about the threat of international terrorism coupled with WMD proliferation was also exported from the United States to international security forums. The international community's premier security forum, the United Nations Security Council, decided, for example, in resolution 1540 that all states should refrain from providing any form of support to non-state actors that attempt to obtain biological and other weapons of mass destruction for terrorist purposes. New laws and other non-proliferation measures were implemented in capitals around the world, and counteroffensives materialized in international risk and security strategies.

Global health security

The World Health Organization (WHO), which has traditionally been reluctant to address security-related issues for fear that its public health mission would be compromised, has increasingly been gaining a profile as a key actor in the security world, and it has exerted significant influence on how perceptions of biological threats have evolved. From the outset, its overriding message has been that, whatever the cause of epidemics or emerging infectious diseases, the response to them will initially be the same: 'In most situations, the public health system will be the first to detect cases and raise the alarm.'[6] In other words, the threat of deliberate use of biological weapons should be thought of as part of a wider spectrum of threats that also includes the threat of disease from natural outbreaks and accidental releases, and the most effective response to these threats is to bolster public health measures.

Following this lead, the Obama administration ushered in an evolution in US thinking about its response to bioterrorism. The administration's first major policy initiative on biosecurity was the *National Strategy for Countering Biological Threats*. While the Bush Administration's efforts had been focused on biodefence, this strategy was focused on prevention. It emphasised linking deliberate disease outbreaks from bioterrorism attacks with naturally occurring disease outbreaks, to create a more 'seamless' and 'integrated' link across all types of biological threats – echoing what the WHO had been pushing multilaterally for years. In his 2011 speech to the United Nations General Assembly, President Obama called upon all countries to 'come together to prevent, and detect, and fight every kind of biological danger – whether it's a pandemic like H1N1, or a terrorist threat, or a treatable disease.'[7] In February 2014, the US spearheaded the Global Health Security Agenda to establish global capacity to prevent, detect and rapidly respond to biological threats.

A test case was brewing even as the initiative was getting off the ground. By August 2014, the WHO declared the Ebola epidemic in Western Africa a 'Public Health Emergency of International Concern.' But as Margaret Chan, the Director-General of the WHO, explained to the United Nations Security Council, this Ebola epidemic was very different to the many big infectious disease outbreaks managed by the WHO in recent years: 'This is likely the greatest peacetime challenge that the United Nations and its agencies have ever faced. None of us experienced in containing outbreaks has ever seen, in our lifetimes, an emergency on this scale, with this degree of suffering, and with this magnitude of cascading consequences.'[8] The Ebola outbreak was characterised not merely as a public health crisis, but as 'a threat to national security well beyond the outbreak zones.'[9]

Two of the Special Issue contributions focus on the Ebola outbreak and the intelligence gaps that existed in the months before the Ebola outbreak became characterised as a national security concern. Political scientist **Robert Ostergard** draws on newly declassified material to piece together how US embassy personnel in Conakry, Guinea perceived the early stages of the outbreak and the local government's response to it, and how they relayed that perception to Washington DC. His contribution demonstrates the significant potential of health intelligence – the concepts, methods, practices and apparatuses assembled to monitor and detect health events – in assessing risks from an emerging infectious disease outbreak. **Rose Bernard and Richard Sullivan**, who work at the intersection of conflict, health and intelligence, elaborate the role of human intelligence in gathering information on a developing Public Health Emergency of International Concern in their contribution to the Special Issue. They demonstrate how modelling and disease tracking for the Ebola outbreak could have been significantly assisted by a standardised ethnographic and anthropological assessment based on human intelligence. In their own words, 'An assessment of the social and cultural context could have identified healthcare and burial practices, as well as population movements over common borders and identifying potential cases. Local healthcare workers could have been asked about the healthcare capabilities and the most necessary equipment suited to the immediate context. Similarly, interviews with individuals could have identified attitudes towards the ETUs, and potentially identified any false drop in cases.' They conclude that the human ecosystem is increasingly the crucial determinate of disease risk and intervention success in complex outbreaks of emerging infectious disease, and that this requires a wide human intelligence perspective that encompasses anthropology, other social sciences, psychology, economics, history and political sciences.

An emerging infectious disease is one that either has appeared and affected a population for the first time or has existed previously but is rapidly spreading in terms of the number of people getting infected or in terms of the new geographical areas affected. Ebola and COVID-19, along with fellow coronavirus diseases Severe Acute Respiratory Syndrome (SARS) and Middle East Respiratory Syndrome (MERS), are examples of diseases that have recently emerged. These new infectious diseases are increasing in frequency, due to a variety of factors including: climate change, the increase in world travel, greater movement and displacement of people resulting from war, the global transport of food and intensive food production methods, humans encroaching on the habitat of wild animals, and better detection systems that spot new diseases. Many emerging infectious diseases are zoonotic in origin, which means that the disease has emerged from an animal and crossed the species barrier to infect humans. More often than not, humans have little or no natural immunity to emerging infectious diseases, so their disruptive impacts on health, society and the economy are difficult to predict. This is one of the reasons infectious disease pandemics are often characterised as disrupters with the highest likelihood and most severe impact on national security.

Two contributions to the Special Issue present detailed historical case studies of emerging infectious diseases that demonstrate the role of particular warning signals in monitoring health security threats. Operational health security intelligence specialists **James Wilson, Garrett Scalaro and Jodie Powell** highlight the role of local media reporting. Using comparative case studies of local media reporting in Philadelphia on the 1918 and 1977/78 influenza pandemics, they argue that warning signals typically appear in local media reporting ahead of reactive public health surveillance. In a second paper **James Wilson** joins **Tracey McNamara**, a veterinary pathologist to highlight the critical role of the astute clinician-observer. Drawing on their own significant involvement in responding to the unfolding West Nile virus epidemic that started in New York in 1999, they emphasise the importance of communication between the veterinary and human health communities, as well as the federal and private sectors.

In a final contribution on emerging infectious diseases to the Special Issue, **Steven Hatfill**, a specialist physician and virologist, analyses a series of emerging infectious disease outbreaks over the past 25 years to explore choke points or major rate-limiting steps in the global pandemic surveillance process to provide timely warning of significant outbreaks. He identifies the challenges of obtaining lab and epidemiological data from affected countries as particularly significant, and argues for establishing independent specialist teams to conduct rapid 'boots-on-the-ground' examinations of developing outbreaks posing a possible threat to international security.

Dual use research of concern

Biological threats are today generally thought of as sitting on a spectrum, running from deliberate disease outbreaks at one end, to emerging infectious diseases and natural disease outbreaks at the other. Squeezed in between these two types of threats is a series of linked threats all based on significant scientific advances in capacities to modify genes and organisms.

Innovations in biotechnology are expanding the toolbox to modify genes and organisms at an unprecedented rate, making it easier to produce increasingly dangerous pathogens.[10] Disease-causing organisms can now be modified to increase their virulence, expand their host range, increase their transmissibility, or enhance their resistance to therapeutic interventions. Low-risk pathogens can also potentially be modified to become high-risk pathogens. In addition to modifying *existing* pathogens, scientific advances are also making it possible to synthetically create known pathogens. Scientific advances are even making it possible to synthetically re-create extinct pathogens like the variola virus which causes smallpox. Entirely new pathogens that have never existed in nature could also potentially be created. These are sometimes referred to as super-pathogens, where characteristics of two, or more, pathogens are combined.

In addition to increased capacities to modify genes and organisms, the global nature of science continues to drive the diffusion of knowledge around the world, with more knowledge hubs and virtual communities, and research occurring in more diverse locations and involving a broader range of actors. Although significant levels of technical skill and tacit knowledge are still required to produce dangerous pathogens, barriers are being reduced, it is becoming easier to misuse the science for a larger group of people, and vulnerabilities are becoming greater.[11] There are generally considered to be at least four new types of biological threats arising from these developments: unintended consequences of research, laboratory accidents, lack of awareness, and negligence.

A set of high profile scientific experiments in the early 2000s, which made mousepox more deadly, chemically synthesised poliovirus from scratch in the lab, and reconstructed the extinct 'Spanish flu' virus from the end of World War I, first drew attention to these threats.[12] Responding to the experiments and the novel threats they represented, a US National Academies of Sciences committee identified a broader set of seven illustrative experiments that raised concern.[13] In the Committee's view, these were the sorts of experiments that should necessitate further review before they are conducted or published. They include those that: (1) demonstrate how to render a vaccine ineffective, (2) confer resistance to therapeutically useful antibiotics or antiviral agents, (3) enhance the virulence of a pathogen or render a non-pathogen virulent, (4) increase the transmissibility of a pathogen, (5) alter the host range of a pathogen, (6) enable the evasion of diagnostic/detection modalities, and (7) enable the weaponisation of a biological agent or toxin. The Committee also recommended the creation of a new National Science Advisory Board for Biosecurity to provide guidance for the review and oversight of such experiments and other dual-use research concerns.

The National Science Advisory Board on Biosecurity (NSABB) was chartered in 2004 by the Executive Office of the President to provide advice to the US Government regarding the review and oversight of dual-use research. In the first years of its existence, the NSABB focused on defining and providing oversight recommendations for dual use research.[14] The Board proposed a split between two kinds of science. 'Dual use research' was used to refer in general to legitimate life sciences research with potential to yield information that could be misused to threaten public health and safety and other aspects of national security. Since nearly all science could be used in this manner, NSABB offered another category: 'Dual use research of concern' (DURC). This denoted 'research that, based on current understanding, can be reasonably anticipated to provide knowledge, products or technologies that could be directly misapplied by others to pose a threat to public health and safety'.[15]

Another set of high-profile experiments attracted attention in 2011. The 'gain-of-function' experiments, which resulted in the creation of laboratory-modified H5N1 'bird flu' viruses that could spread not just between birds but now also between mammals, and, if accidentally or deliberately released, could result in a deadly pandemic, were considered archetype DURC. The gain-of-function research prompted a moratorium, followed by the release of the US Government's *Policy for Oversight of Life Sciences Dual Use Research of Concern* in March 2012, and later the *Policy for Institutional Oversight of Life Sciences Dual Use Research of Concern* in September 2014. The policies built on the criteria for establishing DURC proposed by the National Academies of Sciences and the NSABB, but the US Government limited review to research carried out with one of 15 pathogens deemed to pose the greatest risk of deliberate misuse with most significant potential for mass casualties or for devastating effects to the economy, critical infrastructure or public confidence.[16]

Very few, if any, other countries have to date developed guidance or practices like the US to address the potential for terrorist or criminal use of information based on biology and biomedical research. While the focus of the political response has been on unintended consequences of research, laboratory accidents, lack of awareness and negligence, DURC research would of course also have implications for the threat of deliberately developed biological weapons, where scientific advances could, for instance, be used to enlarge the target of traditional biological weapons from causing disease to directly targeting the immune system, nervous system, genome or microbiome.

Convergence

Technological change is accelerating, not just in the biological sciences but also in other emerging technologies, and this acceleration is impacting biological threats across the spectrum.[17]

Of particular note is the convergence between biology and chemistry, spurred on by advances in neuroscience and toxicology. New pharmaceutical based agents are being developed that share characteristics of both traditional chemical and biological agents. These agents mostly comprise chemicals that have been designed for medical pharmaceutical use but which in overdose, or certain exposure contexts, can cause either incapacitation, permanent injury or death. **David Heslop and Peter Blain** analyse this convergence in their contribution to the Special Issue. Experienced physicians working at the intersection of medicine, academia and defence, they present a risk assessment of pharmaceutical based agents and approaches to threat prevention or mitigation. They highlight in particular fentanyl analogues, now widely available in illicit drug markets, as the major threat potential of pharmaceutical based agents, and urge both law enforcement officers and emergency planners and responders to factor in accidental exposure to, or deliberate use of, these agents into emergency preparedness, resilience, response and recovery plans, as well as training programmes.

Another significant area of convergence is that of genomic technologies with artificial intelligence (AI), automation, robotics and cloud computing.[18] Genomic technologies are driving a vast expansion in genomic data, from gene sequences and entire genomes to data that links genes to specific functions and other types of metadata for humans, animals, plants and microbes. This data is becoming increasingly digitised, and computational power is significantly changing how genomic data is analysed.[19] This integration of AI computation into biology opens up new possibilities for understanding how genetic differences shape the development of living organisms including ourselves, and how these differences make us and the living world susceptible to diseases and disorders, as well as responsive to drugs and treatments.

But the interface of bioinformatics and AI also open up new possibilities for harm. Developments in advanced AI and machine learning could speed up identification of harmful genes or DNA sequences. Advanced AI and machine learning could also potentially enable much more targeted biological weapons that would harm specific individuals or groups of individuals based on their genes, prior exposure to vaccines, or known vulnerabilities in their immune system. Big Data and 'cloud labs' (completely robotized laboratories for hire) facilitate this process by enabling massively scaled-up experimentation and testing, significantly shortening 'design-test-build' timeframes, and improving the likelihood of obtaining specificity or producing desired biological functionality.[20]

There are also traditional cyber risks at the interface of bioinformatics and AI, particularly for the healthcare sector. In their contribution to the Special Issue, **Kim Offner, Elena Sitnikova, Keith Joiner and Raina MacIntyre** review the literature on global cyberattacks against the healthcare sector and examine recent trends in cybersecurity breaches, focusing especially on their own country, Australia. They argue that a culture of cybersecurity maturity must be proactively developed within healthcare systems to help mitigate cyber threats, limit disruption to essential services, and protect patient safety and privacy.

In addition to traditional cyber risks, there are also what have been termed 'cyber-biosecurity' risks, focused on the bioeconomy. These risks include waging adversarial attacks on automated biocomputing systems, biotech supply chains, or strategic cyber-biosecurity infrastructure.[21] Malicious actors could, for example, use AI malware to co-opt networks of sensors and impact control decisions on biotech supply chains with the intent to damage, destroy or contaminate vital stocks of vaccines, antibiotics, cell or immune therapies. In another scenario, AI malware could be used to automate data manipulation with the intent to falsify, erase or steal intelligence within large curations of genomics data. Such data poisoning could affect how pathogens are detected and analysed. It could also affect biointelligence on complex diseases in subpopulations collected over many years.

Intelligence-gathering and biological threat assessments

State-based intelligence activity has traditionally formed the bulk of biological threat assessments. Yet, obtaining accurate intelligence on biological threats from both state and non-state actors is challenging, as highlighted by **Patrick Walsh**, a former intelligence analyst, in his contribution to the Special Issue. His account of 'Five Eyes' health security capabilities emphasises gaps in three core intelligence processes: tasking and coordination, collection and analysis.

Capability gaps have certainly been apparent historically. In terms of state threats, for instance, the size, scope and sophistication of the extensive Soviet biological weapons programme took Western intelligence communities completely by surprise when it began to be uncovered at the end of the Cold War. Western intelligence communities also had to re-evaluate assessments made in the 1990s and early 2000s that Libya and Cuba had active biological weapons programmes, retroactively concluding that earlier judgements were incorrect. The most remarkable failure, however, was the incorrect assessment of Iraq's biological weapons programme before the US invasion of Iraq in 2003. Scholars have demonstrated how the 'anticipatory frame' CIA analysts used in their assessment of the programme fixated the analysts on particular technical pieces of information rather than integrating the more complex social, political and economic dynamics shaping Iraq's biological weapons development: 'factors which ultimately proved to be decisive.'

Today, there is limited public information on possible illicit state-based biological weapons activity. There is no public reporting that any country is maintaining a biological weapons programme. In the US State Department's annual compliance report on arms control, non-proliferation and disarmament treaties – the only publication of its kind – concerns are expressed that the Russian Federation has not 'satisfactorily documented whether [its inherited Soviet offensive] program was completely destroyed or diverted to peaceful purposes.'[22] Three key military institutes involved in the Soviet programme remain closed to outsiders, and it is these that are of particular interest to the USA. Bilateral discussions and confidence-building measures under the Biological Weapons Convention have not clarified the situation and, as a result, the US position is that it cannot confirm the elimination of past illegal biological weapons activities in Russia.[23] Russia's official position is that no offensive biological weapon programme ever existed in the Soviet Union.

The US intelligence community has been most explicit in expressing concerns that an adversary might be harnessing techniques for sequencing, synthesizing and manipulating genetic material for offensive use, and the government is investing heavily in defensive capabilities. The Defense Advanced Research Projects Agency (DARPA), the US military's research wing, asserts that: 'The application of biotechnologies by an adversary is an area where the United States could be most surprised as a nation, but it is also a source of great potential, where the United States could develop a host of new surprises of its own.'[24] The goal to 'harness biology as technology' is one of four main areas of focus for DARPA's strategic investments in 'overmatch' capabilities, according to its website. In Congressional testimony from March 2017, Arthur T. Hopkins, Acting Assistant Secretary of Defense for nuclear, chemical and biological defence programmes, stated that: 'The same tools of synthetic biology that we're concerned about as being capable of being used against us, we are also using in the laboratories to help develop countermeasures.'[25]

This build-up of biodefence infrastructure and capacities, not just in the United States but taking place around the world, means that states are moving closer to being in a position to threaten or perpetrate a biological attack.[26] This situation is worrying from an international security perspective. While states building their biodefence and civil emergency response capacities are not deliberately developing offensive capabilities, states observing the build-ups might feel the need to prepare for a sudden change of mind or change of intent by the leadership of the state building its capacities, and observer states might then begin to investigate the offensive capabilities they fear. Russia, for instance, claims that the US military is establishing a chain of dual-use laboratories on its border, that it is secretly collecting Russian biological material, and that the USA is conducting biological experiments near Russia's borders.[27] Like the USA, Russia is probably preparing for the eventuality that sophisticated biology might be used against its people, animals or crops. Russia's claims that it is aiming to develop 'genetic weapons' suggests the country might even aspire to go beyond defensive measures.[28] A build-up of capabilities would lead to more offensive know-how all round and to more danger of biological attacks against more states.

The focus in the 'non-state actor' category has traditionally been on terrorists. There is, however, relatively little evidence of past terrorist interest in biological agents.[29] Terrorists tend to be conservative and use weapons that are readily available and have a proven track record, not unconventional weapons that are more difficult to develop and deploy.

There are few instances of intent to develop mass casualty capabilities.[30] In one of the earliest incidents, in the 1970s in the USA, a group of teenagers calling themselves RISE fantasized about killing large parts of the world population and then regenerating humankind. They obtained several pathogens and learned how to grow them, but they failed to carry out their planned attacks before being arrested. In the 1980s, also in the USA, the Rajneeshees cult deliberately contaminated salad bars with Salmonella to sicken diners to make them stay away from voting booths during local elections in Oregon. Salmonella rarely kills, and no one died in this attack, but more than 750 people were infected, some of them quite severely. In the 1990s in Japan, the Aum Shinrikyo cult tried to cause mass casualties by developing and disseminating Bacillus anthracis, but the cult's attempts failed and no one was infected with anthrax. The Aum had more success with chemicals. In 1995, the same cult carried out the sarin attack on the Tokyo underground.

The most lethal bioterrorism attack was the 2001 anthrax letters. Codenamed Amerithrax by the FBI, the attack killed five and sickened another 17 people. Five anonymous letters containing a deadly strain of Bacillus anthracis were sent to media outlets and the US Senate within weeks of the 9/11 terrorist attacks on New York and Washington. The letters overtly linked the two attacks, with its messages of '09-11-01 you cannot stop us' and 'this is next', but the attacks were in fact not connected.

During the invasion of Afghanistan in late 2001, US soldiers captured a primitive laboratory known to be used by al-Qaeda operatives. As Vogel notes: 'Although crude and not yet operational, the lab findings suggested that al-Qaeda had acquired an avirulent strain of anthrax bacteria, limited biotech equipment, and some scientific articles. US officials determined that one PhD-level microbiologist from Pakistan was in charge of planning the design and work of the laboratory; he had also visited biotechnology companies and conferences. ... Declassified US government reports about this Afghani makeshift laboratory have indicated that al-Qaeda was unable to obtain a pathogenic culture of the anthrax bacteria, and that there was no evidence of any technical work done at this site, suggesting that al-Qaeda's 2001 bioweapons capabilities never went beyond trivial (Vogel 2013).'[31]

Interrogations of a captured Malaysian biological technician who was seeking to acquire bioweapons materials and equipment for al-Qaeda revealed that the group faced similar hurdles to developing biological weapons as the Aum Shinrikyo cult.

While there are few datapoints, past incidents show that even in the small number of cases where terrorists have actually made a serious effort at bioterrorism, pathogens have been difficult to acquire and use as weapons. The skills required to undertake even the most basic of bioterrorism attacks are often greater than assumed. The incidents also illustrate that bioterrorism can take many forms. Motivations differ significantly. RISE, the Aum Shinrikyo cult and al-Qaeda were motivated by a desire to cause mass casualties. The Rajneeshes were aiming to disrupt an election and focused on incapacitation. The Amerithrax case seems to have been motivated by a desire to make a political statement, drawing attention to the importance of anthrax research and the need to continue to fund it. Another takeaway from past bioterrorism incidents is that it is difficult to predict which pathogens terrorists might employ. It is often assumed that terrorists will use the same agents as were developed in state weapons programmes, but bioterrorists have acquired and used agents of little or no value as weapons of war.

The unique characteristics of biological agents make bioterrorism fundamentally different from other forms of terrorism. Not only are biological agents radically different from other weapons available to the terrorist, but biological weapons are also substantially different from the other weapons of mass destruction: chemical and nuclear weapons. To develop an effective biological weapon, it is necessary to obtain a pathogen suitable for weaponization. That pathogen must be weaponized and then disseminated without itself being affected by exposure to the environment. The pathogen must be capable of infecting the target, causing illness and/or death despite the efforts of the authorities to provide medical treatment, vaccination, quarantine, and so on. While case studies of terrorists evaluating the use of biological weapons are scare, there is one prominent example. The Norwegian right wing extremist, Anders Behring Breivik, who carried out a bomb attack in Oslo and a massacre on the island of Utøya in 2011, stated in a manifesto that he had considered using biological warfare agents, in particular anthrax, but concluded that he did not have the necessary expertise. Instead, he carried out a conventional attack with explosives and firearms.

Today, there is no public reporting that any current terrorist group has the capabilities to inflict mass casualties using biological agents. The characteristics of bioterrorism drawn out from previous incidents – technical barriers, range of motivations, uncertain pathogens/nature of the attack – are likely to remain in the short to medium term.

Fostering engagement between intelligence and academia

State-based intelligence activity is struggling to keep pace with the rate of societal transformation. Intelligence has traditionally been concerned with the assessments of threats which influence tactical and strategic responses, embedded within national security postures. Technological advances, and political and economic upheaval, have at once both undermined and strengthened the state's capacity to observe and analyse, the capacity for secrecy, and the capacity to act at a distance. This represents a fundamental challenge not just for the state and the intelligence community, but for broader conceptions of national security and intelligence and their functions within statecraft.

A significant component in meeting this challenge is the acquisition of outside expertise to gain new insights and mitigate against intelligence failures.[32] In the US, for instance, a National Research Council report, sponsored by the Office of the Director of National Intelligence, recommended that the intelligence community 'should expand opportunities for continuous learning that will enhance collaboration, innovation, and growth in the application of [social and behavioural science] analytical skills.'[33] In Britain, the Chief of MI6 has recently commented on the 'danger of group think' and the requirement to 'stimulate a contrary view'. Lord Butler's report *Review of Intelligence on Weapons of Mass Destruction* identified the need for 'challenge' to the government – a need that is still unmet.[34] The *Blackett Review of High Impact Low Probability Risks*, commissioned by the Cabinet Office and the Ministry of Defence, argued that greater use ought to be made of 'external experts to inform risk assumptions, judgments and analysis'.[35] In January 2018, the British Government's 'Areas of Research Interest' identified the need to 'align scientific and research evidence from academia with policy development and decision-making.'[36] The growing emphasis on intelligence outreach provides an unparalleled opportunity for scholars from a broad range of disciplines to consider the role they might play in these efforts, as well as the various opportunities and difficulties that can shape these relationships.

Perceptions of biological and health security threats have evolved in broad terms over the last century from deliberately introduced disease outbreaks to also incorporate natural disease outbreaks, unintended consequences of research, laboratory accidents, lack of awareness, negligence, and convergence of emerging technologies. This spectrum of threats has led to an expansion of the stakeholders and tools involved in intelligence gathering and threat assessments. Initially limited to groups associated with war, defence, international order and strategy, the field has expanded to also involve groups associated with medicine, health care and the life sciences, as well as groups associated with crime, internal security, public order and police investigations. To strengthen global health security and health intelligence, the traditional state-based intelligence community must actively engage with non-security stakeholders and incorporate space for new sources of intelligence. It is our hope that this Special Issue will contribute to the larger effort of developing a multidisciplinary, empirically informed and policy-relevant approach to intelligence-academia engagement in global health security that serves both the intelligence community and scholars from a broad range of disciplines.[37]

Notes

1. Lentzos, *Biological Threats.*

2. Carus, "A century."
3. Guillemin, *Biological Weapons*; and Wright, "Terrorists and biological weapons".
4. Wright, "Terrorists and biological weapons".
5. See note 3 above.
6. WHO, "Preparedness for Deliberate Use".
7. White House, "Remarks by President Obama".
8. WHO, "Director-General".
9. Ibid.
10. NASEM, *Biodefense*.
11. IAP, *Biological and Toxin Weapons*.
12. NRC, *Biotechnology Research*.
13. Ibid.
14. NSABB, *Proposed Framework*.
15. Ibid.
16. NASEM, *Dual Use Research*.
17. Brockman, Bauer and Boulanin, *Bio plus X*.
18. Dunlap and Pauwels, *Intelligent and Connected*; and Pauwels, *New Geopolitics*.
19. Bajema et al., *Digitization of Biology*.
20. Lentzos and Invernizzi, "Laboratories in Clouds".
21. See note 18 above.
22. US Department of State, *Report on Adherence*.
23. Ibid.
24. DARPA, *DARPA: 1958–2018*.
25. Pellerin, "DOD Officials".
26. Lentzos and Littlewood, "DARPA's Prepare Program".
27. Lentzos, "Russian Disinformation Attack".
28. Hoffman, "Genetic Weapons You Say".
29. Carus, *Bioterrorism and Biocrimes*.
30. Carus, "RISE, The Rajneeshees".
31. Vogel, *Phantom Menace*, 47.
32. Dover and Goodman, "Impactful scholarship"; Dover, Goodman and White, "Two Worlds".
33. NRC, *Intelligence Analysis*.
34. Butler, *Review of Intelligence*.
35. Government Office for Science, *Blackett Review*.
36. HM Government, "Areas of Research Interest".
37. Vogel and Balmer, "Secrecy and Intelligence"; Vogel and Knight, "Analytic Outreach"; and Nolan, "Ethnographic Research".

Disclosure statement

No potential conflict of interest was reported by the authors.

ORCID

Filippa Lentzos http://orcid.org/0000-0001-6427-4025

Bibliography

Bajema, N. E., D. DiEuliis, C. Lutes, and Y. B. Lim. "The Digitization of Biology: Understanding the New Risks and Implications for Governance." *Research Paper No.3, Center for the Study of Weapons of Mass Destruction*. Washington, DC: National Defense University, 2018.

Brockman, K., S. Bauer, and V. Boulanin. *Bio Plus X: Arms Control and the Convergence of Biology and Emerging Technologies*. Stockholm: Stockholm International Peace Research Institute, 2019.

Butler, L. R. 2004. "Review of Intelligence on Weapons of Mass Destruction." *Report of a Committee of Privy Counsellors*, July 14. http://news.bbc.co.uk/nol/shared/bsp/hi/pdfs/14_07_04_butler.pdf

Carus, S. W. *Bioterrorism and Biocrimes: The Illicit Use of Biological Agents since 1900. Center for Counterproliferation Research*. Washington, DC: National Defense University, 1998.

Carus, S. W. "RISE, The Rajneeshees, Aum Shinrikyo and Bruce Ivins." In *Biological Threats in the 21st Century: The Politics, People, Science and Historical Roots*, edited by F. Lentzos. London: Imperial College Press, pp. 171–197, 2016.

Carus, S. W. "A Century of Biological-weapons Programs, 1915–2015: Reviewing the Evidence." *Nonproliferation Review* 24, no. 1–2 (2017): 129–153. doi:10.1080/10736700.2017.1385765.

DARPA. *Darpa: 1958–2018*. Tampa, FL: Faircount Media Group, 2018. https://issuu.com/faircountmedia/docs/darpa_publication/1?ff

Dover, R., and M. Goodman. "Impactful Scholarship in Intelligence: A Public Policy Challenge." *British Politics* 13, no. 3 (2018): 374–391. doi:10.1057/s41293-018-0078-8.

Dover, R., M. Goodman, and M. White. "Two Worlds, One Common Pursuit: Why Greater Engagement with the Academic Community Could Benefit the UK's National Security." In *The Palgrave Handbook of Security, Risk and Intelligence*, edited by Dover, R., H. Dylan and M. Goodman, pp. 461–478. London: Palgrave Macmillan, 2017.

Dunlap, G., and E. Pauwels. *The Intelligent and Connected Bio-Labs of the Future: Promise and Peril in the Fourth Industrial Revolution*. Washington, DC: Wilson Center, 2017.

Government Office for Science. *Blackett Review of High Impact Low Probability Risks*. London: Government Office for Science, 2004. https://www.gov.uk/government/uploads/system/uploads/attachment_data/file/278526/12-519-blackett-review-high-impact-low-probability-risks.pdf

Guillemin, J. *Biological Weapons: From the Invention of State-sponsored Programs to Contemporary Bioterrorism*. New York: Columbia University Press, 2005.

HM Government. "Areas of Research Interest." June 28, 2017. https://www.gov.uk/government/collections/areas-of-research-interest

Hoffman, D. 2012. "Genetic Weapons You Say." *Foreign Policy*, March 27. http://foreignpolicy.com/2012/03/27/genetic-weapons-you-say/

Inter-Academy Partnership. *The Biological and Toxin Weapons Convention: Implications of Advances in Science and Technology*. London: Royal Society, 2015.

Lentzos, F. *Biological Threats in the 21st Century: The Politics, People, Science and Historical Roots*. London: Imperial College Press, 2016.

Lentzos, F. "The Russian Disinformation Attack that Poses a Biological Danger." *Bulletin of the Atomic Scientists* (November 19, 2018). https://thebulletin.org/2018/11/the-russian-disinformation-attack-that-poses-a-biological-danger/.

Lentzos, F., and C. Invernizzi. 2019. "Laboratories in the Cloud". *The Bulletin of Atomic Scientists*, July 2. https://thebulletin.org/2019/07/laboratories-in-the-cloud/

Lentzos, F., and J. Littlewood. "DARPA's Prepare Program: Preparing for What?" *The Bulletin of Atomic Scientists*, July 26, 2018. https://thebulletin.org/2018/07/darpas-prepare-program-preparing-for-what

National Academies of Sciences, Engineering and Medicine. *Dual Use Research of Concern in the Life Sciences: Current Issues and Controversies*. Washington, DC: The National Academies Press, 2017.

National Academies of Sciences, Engineering and Medicine. *Biodefense in the Age of Synthetic Biology*. Washington, DC: The National Academies Press, 2018.

National Research Council. *Biotechnology Research in an Age of Terrorism*. Washington, DC: The National Academies Press, 2004.

National Research Council. *Intelligence Analysis for Tomorrow: Advances from the Behavioral and Social Sciences*. Washington, DC: The National Academies Press, 2011.

National Science Advisory Board for Biosecurity. *Proposed Framework for the Oversight of Dual Use Life Sciences Research: Strategies for Minimizing the Potential Misuse of Research Information*. Washington, DC: NSABB, 2007.

Nolan, B. "Ethnographic Research in the US Intelligence Community: Opportunities and Challenges." *Secrecy and Society* 2 (2018): 1.

Pauwels, E. *The New Geopolitics of Converging Risks: The UN and Prevention in the Era of AI*. New York: United Nations University Centre for Policy Research, 2019.

Pellerin, C. 2017. "DoD Officials Discuss Countering WMD, Threats Posed by Synthetic Biology." *US Department of Defense News*, March 23. https://www.defense.gov/News/Article/Article/1128356/dod-officials-discuss-countering-wmd-threats-posed-by-synthetic-biology/

US Department of State. *Report on Adherence to and Compliance with Arms Control, Nonproliferation, and Disarmament Agreements and Commitments*. Washington, DC: US Department of State, April 17, 2018.

Vogel, K. *Phantom Menace or Looming Danger?* Baltimore, MD: Johns Hopkins University Press, 2013.

Vogel, K., and B. Balmer. "Secrecy and Intelligence: Introduction." *Secrecy and Society* 2 (2018): 1.

Vogel, K., and C. Knight. "Analytic Outreach for Intelligence: Insights from a Workshop on Emerging Biotechnology Threats." *Intelligence and National Security* 30 (2015): 686–703. doi:10.1080/02684527.2014.887633.

White House, Office of the Press Secretary. *Remarks by President Obama in Address to the United Nations General Assembly*. New York: United nations, September 21, 2011. https://obamawhitehouse.archives.gov/the-press-office/2011/09/21/remarks-president-obama-address-united-nations-general-assembly

World Health Organisation. "Preparedness for the Deliberate Use of Biological Agents: A Rational Approach to the Unthinkable." *WHO/CDS/CSR/EPH/2002.16*. Geneva: WHO, 2002.

World Health Organisation. *WHO Director-General Addresses UN Security Council on Ebola*. New York: UN Security Council, September 18, 2014. https://www.who.int/dg/speeches/2014/security-council-ebola/en/

Wright, S. "Terrorists and Biological Weapons: Forging the Linkage in the Clinton Administration." *Politics and the Life Sciences* 25, no. 1–2 (2007): 57–115. doi:10.2990/1471-5457(2006)25[57:TABW]2.0.CO;2.

The West Africa Ebola outbreak (2014–2016): a Health Intelligence failure?

Robert L. Ostergard, Jr.

ABSTRACT

The role of health intelligence (HI) has received little assessment in the West African Ebola outbreak (2014-2016). Using newly declassified information on the outbreak, this research finds significant HI problems that hindered an appropriate response to the outbreak. The Guinean government's low capacity to deal with the crisis, the government's misleading assessments of the crisis, the US embassy's failure to contextualize the information properly in terms of the risks the virus posed, and the US embassy's willingness to accept the Guinean government's assessment without criticism were contributing factors in the HI failure in the opening months of the Ebola outbreak.

Introduction

In the aftermath of the 2014–2016 Ebola virus outbreak in the three West African countries of Guinea, Liberia, and Sierra Leone, the international community, public health officials, and other analysts have dissected the events to discover how the crisis escalated and what could have been done to prevent it. While much of these analyses have focused on institutional responses from the international community, few analyses have examined whether problems focused in the area of health intelligence may have contributed to problematic assessment of the crisis unfolding in West Africa. This research focuses on the role of health intelligence and the assessment of that intelligence in understanding how the outbreak got so far out of control in such a short period of time.

The research unfolds in three parts. First, the paper examines the concept of health intelligence and its usefulness in assessing risks from epidemic outbreaks. Next, it highlights the important problem of risk assessment when the risk comes from a human security issue and not a direct overt military threat. Then it surveys the unfolding events of the Ebola outbreak from March of 2014 when the Guinean government announced that there had been an Ebola outbreak to September of 2014 when the US President Barak Obama declared the outbreak a national security concern to mobilize a US military response. In doing so, this research focuses on newly released classified documents obtained from a Freedom of Information Act request that highlight the Guinean government's insufficient response to the outbreak, and the reaction of US embassy personnel in Conakry to Guinea's response. These documents highlight significant deficiencies in the assessment of the situation as it unfolded during this period of time.

Health intelligence & surveillance

Typically, our information with regard to 'health security' is centered on the notion of public health surveillance. The World Health Organization (WHO) defines surveillance as ' … the continuous, systematic collection, analysis and interpretation of health-related data needed for the planning, implementation, and evaluation of public health practice.'[1] The intent is for surveillance to serve as an early warning system, to document interventions or to track progress toward public health goals, and to monitor the epidemiology of health problems that allow for policymakers to make informed decisions on public health policies and strategies.[2] Even before the West Africa Ebola outbreak and in the plethora of post-Ebola assessments, the term 'health intelligence' has been brought into the discussions about what 'went wrong' and 'how to prevent it.' While the meaning of the term is not so clear, the myriad of subjects and approaches termed 'health intelligence' have potentially important applications for better information and forecasting. Such applications have been the subject of recent research that expands the horizons of the approaches to health intelligence.

In recent research, Shaban-Nejad et al. aligned the notion of health intelligence with artificial intelligence and the theories and models that have applications in patient education, geocoding, health data, social media analytics, epidemic and syndromic surveillance, predictive modeling, and health policy decisions.[3] Morse conceptualized the term as an element of surveillance but focused specifically on 'useable information on events of public health significance.'[4] Morse has characterized existing surveillance systems as disease-specific and passive, maybe reactive, at best.[5] Such systems are hampered by the usual policy problems: (a) health is a low priority for governments, (b) governments are hesitant to release health information because of the political fallout potential, (c) conflicting policy issues such as conflicts between agricultural output and potential health impacts.[6] The presentation of such information has been in such a fragmented state that the effectiveness of the information obtained is reduced.[7]

My intent here is not to review the problems with surveillance systems, but to draw a distinction between surveillance and a broader information gathering process that involves intelligence and its analysis. French and Mykhalovskiy focus on health intelligence as the detection of public health events as they unfold or even before they unfold.[8] Health intelligence thus emphasizes the concepts, methods, practices, and apparatuses assembled to monitor and detect health events.[9] More recently, the movement is toward extending health intelligence beyond surveillance into more contemporary activities such as blogging and data mining social media networks. These activities capture the nature of pandemic surveillance and health intelligence by transcending a static conceptualization of metrics in data counts to

> ... reflect a broader set of time-space relations that are characteristic of contemporary thinking about pandemics. On the one hand, these relations involve a high degree of sensitivity to the spatial dimensions of health events, especially their potential to extend beyond local settings. On the other hand, they are beset by deep anxiety about the timeliness of response, the outcome of which is an immense effort to detect, pre-empt or rapidly respond to health events to prevent them from having trans-local effects.[10]

These approaches and definitions have a common thread through them; namely that they represent a need for more, better, and earlier forms of information and for decision makers to act upon that information. From outbreak surveillance to prediction of such outbreaks, the objective of surveillance and health intelligence is to mitigate *risk* on a number of levels. How we understand risk in this context is worth reviewing.

Risk and perceptions of threat

Risk perception is at the center of decision making for political leaders confronting epidemic outbreaks.[11] The scope and depth of the risk from any human security issue arises as a function of two factors: the perceived importance (saliency) associated with the risk and the likelihood of the state incurring significant losses (however those losses may be defined by the leaders). The scope of the issue that the leader is most concerned with includes the principle focus of the state's objective security characteristics: territory, the state, and population. The value or importance of these targets is both calculated, meaning that states may be able to quantify the potential losses due to the event or action, and symbolic, in that these targets are the personification of the state and its legitimacy to act on behalf of its population to confront those risks (the principal-agent issue).

When problems that are typically in a sphere of domestic public policy affect the population (such as a public health problem), the leader's perception of whether the problem constitutes a risk for the state may hinge on how the risk to the population will affect the state's capacity, the time-frame of the risk itself, and its immediacy (i.e. whether the risk to the population is an immediate short-term or a distant long-term risk). What these types of issues have in common is that they have a *potential* to damage the state's capacity to function. State capacity embodies the capability to carry out specific governmental functions including, its own survival (first and foremost), protection of its citizens from physical harm, economic prosperity and stability, effective governance, and territorial integrity. The most recent coronavirus pandemic presents a prime example of how a state's leadership risks political damage if its judgement of the risks associated with the outbreak are not attentive to the perceptions of other states and its own population. The inability of China's government to contain the outbreak has caused not only substantial harm to its governing credibility inside of China, but also to its global relations as the international economy slows down in response to supply chain disruptions and the increasing risks to the stability of China's markets.

For decision makers to perceive a non-military risk to the state or to the state's capacity, the potential, recognized loss, or disablement of the state and its population has to be substantial and sustained to the extent that the state's capacity and the functions related to its capacity are significantly hindered or even abrogated. For this to happen, in the short term, the state must face a cataclysmic incident or action that highlights the state's vulnerability to the risk and poses a significant risk of population destruction or displacement. History is replete with examples that reflect this situation to varying degrees.

Volcanic eruptions, earthquakes, and even hurricanes have effectively crippled states and cities. Such events are almost self-evident in terms of how they can affect the population, the state and the state's capacities and capabilities. The key factor here is that these types of incidents are typically risks that are acute (i.e., short-term causal though the ramifications of those events may extend temporally well beyond the actual event itself to create long-term consequences). The incident itself is seen as the immediate risk, and decisions are predicated upon dealing with the immediate risk. The decision makers' perceptions of such incidents are reflected in preparations and contingencies made to the extent that the immediate crisis can be weathered. In other words, there is a temporal end to the incident and decisions can be made to manage the risks during the incident and to minimize likely losses in its wake.

At any given moment, leaders may perceive an outbreak, particularly in its initial stages, as non-threatening at time t; given changing circumstances, they may reconsider that judgment at time $t + 1$. Issues that leaders perceive to be a security risk require a rapid response from them, particularly if they have downplayed the initial threats from the outbreak. As leaders address the incident, these issues may become less of a risk, instilling more confidence in the affected population and causing the leaders to reassess their risk from the outbreak as it dissipates. Thus, the immediacy and the perception of the risk to the regime ultimately are significant factors in determining whether leaders may perceive an issue as passing the threshold into the realm of a security risk. The 2014–2016 Ebola outbreak represents a strong case for how a mild and low-level outbreak quickly evolved into a major security threat to individual states and the international system. To understand this process fully, we need to understand the role of global health intelligence in the period leading up to the point where states declared Ebola a national and international security threat and emergency.

Intelligence and global health intelligence

Risk is based on information; how information is handled is critical. Just as critical is the interdisciplinary knowledge needed to make an appropriate assessment of information. As some have previously noted, intelligence is part science (the tools to gather information at all levels), but also part art, how we interpret that data and information.[12] To understand this part of the picture, we need to draw upon our understanding of intelligence and information gathering and flows.

In traditional intelligence studies, warning intelligence characterizes a continuous process of data collection and reporting of actions being taken by states or groups that could be a danger. The objective is to render a judgment on whether policymakers need to be aware of risks to a state's interests.[13] These assessments are strategic indicators or warnings that characterize long-term risks or to draw attention to immediate problems with the earliest possible warnings. Information comprehensiveness and recentness are central to this assessment.

Warnings and other attempts to garner attention to a potential risk is largely an assessment of probabilities along a continuum. The more information analysts have, the less uncertainty and greater confidence analysts will have in their conclusions. That these are probabilities is a key indicator that there is a slide into the realm of artful interpretation, meaning that there are few, if any, absolutes; there are only greater and lesser probabilities of occurrence. Within this continuum lies one great danger amongst many, namely that the more information that is gathered, the greater the probability that a key piece of information may never see the light of day – the problem of information overload where our abilities to gather information are far exceeding our capacity to process that information for meaning and context. Grabo has pointed to other factors that are just as important in this process.[14] These factors include: realistic assessments of probable outcomes from intelligence systems; knowledge of history, precedent, and doctrine with an understanding of their limitations to probabilities of outcomes beyond what is known at that moment; warnings do not exist unless and until analysts have conveyed them to policy makers; policy makers receive highly condensed information; intelligence warnings must be loud and frequent for them to penetrate bureaucratic walls and information flows. This latter point highlights the context of security theory, as these intelligence pronouncements are not about 'securitizing an issue' – that is for policy makers. Instead, they are about voice in a governmental decision-making process designed to prioritize the most critical issues ahead of others, and often, to leave long-term issues to be kicked down the road.

Perhaps the most difficult compounding element in the art of the analysis is understanding context, culture, and environment. In 1962, satellite photos gave the United States pictures of buildings on the island of Cuba; imagination and knowledge informed analysts that Cubans do not play soccer; they play baseball.[15] The parallels between intelligence gathering on a perceived enemy and gathering intelligence on a natural disaster or process is difficult as our knowledge of the enemy differs from our knowledge of the laws of nature and biological evolution. What they do have in common is lots of room for uncertainty and little room for miscalculation as the costs can be equally high.

Despite the distinctions traditional intelligence and health intelligence, the two have a basic common principle, which is to gather information and to assess that information for potential risks to states and even to the global system. It extends beyond simply monitoring a situation or a problem, but to assessing the risk to states and their populations. Such assessments in the area of health intelligence have encountered problems not unfamiliar to traditional intelligence assessments. While data collection and information have improved, our processing of that information and the interpretation of that information is lagging behind in understanding the environment of health crises and the political, social, and economic factors that influence their direction and outcome beyond a natural progression to the crisis. The nature of these problems in health intelligence can be seen in the West Africa Ebola outbreak (2014–2016).

The West Africa Ebola outbreak, 20142016

Health and policy analysts are still dissecting how an Ebola outbreak in a small village produced the largest number of infections and casualties in the known history of the virus. In a Freedom of Information Act request to the US Department of State (USDOS) and US Department of Defense, communications between the USDOS and the US Embassies in Guinea, Liberia, and Sierra Leone reveal, to an extent, how the events unfolded in the outbreak, and some of the perceptions and insights of both embassy personnel and the myriad of US agencies with whom they had been communicating. While in no way do these documents present the entire picture of what happened in West Africa, they do provide a preliminary insight into the information conveyed to the USDOS, which had the lead in the US response to events in West Africa. For this review, I will focus on communication between the US Embassy in Conakry, Guinea and the USDOS during the period of March 2014, when the government of Guinea acknowledged an Ebola outbreak in the country, and September 2014 when US President Barak Obama declared Ebola to be a 'national security priority' that necessitated the mobilization of US military forces for intervention into West Africa under operation United Assistance. Before getting to this account, it is necessary to understand what policy makers and embassy personnel should have understood as the nature of Ebola and its potential lethality because this is the basis for commentary found in the communiques between embassy personnel and the USDOS.

Background to the Ebola virus

Ebola Virus Disease (Ebola) is the kind of virus that writers and screenwriters have etched into the minds of people around the world. From Richard Preston's 1995 book *The Hot Zone* to Wolfang Peterson's film *Outbreak*, Ebola has become the quintessential viral nightmare, real or imagined.[16] That popular perception has been the basis for attention-getting headlines when the African continent has faced outbreaks of the dreaded virus. While there are other similar viruses (such as Lassa Fever, Marburg hemorrhagic fever, and Crimean-Congo hemorrhagic fever), Ebola is especially rare and deadly in people, with no known cure and vaccines largely in trial, but heavily deployed in the current Ebola outbreak in the Democratic Republic of Congo.[17]

Ebola Virus Disease (Ebola) is a hemorrhagic fever that resides in animals in African forests. The virus infects humans after they come into close contact with Ebola infected animals; this infection is known as a zoonotic spillover event.[18] Currently, researchers believe that fruit bats are one of the primary reservoirs for the virus.[19] Diseased animals infect humans when they come into close contact; for example, humans that consume bat meat, a primary bushmeat in parts of Africa, are highly susceptible to viral transmission.[20] Infected humans can then transmit Ebola to other people through direct contact with broken skin, mucous membranes, and bodily fluids, such as blood or secretions.[21] Ebola is a highly infectious virus; even the most limited exposure to an infected individual can result in the transmission of the disease. However, infectious disease specialists emphasize that transmission is difficult, and that direct contact with infected bodily fluids must occur. Thus, transmission frequently occurs in hospitals or clinics where infected individuals are receiving treatment and in homes where infected individuals are being cared for by their loved ones.[22]

An Ebola infection follows a common pattern. An individual infected with Ebola will initially suffer from flu-like symptoms occurring in two distinct phases. The dry phase lasts approximately three days and symptoms include fever, nausea, headaches, and muscle and joint pain. This phase is followed by the wet phase, which includes vomiting and diarrhea that quickly evolves into hemorrhagic symptoms, including rashes, internal and external bleeding, and impaired kidney and liver functioning.[23] The incubation period is typically between five and eighteen days but may range from two to twenty-one days depending on the type of Ebola virus contracted.

To diagnose Ebola officially, a laboratory test is required, and this requires a biosafety level four laboratory.[24] Without this test, diagnosis can be difficult, but the World Health Organization claims that epidemiological elements should suggest Ebola and decision makers should react accordingly.[25] These epidemiological elements include the geographic location, the fatality rate, the reported course of symptoms, and the characteristics of transmission. Once an individual is diagnosed with Ebola, they must be isolated for treatment to limit the likelihood of transmission. Additionally, health care workers must take special precautions during and after treatment to avoid contracting the virus. For example, all healthcare workers must wear protective clothing that is disinfected or destroyed after use, medical instruments must be thoroughly disinfected or disposed of after use, and all bedding and linens must be covered in plastic and soaked in disinfectant. Finally, health care workers must collect information about potential contact cases and complete follow-ups with them for twenty-one days.[26]

Between 1976 and 2012, Ebola killed approximately 1,600 individuals in six African countries. Ebola outbreaks appear to originate independent of any particular season.[27] Significantly more females are infected, likely due to women's caretaking responsibilities and role in burial rituals.[28] Rural outbreaks often remain small and may go undetected but spread very quickly when patients enter health care facilities with poor hygiene. Urban outbreaks are generally much larger and much more difficult to contain.

Since 1976 when Peter Piot and his team discovered the Ebola virus in modern day Democratic Republic of Congo, and prior to the 2014–2016 Ebola epidemic in West Africa, there were 22 outbreaks of Ebola encompassing 2387 cases and 1590 deaths, with a case fatality rate of 67 percent across all cases and viral variants and for the variant of Ebola that emerged in West Africa (Zaire), the average case fatality rate was 77 percent.[29] In short, across all incidents going into the 2014 outbreak, a person had a 1 in 3 chance of surviving an Ebola infection generally, and less than a 1 in 4 chance of surviving an Ebola (Zaire) infection. Prior to the 2014–2016 outbreak, the medical community had formed a consensus that because Ebola resulted in death quickly, widespread transmission and an international outbreak were unlikely.[30]

Ebola in Guinea

Ebola produces what is known as an acute or flashpoint epidemic. Acute epidemics correspond with a rapid, and high incidence and mortality rate. The spread is generally attributed to the nature of transmission. Within this context, acute epidemics are generally crises for governments and require a comprehensive, short-term response to mitigate the potential risk to the state and its population. Acute epidemics embody a swift capability to manifest as security risks for governments. These risks are attributed to the ability for acute epidemics to affect a large population in a relatively short amount of time. Ebola is a modern-day example of an acute epidemic symbolizing such results.

On 6 December 2013 a child in Guéckédou, Guinea died after becoming severely ill from a mysterious disease. However, it was not until 10 March 2014 that local officials notified the Guinean Ministry of Health of an unidentified, highly deadly, multiple cluster disease outbreak. In Guéckédou, medical authorities had hospitalized eight people; three subsequently died and additional deaths were reported among family members.[31] After dispatching an investigative team to Guéckédou, on March 22nd, the government confirmed that Ebola was present in the country and that West Africa had its first Ebola outbreak in history.[32] At this point, the government confirmed six Ebola cases, 49 suspected cases, and 29 deaths, but it was clear that the outbreak had moved out of the Guéckédou area, with cases being reported or suspected in the capital Conakry and in neighboring Sierra Leone.[33] On March 29, officials identified the Ebola strain as the Zaire strain.[34] The next day, the World Health Organization (WHO) confirmed that Ebola was also present in Liberia near the Guinean border. At the end of March, authorities confirmed 111 suspected cases, 79 deaths with a 71% case fatality rate in the prefectures of Guéckédou, Macenta, and Kissidougou (approximately 53 miles north of Guéckédou). The expanse of the outbreak in a short period of time led the WHO to declare the epidemic to be a 'public health emergency of international concern,'though the organization would later be criticized for its delayed response in declaring the emergency.[35]

The first reported communication of the US embassy in Conakry to the USDOS was on 24 March 2014. Some background on embassy operations is useful at this juncture. All US embassies can establish an Emergency Action Committee (EAC) comprised of subject-matter experts from the embassy or mission and are appointed by the embassy's Chief of Mission (usually the ambassador). The EAC meets to discuss the status of any emerging situation in-country, including the possible drawdown and evacuation of the embassy, vulnerability and risk assessments, assessing the embassy and host government's capabilities and limitations for emergency response and drafting the embassy's emergency action plan (EAP) that outlines 'tripwires' within the emergency that may require the embassy to take additional steps. It is important to note that the decision to drawdown or withdraw US embassy personnel is a political decision. Its importance lies in the perception that the host and other states may interpret the drawdown or evacuation as a lack of confidence in the host state and that the US lacks confidence in the ability of the host state to contend with the emergency at hand.[36] The USDOS approves all final EAPs and embassy personnel must review EAPs on an annual basis.[37] Information regarding EACs and EAPs is generally classified and the chapters of the document that govern their creation, work, and execution is classified.[38]

The US embassy reported to the USDOS that their EAC had met to discuss the Ebola outbreak and the Guinean government's decision to declare the situation as a formal outbreak. The communique provided initial insight into the embassy's posture on the epidemic, which was that the epidemic was essentially manageable. Embassy consultation with the foreign service health practitioner and the Peace Corp's senior medical officials had reported to embassy personnel that Ebola,

> ... while highly lethal, with mortality rates ranging from 80-90%, is very difficult to transmit unless in direct contact with infected persons. Moreover, the period of transmissibility is short, given the rapid evolution of the disease after onset of symptoms. Given the transmission vector, Post's medical professionals echoed published advice from the WHO, CDC and other global health institutions that employing universal precautions (avoiding symptomatic individuals, health professionals need to wear masks, gloves and other protective gear when treating symptomatic individuals) is sufficient defense against the disease infecting Mission personnel.[39]

The embassy further conveyed that the international community had mobilized to support the Guinean government's response. The embassy characterized that response as 'aggressive' with steps taken including free treatment in isolation centers, airing of prevention messages on radio, television and social media, limiting corpse disposal to medical practitioners and the Guinean Red Cross, victim tracing, and additional testing of affected persons.

The embassy communique focused on Ebola transmission. But as noted previously, while difficult, without proper equipment and training, transmission becomes much easier. What is also missing from the first communique is an assessment of the Guinean government's known capacities to contend with such an epidemic and the cultural problems that had emerged in previous Ebola outbreaks. The state had been wracked with political violence and ethnic divisions. In 2013, Guinea held elections to replace the transitional government that had been in power since the military gave up rule of the country. Alpha Conde became the first democratically elected leader in the country's history. However, the opposition and international observers said that the elections suffered from severe irregularities. In September of 2013, the Guinean Supreme Court upheld Conde's election, prompting an extended period of uprisings and protests against the government.[40] However, there were other societal factors which intensified tensions in Guinean.

Corruption is historically prevalent in Guinea and is still an endemic problem. This issue, coupled with the exacerbated ethnic tensions in Guinea, 'deepened a concentration of power in the executive branch, and generated considerable frustration within Guinean civil society and the country's international partners.'[41] These background issues helped set the stage for internal division; at a time when strong leadership was needed to coordinate the Ebola response in Guinea, the opposition to the president had called into question his legitimacy and questioned his motives during the outbreak. Moreover, Guinea's infrastructure is virtually non-existent to the extent that US military forces would cite infrastructure as a major hurdle to providing relief and requiring special training for the possibility of vehicle rollovers.[42] Guinea's health infrastructure is one of the poorest in the world, with few doctors, medical facilities, and hospitals present in the country. These would become significant contributory factors to the rapid deterioration of the government's handling of the epidemic.

On April 1, the US embassy in Conakry reported that the CDC had advised them that the virus transmission was by fruit bats and monkeys and that there was no public health utility in 'closing' borders. The communique emphasized concerns over media sensationalism and the rumors swirling around the epidemic. The embassy further reported that 'The EAC judgment is that none of our trip wires have been crossed. The nearest border post with Senegal is a 17-hour drive from Conakry, and even if the border were completely closed, none of our emergency planning relies on overland access to Senegal. That said, we recognize that Ebola is frightening in ways that have nothing to do with the statistical probability of infection. We will continue to listen to the experts and continue to try to reassure the American community.'[43] The US Agency for International Development (USAID) committed 538,000 USD to provide supplies and equipment to the effort.[44] On the same day, the border between Guinea and Guinea-Bissau closed against the expressed guidance of the World Health Organization and US Centers for Disease Control. At this point, approximately 97 confirmed cases of Ebola had been diagnosed.

A week later, on April 8, the US embassy reported that the Guinean government is

> ... doing a pretty good job – with the support of a wide range of international actors – in responding to the recent outbreak of Ebola fever. The less good news is that while the outbreak may be under control, or at least on track to be under control, the panic it has caused remains a greater threat than the disease itself. We went into this outbreak with a focus on the medical response but have since spent the balance of our time on trying to calm a nervous population, including our own community. CDC and M/MED have been consistent in their message that the public health risk is minimal, limited to those in direct contact with acutely ill or recently deceased Ebola patients and those who consume the raw or under-cooked meat of fruit bats or non-human primates. Based on this guidance, we have made no changes to our security posture".[45]

In the same communique, the US embassy demonstrated that its analysis was lacking situational context of the well-known conditions that had existed in Guinea and would hinder the government's ability to confront the epidemic.

> ... we have been guided by our former RMP/P ... who told our community over a year ago that fear is not tied to statistics; indeed, from an actuarial point of view he noted that most of us are afraid of the wrong thing ... great white sharks versus bath tubs, for example. According to the CDC, there have been 2,000 Ebola deaths since 1978; given the prevalence of typhoid, cholera, meningitis and – above all – malaria, Ebola is a statistically irrelevant threat. However, thanks to Hollywood, a not-insignificant societal disdain for the Forest Region among other Guineans, and some high-visibility cases of panic by people and organizations who should know better, we're faced with a messaging challenge more than an epidemiological one at this point.[46]

Further information in the April 8 communique emphasized the need for the government and the President to remain positive, noting that Conde had been privately critical of the relief agency Medicines Sans Fronteirs (MSF) for what he considered to be alarmist statements about the outbreak, of Emirates Airlines for cancelling flights to Conakry, of Senegal for temporarily closing its border, and of angry Guineans who were attacking medical personnel. The embassy was particularly concerned with keeping air flights into Conakry running. 'A number of measures have been put into place, including medical students doing the initial questioning of outbound passengers backed up by medical instruments in case someone with symptoms appears. (Note: these are in fact placebos, but if it keeps the airlines operating, we can live with it.) Our operations have not been affected.'[47] The use of placebo medical equipment is particularly disturbing ethically and practically, and highlights how ill-equipped the government was to deal with the outbreak. Moreover, the government of Guinea played a game of Russian roulette with the placebo medical equipment; should such information had become known, public and international confidence in the government's ability to handle the crisis would have plummeted. However, these issues were not the subject of the embassy's communication; the primary concern was in keeping the airlines running.

Moreover, the embassy was supportive of opposition leaders in Guinea that struck a unifying message with the government. The communique referred to opposition leader Cellou Dalein Diallo of the Union of Democratic Forces of Guinea (UFDG) party as 'responsible' when he described the crisis as a period of 'national mourning,' but criticized opposition leader Sidya Toure of the Union of Republican Forces (URF) as 'less helpful' when he criticized the government for not anticipating the disease's spread. The UFR chief deputy Mohammed Tall said that "as usual, the government has been lazy in reacting to this. It did not take the situation seriously. We have known about it since early February (and perhaps the first cases started as early as January), if they had acted earlier, it could have saved lives instead of spreading. Now we are working from behind. The government needs to get out there and raise awareness still. Kids are still afraid to go to school. Yet the RPG [Rally of the Guinean People] party is holding meetings like nothing has happened."[48] The embassy further emphasized its criticism of opposition leaders in its April 1–13 political and economic summary report of Guinea.[49] Such analysis ignored opposition leaders' legitimate complaints of the government's performance in handling the crisis.

The embassy's emphasis on a unified message from the government and the containment of rumors and hype were key features of how the embassy perceived the risk in Guinea. This approach was limiting in terms of understanding the scope of the *potential* problem, but it was not unfounded. Rumors and false information had been a problem in previous Ebola outbreaks and had been emerging amongst large segments of Guinea's illiterate and uneducated population. Such an environment lends itself to political entrepreneurship and opportunism in a highly fractured political environment like that which had existed in Guinea. However, the underlying problem in Guinea, the epidemic and the government's capacity to contain it, appeared to be assumed in the communication given the embassy's assessment of the government's performance to this point as 'good.' As the embassy said, "Ebola is scary in a primordial sense, but hopefully our public diplomacy can help us all go back to being scared of boring things like mosquitos and automobiles."[50]

The return to mosquitos and automobiles appeared to be where the embassy believed Guinea was in its April 14-May 10 political summary report of Guinea. Eight paragraphs into the report, the embassy addressed the Ebola outbreak, which 'seem[ed] to be contained, with the few new cases limited to people who were monitored because they were known to have come in contact with other victims.'[51] The embassy reported that MSF representatives were confident that the epidemic had been contained in two of the four outbreak zones. This assessment was offered despite also reporting that MSF, the WHO, and the Ministry of Health were monitoring up to 300 people in Guéckédou for Ebola, all of whom had been in contact with Ebola victims. The embassy's assessment was not necessarily wrong, but was too optimistic given the environment, the location of the outbreak as having porous roadways and dotted with small villages, and the number of people still under watch for Ebola.

Thus, by the end of April, the Guinean government was confident that the Ebola outbreak was under control. President Alpha Conde believed that the outbreak was being contained. While cases were on the decline, the president's optimism seemed unwarranted. As Figure 1 shows, confirmed and probable Ebola cases were declining, but would not hit a bottom until May 18 when only eight new confirmed and probable cases emerged. However, the next week, that number almost tripled. Thus, in May, a handful of confirmed cases remained in Guinea and no new cases had been reported for over three weeks in Liberia; Senegal had reopened its borders with Guinea.[52] However, by the middle of May, Guinea reported new Ebola cases, but from a different part of the country. The data would later show this was the beginning of one of many upsurges in Guinea's Ebola outbreak (Figure 1).

On June 12, in its summary report for May 11 to June 9, the embassy reported that Ebola cases in Guinea increased in number and in geographic distribution. MSF and the WHO reversed the

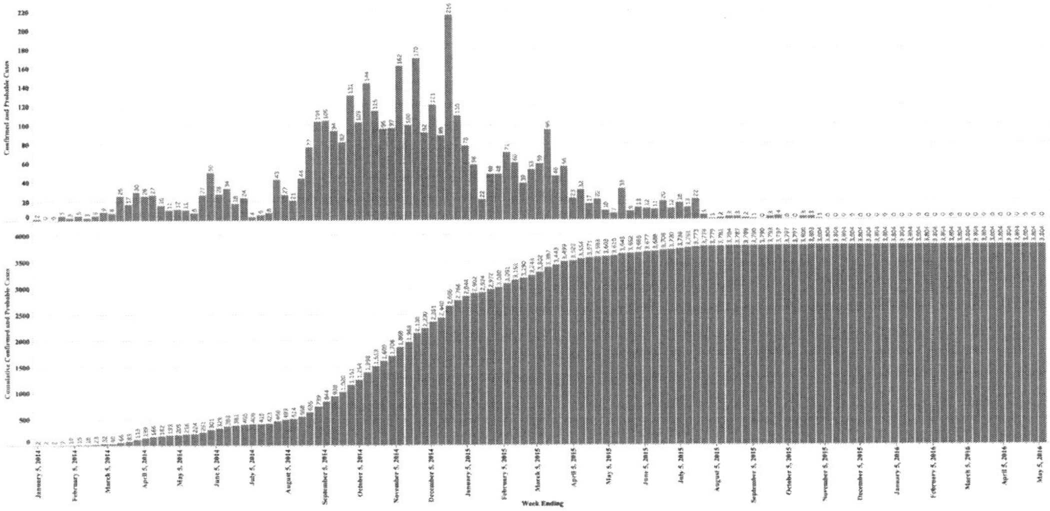

Figure 1. Weekly Confirmed, Probable, and Cumulative Ebola Cases: Guinea January 2014-May 2016

drawdown of personnel as new cases appeared. The embassy reported that between May 29 and June 3, Guinea's Ministry of Health had reported 344 cumulative cases of Ebola, including 215 deaths and 207 confirmed laboratory cases. The epidemic had spread to districts, not just in the South, such as Guéckédou and Macenta, but also in the western part of the country.[53] The next day, the US embassy reported in a preparation document for a visit by a US Principal Deputy Assistant Secretary (PDAS), that the government had experienced 'setbacks' due mainly to cultural factors in the Forest Region of the country, and that 'fault lines' had opened between the government and international actors United States Embassy, Conakry.[54]

The embassy recognized that the epidemic was beginning to get out of control on June 20 in its first Ebola-specific communique since April, 'Despite earlier forecasts that the tide of the outbreak was receding, it has proven harder to contain than initially anticipated'.[55] The embassy reported that the US ambassador had been engaged in public activities with the president to draw attention to the outbreak, but that health workers were having problems gaining access to communities with people who had been exposed to the virus. Linguistic and cultural barriers had proven to be obstacles in helping the people particularly in the Forest Region, where deeply held cultural practices for funerals had been a persistent source of contamination.[56]

On July 16, the embassy further reported that the government was struggling to bring the outbreak under control. The embassy reported that well-equipped hospitals were underutilized because of local fears and the eruption of violence against health personnel. The Guinean government had begun working with a WHO anthropologist to try to reframe the way in which messaging to the public was conducted. Resistance, the embassy reported, had been passive (not talking to medical personnel) and active (attacks on health care workers, roadblocks, and car stonings). The embassy reiterated its work toward avoiding public criticism from the government and international actors, declaring such statements as counterproductive toward the goals of containing Ebola. The embassy noted that MSF, for a long time, had been the sole provider of treatment centers during Ebola outbreaks in Africa, but that they were spread thin in Guinea and West Africa more broadly given the spread of the virus to multiple countries.[57] The embassy also highlighted key mistakes in the early messaging of the epidemic, with relief organizations saying there was no cure for Ebola, but that they should send their loved ones infected with Ebola to hospital centers. The WHO anthropologist highlighted that this mixed message promoted traditional healers as the 'stars' of the outbreak for local populations, but created another vector of transmission as traditional healers touched infected patients without protection.[58]

In its July 22 political summary to the USDOS, the embassy highlighted the declining trend in cases, but added some caution by highlighting concerns. The most prominent of those concerns was that there may be undiagnosed Ebola cases in small and remote villages and that some villages had been actively blocking national and international health workers from entering to monitor and trace contacts. Migration across the borders also had been making it difficult to determine the origin of cases among Guinea, Liberia, and Sierra Leone.[59] By August 15, however, the tone and urgency of the situation in Guinea changed swiftly.

On August 15, the US embassy issued a request for emergency assistance, five months after the outbreak was declared an epidemic in the country. The embassy reported that on August 1, President Conde and the other heads of state of the Mano River Union (Guinea, Sierra Leone, Liberia, and Cote d'Ivoire) formally acknowledged the need for a concerted intervention to address the Ebola epidemic and welcomed international support. The government of Guinea had declared a national health emergency on August 14, which came in the wake of the WHO's declaration of the outbreak as a public health emergency of international concern. The US Charge d'Affaires Ervin Massinga declared a disaster and requested relief assistance for the country of Guinea with the USAID Office of US Foreign Disaster Assistance to provide and coordinate appropriate emergency response activities to address the outbreak.[60] The embassy further reported that the government of Guinea formally requested international assistance in medical expertise and logistics to increase case detection, isolation units, transferring patients to health facilities, contact tracing of person exposed to Ebola, burial and corpse management, sample collection, and messaging and awareness campaigns to prevent further transmission.[61] The embassy reported to the USDOS that the Ebola outbreak had moved beyond the Government of Guinea's capacity to handle. The embassy further requested coordination with other US government agencies in developing a full government humanitarian response.

On August 19, the embassy issued its Ebola update to the USDOS highlighting the beginning of USAID assistance with a disaster assistance response team (DART). The embassy reported the situation in Guinea to be stable, but vulnerable to upswings due to active viral transmission across the region. The Ministry of Health in Guinea had revised its budget estimate for the National Response Plan to 49 USD million, an increase of 38 USD million dollars for activities through the end of December.[62] Interestingly, in the commentary to the report, the embassy made the following observation:

> Comment: The arrival of the DART element in Conakry, along with enhanced CDC technical resources provided to the sub-regional coordination body, have been well-received and much appreciated by a system under heavy strain by the regional caseload. These new resources are helping to bridge the gap produced by on-going Guinean governmental confusion and weakness, such as poor implementation of decisions and an unsteady grasp by senior decision makers of how policies are being put in place in the field. The biggest hurdles in the coming weeks and months will be to coordinate the standing up of the tri-border isolation zone, both by the governments and the international organizations here to confront the epidemic. End comment.[63]

The observations of the problems of 'Guinean governmental confusion and weakness ... ' were not new to the country; they were endemic problems in the country, particularly since the 2013 upheaval in Guinea's politics. However, this commentary was the first time in the communiques since the outbreak began that embassy personnel had expressed a lack of confidence in the Guinean government's ability to confront the epidemic. In fact, embassy personnel had been critical of opposition leaders who expressed similar, though less politically tolerant, commentary.

On August 28, the US embassy highlighted the Guinean government's pushback on international travel restrictions and the complaints about it from the political class in Guinea. However, the embassy emphasized the ineffective government policies on border and transportation issues. Embassy personnel claimed that the Guineans had not deployed health screeners, keeping the border crossing closed to people and goods. They further expressed the idea that government officials may not be aware of the problem, which would speak to the need to improve intra-governmental coordination.[64] Such border closings could have created issues of food security and food supplies within the region, which occurred when Senegal closed their border in May. However, the embassy further highlighted the problems with Guinea's government response.

> Comment: The border and air links closure issue has predictably tracked the international level of fear associated with Ebola. The President and his key Ministers know this, and have come out aggressively to counter fear-based policymaking criteria that are undermining the economy and becoming a massive policy distraction while the government is still tightening up its intra-governmental efforts to squarely attack the Ebola outbreak head-on. We will continue to be active in assisting them, as will our international partners who are shouldering much of the burden in managing the Ebola fight. However, the issue with the land border with Sierra Leone is concerning – the government's top officials are seemingly unaware of what's going on 100km away from the capital. Given that a senior Minister of State confided that he does not have confidence the country's prefets and sub-prefets are all in the field and doing their jobs, the picture is of a government still unable to bring its full weight to bear in attacking the outbreak. End Comment.[65]

The US embassy had made it clear to the USDOS that Guinea's performance in confronting the outbreak was subpar. In its communique of September 4, the embassy provided an analysis of a high-profile visit to the region in which the US CDC Director Thomas Frieden confronted President Conde about the government's response. President Conde was on a '... private trip after a particularly heavy international travel schedule'.[66] Though President Conde had been traveling, Dr. Frieden, in a telephone conversation with President Conde, fielded concerns from President Conde that the WHO had been 'exaggerating' potential number of victims in recent public statements. Dr. Frieden told President Conde that the situation in the region, particularly with the epidemics in Sierra Leone and Liberia, may even be worse than what the WHO had stated publicly. President Conde then assured Dr. Frieden that his government would do what was needed to stop the outbreak, while asking for further assistance from the US. But it was clear that the Guinean government was merely speaking to action, and that it was unsure how to proceed. The embassy reported to the USDOS that

> The government's lack of clarity on how the system is to work was vividly on display when Dr. Frieden asked a "hypothetical" question (taken from an actual issue in the field) concerning how the new structure would manage a broken radio tower vital to disseminating Ebola information. The response, essentially four different approaches from four different senior leaders, half of whom said the matter would have to be referred to Ministries and ultimately Ministers for final action, showed our Guinean partners know they need a more effective decision-making system but don't have a universal grasp on how it would work.[67]

Later in September, following Dr. Frieden's visit to West Africa, the Obama administration declared the situation in West Africa to be a 'national security priority' and began the process of mobilization of US armed forces for assistance in West Africa. By the end of September, US troops entered Liberia under Operation United Assistance to provide logistical and medical support to all three countries.

Analysis and conclusion

The West Africa Ebola outbreak was a disaster whose onset cannot be blamed on any actor, but whose spread was exacerbated by the actions and inactions of a multitude of domestic and international actors. This research has examined a narrow, early segment of this crisis, focusing on the actions of the Guinean government and the interpretation of those actions by US embassy personnel in Conakry. Three issues have become clear in this examination.

First, the Guinean government under represented its capacity to handle the outbreak to not just US embassy personnel, but also to the international community. In fact, Guinean President Alpha Conde actively downplayed the severity of the outbreak, attacking domestic opposition leaders and NGOs that dared to suggest the government's response was lacking.

Second, US embassy personnel did not have a full understanding of the nature of the Ebola virus, the cultural context in which it may spread, and the capacity of the Guinean government to handle the crisis. This point represents an information failure that was avoidable through training and additional health briefings that could have been provided at the onset of the outbreak. West Africa had never seen Ebola; more information should have been sought, but the embassy seemed content to accept the Guinean government's biased assessment early in the crisis. Given the specialized equipment, personnel, and procedures needed to handle a level four biohazard and Guinea's lack of medical facilities and capacity, the embassy should have been more active in raising the alarms about the risks for the crisis to escalate beyond the government's capacity to control it. Later in the crisis, the embassy reported on the sheer inability of the government to make fundamental decisions during the crisis. This problem did not emerge as a facet of the crisis; it was an endemic condition inside of a government that had low legitimacy and low political capacity before the onset of the crisis. Thus, the assessment of the government's ability to confront the outbreak should have been couched within a skeptical framework.

Third, by the time the Guinean government requested assistance, it was too late to contain the virus; it had already spread to other countries that also had low and weak capacities in the face of an overwhelming potential caseload of Ebola victims. It may be possible to claim that the Guinean government had reassessed risks as the crisis evolved, but it was clear from the crisis onset that the government would not be able to contain the problem once the virus spread out of the vicinity of Guéckédou. This point is particularly important given the geographic area of Guéckédou being right on the border with Liberia and Sierra Leone. US embassies in Monrovia and Freetown reported specifically on their respective host governments' inability to contain the Ebola outbreaks and forewarned of the need for assistance.

When taken together, these points represent a health intelligence failure in the reporting of information, the assessment of that information, and in the imagination of what that information could mean in a state with weak institutional, economic, and political capacities. The remaining question to be addressed is why did the failure occur? More importantly, why did the Guinean government under President Alpha Conde downplay the severity of the outbreak? Additional research will be needed to provide an adequate answer to this question.

Notes

1. World Health Organization, "WHO | Public Health Surveillance."
2. World Health Organization.
3. Shaban-Nejad, Michalowski, and Buckeridge, "Health Intelligence."
4. Morse, "Global Infectious Disease Surveillance And Health Intelligence," 1070.
5. Grabo, *Anticipating Surprise*, 1–3.
6. Morse, "Global Infectious Disease Surveillance And Health Intelligence," 1072.
7. Morse, 1072.
8. French and Mykhalovskiy, "Public Health Intelligence and the Detection of Potential Pandemics," 174.
9. Donaldson and Wood, "Surveilling Strange Materialities"; Fisher and Monahan, "The 'Biosecuritization' of Healthcare Delivery"; French, "Woven of War-Time Fabrics"; and Weir and Mykhalovskiy, *Global Public Health Vigilance*.
10. French and Mykhalovskiy, "Public Health Intelligence and the Detection of Potential Pandemics," 175.
11. I use the term 'risk' here instead of threat. Risk represents danger and the potential exposure to that danger. Threats imply that someone has intended harm. This distinction is subtle but important as traditional security issues imply an opposite or an 'other' that engages strategically or tactically; human security that may emanate from more natural processes like epidemics or earthquakes do not have a strategic or tactical 'other;' they just exist.
12. Laqueur, "The Question of Judgment."
13. See note 5 above.
14. Grabo, 13–16.
15. Caddell, "Corona over Cuba."
16. Preston, *The Hot Zone*; and Peterson, *Outbreak*.
17. The Centers for Disease Control lists 20 separate viral hemorrhagic fevers, each with their own genetic differentiations and sub-variants. For additional information, see The Centers for Disease Control's website for viral hemorrhagic fevers: https://www.cdc.gov/ncezid/dhcpp/vspb/diseases.html (accessed 12 December 2018).

18. Richards, *Ebola*.
19. Feldmann and Geisbert, "Ebola Haemorrhagic Fever"; Kinsman, "A Time of Fear"; Kuhn, *Filoviruses*; and Leroy et al., "Fruit Bats as Reservoirs of Ebola Virus."
20. Zhang and Wang, "Forty Years of the War against Ebola."
21. World Health Organization, "Ebola Virus Disease."
22. See note 18 above.
23. World Health Organization, "Ebola Haemorrhagic Fever in Sudan, 1976"; and World Health Organization, "Ebola Virus Disease."
24. World Health Organization, "WHO Recommended Guidelines."
25. See note 2 above.
26. See note 21 above.
27. See note 20 above.
28. Francesconi et al., "Ebola Hemorrhagic Fever Transmission."
29. See note 21 above.
30. Bullard, *A Day-by-Day Chronicle*.
31. Baize et al., "Emergence of Zaire Ebola Virus Disease."
32. The 1994 outbreak in Cote D'Ivoire was the only Tai Forest Ebola incident and originated with a primate autopsy. The incident was isolated to one individual.
33. Medicines Sans Frontieres, "Guinea"; Lazuta, "Emergency Ebola Intervention"; Samb, "Ebola Kills Dozens In Guinea."
34. See note 30 above.
35. Bullard.
36. Kampen, "To Stay or Not to Stay," 10.
37. Kampen, 8.
38. "Foreign Affairs Manual."
39. United States Embassy, Conakry, "Guinea."
40. Africa Research Bulletin, "GUINEA."
41. Human Rights Watch, "World Report 2014."
42. Joint and Coalition Operational Analysis (JCOA), "Operation United Assistance"; and Newman, "Face of Defense."
43. United States Embassy, Conakry, "Guinea EAC on Ebola, April 4."
44. United States Embassy, Conakry.
45. United States Embassy, Conakry, "Ebola in Guinea."
46. See note 44 above.
47. Ibid.
48. Ibid.
49. United States Embassy, Conakry, "Guinea's Political & Economic Summary Report."
50. See note 45 above.
51. United States Embassy, Conakry, "Guinea's Political Summary Report."
52. Bullard, *A Day-by-Day Chronicle*, 18.
53. United States Embassy, Conakry, "Guinea's Political Summary Report."
54. United States Embassy, Conakry, "CONAKRY."
55. United States Embassy, Conakry, "Guinea," 18.
56. United States Embassy, Conakry, "Guinea."
57. United States Embassy, Conakry, "West African Ebola Outbreak."
58. See note 44 above.
59. United States Embassy, Conakry, "Guinea's Political Summary Report," 11.
60. United States Embassy, Conakry, "Guinea."
61. See note 44 above.
62. United States Embassy, Conakry, "Guinea."
63. See note 44 above.
64. United States Embassy, Conakry, "Guinean Government, Embassy Push Back."
65. See note 44 above.
66. United States Embassy, Conakry, "Conakry."
67. See note 44 above.

Acknowledgements

I would like to thank my research assistants Keeley Eshenbaugh, Jordyn Green, Thomas Wackman, Christopher Jacox, and Holly Scala for their invaluable help with this manuscript. I would also like to thank Ken Brooke of Congressman

Mark Amodei's staff and Eric Herzik for their support in completing this project. I am also thankful to University of Nevada Scholarly and Creative Activities Committee for its financial support in completing this research.

Disclosure statement

No financial conflicts.

ORCID

Robert L. Ostergard, Jr. http://orcid.org/0000-0001-7902-3827

Bibliography

Baize, S., D. Pannetier, L. Oestereich, T. Rieger, L. Koivogui, N. Magassouba, B. Soropogui et al. "Emergence of Zaire Ebola Virus Disease in Guinea." *New England Journal of Medicine* 371,no. 15 (October 9, 2014): 1418–1425. doi:10.1056/NEJMoa1404505.

Bullard, S. G. *A Day-by-Day Chronicle of the 2013-2016 Ebola Outbreak*. Springer, Cham, Switzerland 2018.

Bulletin, A. R. "GUINEA: Election Results Upheld." *Africa Research Bulletin: Political, Social and Cultural Series* 50, no. 11 (December 1 2013): 19916.

Caddell, J. W., Jr. "Corona over Cuba: The Missile Crisis and the Early Limitations of Satellite Imagery Intelligence." *International and National Security* 31, no. 3 (2016): 416–438.

Donaldson, A., and D. Wood. "Surveilling Strange Materialities: Categorisation in the Evolving Geographies of FMD Biosecurity." *Environment and Planning D: Society and Space* 22, no. 3 (June 1, 2004): 373–391. doi:10.1068/d334t.

Feldmann, H., and T. W. Geisbert. "Ebola Haemorrhagic Fever." *The Lancet* 377, no. 9768 (2011): 849–862. doi:10.1016/S0140-6736(10)60667-8.

Fisher, J. A., and T. Monahan. "The 'Biosecuritization' of Healthcare Delivery: Examples of Post-9/11 Technological Imperatives." *Social Science & Medicine* 72, no. 4 (February 1, 2011): 545–552. doi:10.1016/j.socscimed.2010.11.017.

"Foreign Affairs Manual: U.S. Department of State." Accessed August 26, 2019. https://fam.state.gov/

Francesconi, P., Z. Yoti, S. Declich, P. A. Onek, M. Fabiani, J. Olango, R. Andraghetti et al. "Ebola Hemorrhagic Fever Transmission and Risk Factors of Contacts, Uganda." *Emerging Infectious Diseases* 9,no. 11 (November 1, 2003): 1430–1437. doi:10.3201/eid0911.030339.

French, M., and E. Mykhalovskiy. "Public Health Intelligence and the Detection of Potential Pandemics." *Sociology of Health & Illness* 35, no. 2 (2013): 174–187. doi:10.1111/j.1467-9566.2012.01536.x.

French, M. A. "Woven of war-time fabrics: the globalization of public health surveillance." *Surveillance & Society* 6, no. 2 (2009): 101–115.

Grabo, C. M. *Anticipating Surprise: Analysis for Strategic Warning*. University Press of America, Lanham, 2004.

Joint and Coalition Operational Analysis (JCOA). *Operation United Assistance: The DOD Response to Ebola in West Africa*. Washington, DC: United States: US Department of Defense, January 6, 2016. https://www.jcs.mil/Portals/36/Documents/Doctrine/ebola/OUA_report_jan2016.pdf

Kampen, S. M. "To Stay or Not to Stay: Non-Combatant Evacuation Operations and Their Impact on Host Nation/Regional Stability." Joint Forces Staff College, 2014. https://pdfs.semanticscholar.org/a20c/730dfdeb717fc9a5e61cd143259af75099e6.pdf

Kinsman, J. "'A Time of Fear': Local, National, and International Responses to A Large Ebola Outbreak in Uganda," 2012.

Kuhn, J. *Filoviruses: A Compendium of 40 Years of Epidemiological, Clinical, and Laboratory Studies*. Vol. 20. Springer Science & Business Media, Vienna, 2008.

Laqueur, W. "The Question of Judgment: Intelligence and Medicine." *Journal of Contemporary History* 18, no. 4 (1983): 533–548.

Lazuta, J. "Emergency Ebola Intervention Launched in Guinea | Voice of America - English." Accessed August 25, 2019. https://www.voanews.com/africa/emergency-ebola-intervention-launched-guinea

Leroy, E. M., B. Kumulungui, X. Pourrut, P. Rouquet, A. Hassanin, P. Yaba, A. Délicat, et al. "Fruit Bats as Reservoirs of Ebola Virus." *Nature; London* 438, no. 7068 (December 1, 2005): 575–576. doi:10.1038/438575a.

Medicines Sans Frontieres. "Guinea: Ebola Epidemic Declared, MSF Launches Emergency Response." Médecins Sans Frontières (MSF) International. Accessed August 25, 2019. https://www.msf.org/guinea-ebola-epidemic-declared-msf-launches-emergency-response

Morse, S. S. "Global Infectious Disease Surveillance And Health Intelligence." *Health Affairs* 26, no. 4 (2007): 1069–1077. doi:10.1377/hlthaff.26.4.1069.

Newman, K. "Face of Defense: Soldiers to Support Operation United Assistance." U.S. Department of Defense, October 17, 2014. https://www.defense.gov/Explore/News/Article/Article/603473/face-of-defense-soldiers-to-support-operation-united-assistance/

Peterson, W. *Outbreak*. Warner Brothers, Burbank, 1995.

Preston, R. *The Hot Zone: The Chilling True Story of an Ebola Outbreak*. Random House, New York, 2012.

Richards, P. *Ebola: How a People's Science Helped End an Epidemic*. London: Zed Books Ltd., 2016.

Samb, S. "Ebola Kills Dozens in Guinea, May Have Spread to Sierra Leone | HuffPost." Accessed August 25, 2019. https://www.huffpost.com/entry/ebola-guinea_n_5014500

Shaban-Nejad, A., M. Michalowski, and D. L. Buckeridge. "Health Intelligence: How Artificial Intelligence Transforms Population and Personalized Health." *Npj Digital Medicine* 1, no. 1 (October 2, 2018): 1–2. doi:10.1038/s41746-018-0058-9.

United States Embassy, Conakry. 2014. "Conakry: CDC Director Frieden Visit." Communique. Conakry, Guinea, September 4.

United States Embassy, Conakry. 2014. "CONAKRY: Scenesetter for PDAS Jackson, from Alex Laskaris." Communique. Conakry, Guinea, June 13.

United States Embassy, Conakry. 2014. "Ebola in Guinea; Managing a Disease Is Easier than Managing Dread." Communique. Conakry, Guinea, April 8.

United States Embassy, Conakry. 2014. "Guinea: Disaster Declaration for Ebola Virus Disease (EVD)." Communique. Conakry, Guinea, August 15.

United States Embassy, Conakry. 2014. "Guinea EAC on Ebola, April 4." Communique. Conakry, Guinea, April 1.

United States Embassy, Conakry. 2014. "Guinea: Ebola Update as of June 18." Communique. Conakry, Guinea, June 20.

United States Embassy, Conakry. 2014. "Guinea: Ebola Virus Disease (EVD) Situation Update." Communique. Conakry, Guinea, August 19.

United States Embassy, Conakry. 2014. "Guinea: March 22 EAC on Ebola Epidemic." Communique. Conakry, Guinea, March 24.

United States Embassy, Conakry. 2014. "Guinean Government, Embassy Push Back on Disruptions of Air Service, but Transportation Links Still Jeopardized." Communique. Conakry, Guinea, August 28.

United States Embassy, Conakry. 2014. "Guinea's Political & Economic Summary Report: April 1-13, 2014." Communique. Conakry, Guinea, April 30.

United States Embassy, Conakry. 2014. "Guinea's Political Summary Report: April 14 to May 10, 2014." Communique. Conakry, Guinea, May 16

United States Embassy, Conakry. 2014. "Guinea's Political Summary Report: June 21 to July 11, 2014." Communique. Conakry, Guinea, July 22

United States Embassy, Conakry. 2014. "Guinea's Political Summary Report: May 11 to June 9, 2014." Communique. Conakry, Guinea, June 11.

United States Embassy, Conakry. 2014. "West African Ebola Outbreak: Fighting the Virus on the Ground, despite Confusion and Mistrust." Communique. Conakry, Guinea, July 16.

Watch, H. R. 2014. "World Report 2014: Rights Trends in World Report 2014: Guinea." Human Rights Watch, January 8. https://www.hrw.org/world-report/2014/country-chapters/guinea

Weir, L., and E. Mykhalovskiy. *Global Public Health Vigilance: Creating a World on Alert*. Routledge, New York, 2010.

World Health Organization. "Ebola Haemorrhagic Fever in Sudan, 1976." *Bulletin of the World Health Organization* 56, no. 2 (1978): 247–270.

World Health Organization. *WHO Recommended Guidelines for Epidemic Preparedness and Response: Ebola Haemorrhagic Fever (EHF)*. Geneva: World Health Organization, 1997.

World Health Organization. "Ebola Virus Disease." Accessed August 25, 2019. https://www.who.int/news-room/fact-sheets/detail/ebola-virus-disease

World Health Organization. "WHO | Public Health Surveillance." WHO. Accessed August 25, 2019. http://www.who.int/topics/public_health_surveillance/en/

Zhang, L., and H. Wang "Forty Years of the War against Ebola." *Journal of Zhejiang University. Science. B* 15, no. 9 (September 2014): 761–765. doi:10.1631/jzus.B1400222.

The use of HUMINT in epidemics: a practical assessment

Rose Bernard and Richard Sullivan

ABSTRACT

In this article we explore the potential applications for Human Intelligence (HUMINT) operations in Public Health Emergencies of International Concern (PHEICs) and epidemics. We examine the complex circumstances surrounding outbreaks and how these require the synthesis and analysis of new sources of information and intelligence. We explore the benefits from these tactics by examining intelligence gaps and their consequences during the initial stages of the Ebola outbreak of 2014–2016. Finally, we look at what parameters and circumstances would be needed for the application of HUMINT operations in PHEICs and attempt to understand some of the constraints to its use.

Introduction

The securitisation of health and the blurring of boundaries between national security and infectious diseases is a trend which has been discussed since the early 1990 s, and which has increasingly framed discussions around global health in the past ten years. In these discussions the narrative has ranged widely, from the threat of biological weapons to the erosion of the concept of 'security at the border' by international air travel.[1] This shift has had a significant impact on the way that security is practiced both at a policy level, where contemporary geopolitics is now increasingly considering matters of national and transnational health and where public health and medical experts are increasingly involved in health security policy, as well as the practical, which has involved government intervention in the production of vaccines and medical trade policy.[2]

This securitisation of health reached its most obvious manifestation in the deployment of armed forces to assist Guinea, Sierra Leone, and Liberia following the designation of the ongoing Ebola Virus Diseases (EVD) outbreak as a Public Health Emergency of International Concern (PHEIC) by the World Health Organisation (WHO) on 17 July 2014. On 3 September 2014 Médecins Sans Frontières (MSF) called for the deployment of government civilian and military assets, and so the United States and the United Kingdom deployed in total 3,750 troops to Liberia (US – Operation United Assistance), and Sierra Leone (UK – Operation Gritrock). Other countries also deployed military forces – in October 2014 China deployed a unit of the People's Liberation Army (PLA) alongside 480 medical staff. The UK and the US military deployments, in addition to being the biggest, contained the highest proportion of combat troops – who are often inexperienced in managing populations and insecurity in complex, high risk disease outbreaks – to medical staff.[3]

Rather than being framed as a new phenomenon, the deployment of the military within the context of PHEICs should be framed as part of the trend of growing military involvement in complex humanitarian emergencies (CHEs). However, just as the military had to adapt to stability operations and CHEs, epidemics and PHEICs have their own specific operating environments and requirements. These include, broadly, the nature of military involvement: in CHEs, or in events involving natural disasters, the military's role is often obvious and visible and can be connected to the provision of logistics and services such as the provision of basic infrastructure and the provision of logistics services for NGOs. Involvement in the extraction of individuals following a natural disaster and the provision of logistics for rescue services are similarly relatively logical and normative: vulnerable populations are in visible and obvious danger from events outside their control (floods, fires, situations involving lost power) and the military can remove them from that situation. However, in the case of epidemics this focus changes from infrastructure to individuals, where the threat is less obvious to the outsider: in epidemics the military might deal with contact tracing, identifying the sick, gathering data, providing medical treatment to a population which may not want it or who may perceive it not to be medical treatment at all, and a potential involvement with containment measures. This means the military must move beyond the traditional logistical roles of command, control, communication (C3), to command, control, communication and intelligence (C3I) roles. Any group deployed during a PHEIC, whether military or civilian, must also confront the factors which could hinder or assist the ability to contain the outbreak: specific cultural or social practices, population movement, and population attitudes towards foreigners and security forces.

As the military began to deploy in West Africa during the Ebola PHEIC the parameters of their involvement became a consistent area of conflict. When MSF called for the deployment of military troops it set out specific areas of military involvement to exclude quarantine, crowd control, and containment, and to only include clinical care/patient management and logistics.[4] However, when combined with conditions placed by the government on deployment, which focused on force protection and largely prohibited direct contact or involvement with patient management these conditions hampered the military's ability to take effective action.[5]

More broadly high-risk infectious disease outbreaks have become more complicated in information poor, non-permissive conflict ecosystems. This creates significant intelligence gaps and a tendency to rely on stand-off sources from open source (OSINT), geospatial intelligence (GEOINT) and signals intelligence to epidemiological modelling. However, the human ecosystem is increasingly the crucial determinant of disease risk and intervention success in complex outbreaks.[6] This requires a wide HUMINT perspective that encompasses anthropology, other social sciences, psychology, economics, history, and political sciences.

In this article we therefore consider an area of traditionally military capability which has been widely ignored during PHEICs but which nevertheless is largely used to fill in the intelligence gaps that NGOs now face: human intelligence (HUMINT). We look at what these capabilities include, how they have been used in other humanitarian-military deployments such as CHEs, and how they could be used in PHEICs when the full deployment of military troops may be neither available nor appropriate. Specifically, we examine the March-August 2014 period of the EVD outbreak, where all involved parties missed an opportunity to control the outbreak, and how the application of HUMINT during this period could have assisted in creating a greater understanding of the potential course of the outbreak and might have helped increase preparation for the coming epidemic.

HUMINT and common misconceptions

HUMINT is 'any information that can be gathered from human sources', whether gathered overtly or covertly and which can include a variety of sources, from the stereotypical covert human intelligence source (CHIS), to overt contacts with foreign governments and travellers in-country.[7] There is significant opposition by NGOs and humanitarian organisations to using intelligence collection methods in humanitarian operations in general,[8] but HUMINT, along with its partner intelligence collection capability SIGINT, appears to provoke particularly strong reactions: as Par Eriksson points out these are often due to emotional reactions – 'That a faction would accept a UN reconnaissance patrol consisting of special forces with blackened forces is hard to believe, but it would be less upset by the use of unmanned reconnaissance aircraft (UAV) even though such a device probably is able to collect more intelligence than the patrol'.[9] The reactions to the use of HUMINT and SIGINT can be contrasted against the use of OSINT and GEOINT, and the adoption of crowdsourced geospatial intelligence by NGOs post natural disasters.[10]

The adverse reactions to HUMINT are likely due to misunderstandings of HUMINT as a covert surveillance or 'undercover operation' capability. In fact, while all HUMINT operations conducted by intelligence, military, or law enforcement do entail the same operational structure and intelligence cycle, it can in many cases be more analogous to synchronised anthropology, with an emphasis on open source rather than clandestine collection and anthropological problems such as local economies, social cooperation, and mapping people and population movements.[11] Although they don't necessarily call it HUMINT, the discipline of HUMINT is practiced by many NGOs and civilian organisation who speak to individuals in a crisis to gain a better understanding of the context and issues. It is practiced by journalists, and by doctors treating patients in outbreak-affected areas seeking to get a better idea of the spread of a disease.

For any relief operation to be successful, real time intelligence which can provide intelligence on areas of conflict, logistics routes for relief workers, attitudes to healthcare or relief workers, practical understanding on the local capabilities of hospitals, and potentially the origins of any attack or disaster is invaluable.[12] To this end, HUMINT has received particular priority in stability missions.[13] Relationships with local civilians and the local military and civilian officials can identify the shifts in attitudes towards military and relief workers, as well as identifying solid piece of intelligence such as location.[14] It is worth noting that all these can be obtained overtly, and without the use of CHIS, from strong relations with people on the ground, formal and informal debriefings of affected individuals, and working with local officials

HUMINT and its application to PHEICs

What, therefore, can HUMINT provide in the particular context of PHEICs? From examining non-covert or intrusive HUMINT capabilities, we assess that the intelligence requirements which can be answered through the use of HUMINT capabilities in a PHEIC are contract tracing; population movement, and the location of vulnerable populations; socio-cultural practices which could affect the spread of diseases; attitudes towards medical interventions; attitudes towards governments and NGO interference; and, clarification of attribution. the following intelligence requirements can be answered through the use of HUMINT.

The practical advantages of these can be seen by examining the period of March-August 2014, during the first stage of the EVD outbreak, where although the first cases of EVD were identified in March 2014 by the MSF, with the first case likely occurring in December 2013, by May the outbreak was generally assumed to be over. This decline in reported cases believed to be due to the outbreak burning itself out, in line with previous EVD occurrences.[15] However, in August, reported cases increased again, overwhelming the fragile health services and creating circumstances where medical and public health interventions were no longer sufficient to control the epidemic. The EVD PHEIC of 2014–2016 is now believed to be an exceptional case due to a combination of political, social, cultural and physical factors.

The location of the initial outbreak and the population resident within that location: the first infections occurred at the borders of three countries with a single ethnically and linguistically homogenous population – the Kissi – who moved unrestricted across so-called common borders by road and river.

The location of the initial outbreak also occurred in an area where traditional and routine practices, such as the laying on of hands and washing of the sick, the dying, and the dead, contributed to the rate of infection (Ebola is considered to be at its most infectious in the immediate period after the death of the host).

The initial reports of symptoms were similar to other diseases endemic to the area, leading to the misdiagnosis of a number of cases and early disagreements on the spread of the epidemic.

There was limited access to basic care facilities, and few health care workers (HCWs) had access to appropriate safety equipment or appropriate training, meaning that a high percentage of HCWs fell ill, further decreasing the health care infrastructure.

There was a significant mistrust of governments and foreigners – Guinea had undergone a period of political coups, and both Liberia and Sierra Leone were emerging from a series of prolonged civil wars – and so HCWs found it difficult to provide healthcare interventions and there was a significant mistrust of the ETUs set up at the time.

The failure to provision or prepare an adequate response to these circumstances was largely a failure of information and intelligence – both the ability to share the information between responders and the ability to collect it, analyze it and disseminate those findings in a timely manner. These HUMINT intelligence failures were fivefold.

There was no initial contextual reporting on socio-cultural factors affecting the infection rate

Early responders to the crisis were unaware or insufficiently briefed on the particular cultural context of the event, both in terms of cultural funereal practices which spread the infection, and the political context and hostility to government workers. This incomplete assessment of the operational environment prevented adequate modelling of the severity of the outbreak, and also inhibited later deployments of responders, both civilian and military.[16]

Collection of case numbers

despite reports of a sharp decline in cases, infections increased during August. While a decline in case numbers is commensurate with previous Ebola outbreaks, previous response efforts also indicated that case numbers in fact typically increase in August, something which an intelligence overview should have highlighted. Furthermore, in the case of the 2014–2016 EVD outbreak, it now appears more likely that the decline in cases was the result of a decline in reported cases, as HCWs were chased out of towns and villages, and the rumour that Ebola Treatment Units (ETUs) were where people went to die began to spread, discouraging people from reporting to them. As ETU and HCW statistics were one of the main sources of infection numbers, this artificially created a drop in case numbers. Given the bias of previous outbreaks and the lack of socio-cultural assessment this drop was assumed to be correct.[17]

Disease modelling was limited

Original modelling in Operation United Assistance didn't account for social practices that increased exposure to and affected the rate of the transmission of the disease, or the regular movement of people across unregulated borders between Guinea, Liberia, and Sierra Leone (Joint and Coalition Operational Analysis, 2016). Researchers attempting to model the transmission of the disease also lacked the contextual data which could have assisted in identifying the geographical spread, such as the regular routes and destinations of people moving in infectious borders, maps of human mobility, and data on human population distributions.[18]

Information wasn't shared across borders

In March 2014 a team drafted by the WHO and conducting their own HUMINT investigation although without referring to it as such, interviewed health officials and family members in Guinea on the border with Sierra Leone. One of the results of this report was the identification that individuals had been exhibiting Ebola-like symptoms for months. The investigators also found evidence of cases in Sierra Leone; however, this wasn't reported to the Sierra Leone offices, and Sierra Leone reported no official cases until May 2014, by which time it was too late to contain. This unreported outbreak was likely responsible for the speed with which Ebola spread in Sierra Leone and for the second wave of cases in Liberia.[19]

There was little communication between responders at the outset

During the initial outbreak there were a number of rumours regarding the potential mutation of the virus prevalent among first responders. These rumours, which occurred before a sample had been obtained and analysed, suggested that a mutation of the virus had caused a change in its basic reproduction number, leading to fear and confusion in the initial response. Additionally, lessons from previous epidemics were not communicated: population movements had been a known issue in tracking earlier Ebola epidemics, but this was not incorporated into strategic planning at the outset of the 2014 outbreak.[20]

While these issues are easy to detect and identify with hindsight, they demonstrate that all modelling and disease tracking could have been assisted by a standardised ethnographic and anthropological assessment which would typically be based on HUMINT. An assessment of the social and cultural context could have identified healthcare and burial practices, as well as population movements over common borders and identifying potential cases. Local healthcare workers could have been asked about the healthcare capabilities and the most necessary equipment suited to the immediate context. Similarly, interviews with individuals could have identified attitudes towards the ETUs, and potentially identified any false drop in cases. Furthermore, proactive assessments capturing lessons 'learned' from prior epidemic responses in these particular contexts are also critical, as they can be used to identify intelligence gaps or pre-existing problems with data collection and assessment.

A PHEIC-specific HUMINT framework

Understanding these intelligence failures and the importance of an all-source intelligence analysis in the case of a suspected epidemic means we must consider how this would practically manifest. The intelligence cycle – direction, collection, processing, analysis, and dissemination – is crucial during any operation and in any process where intelligence is useful, and a standardised framework would be needed as part of any HUMINT operation. Although NGOs may currently use HUMINT – whatever they call it – by not treating these investigations as traditional HUMINT operations, they are missing the structure of the intelligence cycle, which is necessary for all intelligence creation and sharing in whatever format.

First, direction. In order to prevent NGO fears that military or intelligence organisations may overstep their boundaries and use the intelligence collected for their own purposes, intelligence requirements must be set to focus the investigation. Additionally, this would include all factors which could affect the cycle of an epidemic and which could prevent the lack of basic anthropological information available in the early stages of any outbreak. Traditional peacekeeping operations have three typical intelligence requirements: the ethnic situation, the socio-economic situation, and the attitudes of local leaders and civilians.[21] In the case of an epidemic these could easily be both broadened out and focused: the ethnic situation "*including or specifically addressing cultural practices which could affect the spread of disease*; the ethnic situation *including specific movements of populations and geographical routes which could affect the spread of disease*; the socio-economic situation *including the state of the healthcare system, and attitudes towards health care workers and state interventions*; the attitude of local leaders and civilians *to both foreign health care workers and NGOS as well as any potential containment methods; the length of the current outbreak; and the number of non-officially identified cases* (cited from Eriksson, Intelligence in Peacekeeping Operations)" . These could ideally be integrated with more specific quantitative epidemic intelligence requirements: the identification of the pathogen, case numbers, alignment with previous epidemic or outbreak spread, and transmission paths. This could provide the combination of both disease specific and context specific factors.

The second phase of the intelligence cycle is the collection of the information needed to answer the intelligence requirements. It is worth noting that none of the interventions or assessments necessitate the involvement of military personnel. In fact, NGO and HCW relationships with the local community often make them the best sources of information: the perceived neutrality of NGOs mean they have access to locations where foreign military assets do not, and people are often inclined to have more trust in a recognised NGO than in a military. However, for the processing and analysis phase, it is likely that trained analysts will be needed: HUMINT often generates a huge amount of material, and analysts trained in the synthesis of information and intelligence from a variety of sources would provide a much more integrated platform as well as taking pressure of the likely already stretched resources of NGOs. The effective deployment of a structured framework could also mitigate against the deployment of a full military operation, which could be ineffective, expensive, and hinder the response activities of any NGOs present.

Finally, dissemination is an area where military and intelligence framework is likely to assist NGOs. As demonstrated in the early months of the Ebola outbreak, the inability to share intelligence on things like case spread can lead to catastrophic results. Dissemination to relevant parties is built into the intelligence cycle and cannot be missed out; it is also likely that the military may have methods of communication which other countries or organisations which may not be available to NGOs.

All this is not to say that NGOs have not been, or do not conduct intelligence operations and successfully gather actionable intelligence which is then used to the benefit of all. However, the integration of the intelligence cycle, and the systematic way in which one phase follows the next, would allow the procedure to become much smoother. If such a practice were implemented whenever an outbreak was suspected, then it is highly likely that such intelligence failures could be avoided or mitigated against.

The other main barrier to this practice is the cultural and political differences between NGOs and military organisations, both of which groups have very reasonable motives for mistrusting the other. Much has been written on this division.[22] Ideally, these concerns would be allayed at the direction stage of the cycle, where parameters can be set out by all organisations for methods used to collect information, the type of information which can and cannot be collected, and who the final intelligence and analysis should be disseminated to.

Finally, there are legal questions to be considered. The legal barriers for the use of intelligence assets in outbreaks have been discussed, and are constrained by the differing paradigms of health security and national security.[23] In order to deploy any intelligence assets, even those simply used for analysis, a legal framework would have to be set in place, including guidelines for resource deployment and considering the questions of proportionality and necessity – the conditions which all intelligence operations are considered or legislated for, for example, under the Regulation of Investigatory Powers Act in the UK.[24] Is the operation planned proportionate to the threat, and is it necessary – are there actionable gains to be made which could not be provided by other means? Ultimately, these questions would have to be considered by both NGOs and the military in any deployment or collaboration.

Conclusion

Although not all of these questions can be answered in a single article, we have discussed here the utility of an actionable framework for the use of HUMINT in operations, and demonstrated how bringing an operational structure to the use of investigation done by HCWs in a suspected outbreak could mitigate against a situation where an outbreak is missed or its impact is underestimated. Deploying a standardised set of intelligence requirements to include both social and cultural landscape questions, and analysing these in conjunction with epidemic factors within an outbreak would provide a much clearer picture of the potential impact. Using all source analysts accustomed to combining this information would take resource from strained NGOs and provide a professionalised cycle which could include ensuring that any reports are correctly disseminated to all necessary parties, including those across borders. In order for such a framework to be successful, NGOs and military resources would need to consider their mutual relationships, and legal and operational parameters would need to be put in place. Nevertheless, the use of a standardised assessment could significantly improve the management of future outbreaks.

Notes

1. Elbe, *Security and Global Health*, 50.
2. Elbe and Nakray, "Security and Global Health," 1.
3. Rajagopalan, "China to send elite army unit."
4. Benton, "Whose Security?," 25–50.
5. Joint and Coalition Operational Analysis, "Operation United Assistance."
6. Nguyen, "An Epidemic of Suspicion," 1298–9.
7. CIA, hxxps://www.cia[.]gov/news-information/featured-story-archive/2010-featured story-archive/intelligence-human intelligence[.]html.
8. See, for example Abilova and Novosseloff, "Demystifying Intelligence in UN Peace Operations"; and Dorn et al., *Intelligence in peacekeeping.*
9. Eriksson, "Intelligence in Peacekeeping Operations," 1–18.
10. See, for example, Zook et al., "Volunteered Geographic Information and Crowdsourcing Disaster Relief," 6–32.
11. Albro, *Implications of the uses of Ethnography.*
12. Sundnes, "Civilian-Military Cooperation," 27–28.
13. Cline, "Operational Intelligence in Peace Enforcement," 179–94.
14. See note 9 above.
15. Henwood, "Ebola in West Africa," 15–29.
16. Joint and Coalition Operational Analysis, *Operation United assistance.*
17. Sack et al., "How Ebola Roared Back."
18. Althaus, "Modeling the Ebola Epidemic," 47–60.
19. See note 17 above.
20. Coltart et al., "The Ebola Outbreak, 2013–2016," 372.
21. See note 9 above.
22. See, for example Aall, "NGOs, Conflict Management and Peacekeeping," 121–41; Abiew, "NGO-Military Relations in Peace Operations," 24–39; and Harris and Dombrowski, "Military Collaboration with Humanitarian Organizations in Complex Emergencies," 155–78.
23. Bernard et al., "Intelligence and Global Health," 509–14.
24. Legislation[.]gov.uk, "Regulation of Investigatory Powers Act 2000."

Disclosure statement

No potential conflict of interest was reported by the authors.

Funding

This publication is funded through the UK Research and Innovation GCRF RESEARCH FOR HEALTH IN CONFLICT (R4HC-MENA); developing capability, partnerships and research in the Middle and Near East (MENA) ES/P010962/1.

ORCID

Rose Bernard http://orcid.org/0000-0003-2395-5371
Richard Sullivan http://orcid.org/0000-0002-6435-1825

Bibliography

Aall, P. "NGOs, Conflict Management and Peacekeeping." *International Peacekeeping* 7, no. 1 (2000): 121–141. Informa UK Limited. doi:10.1080/13533310008413822.

Abiew, F. "NGO-Military Relations In Peace Operations." *International Peacekeeping* 10, no. 1 (2003): 24–39. Informa UK Limited. doi:10.1080/714002394.

Abilova, O., and A. Novosseloff. 2016. "Demystifying Intelligence In UN Peace Operations: Toward An Organizational Doctrine." International Peace Institute. https://www.ipinst.org/wp-content/uploads/2016/07/1608_Demystifying-Intelligence.pdf

Albro, R. 2010. "Implications Of The Uses Of Ethnography In DOD Contexts." *Presentation American University,* Washington, USA.

Althaus, C. "Modeling The Ebola Epidemic: Challenges And Lessons For The Future." In *Ebola's Message: Public Health And Medicine In The Twenty-First Century*, edited by N. Evans, T. Smith, and M. Majumder, 47–60. Cambridge: The MIT Press, 2016.

Anon. 2019. "Welcome To The CIA Web Site — Central Intelligence Agency." *Cia.Gov*. https://www.cia.gov/index.html

Anon. 2019. "Regulation Of Investigatory Powers Act 2000." *Legislation.Gov.Uk*. http://www.legislation.gov.uk/ukpga/2000/23/contents

Benton, A. "Whose Security? Militarization And Securitization During West Africa's Ebola Outbreak." In *The Politics Of Fear: Médecins Sans Frontières And The West African Ebola Edpidemic*, edited by M. Hofman and S. Au, 25–50. Oxford: Oxford University Press, 2017.

Bernard, R., G. Bowsher, C. Milner, P. Boyle, P. Patel, and R. Sullivan. "Intelligence And Global Health: Assessing The Role Of Open Source And Social Media Intelligence Analysis In Infectious Disease Outbreaks." *Journal Of Public Health* 26, no. 5 (2018): 509–514. Springer Nature. doi:10.1007/s10389-018-0899-3.

Cline, L. "Operational Intelligence In Peace Enforcement And Stability Operations." *International Journal Of Intelligence And Counterintelligence* 15, no. 2 (2002): 179–194. Informa UK Limited. doi:10.1080/08850600252869010.

Coltart, C., B. Lindsey, I. Ghinai, A. Johnson, and D. Heymann. "The Ebola Outbreak, 2013–2016: Old Lessons For New Epidemics." *Philosophical Transactions Of The Royal Society B: Biological Sciences* 372, no. 1721 (2017): 20160297. The Royal Society. doi:10.1098/rstb.2016.0297.

Dorn, A., D. Charters, A. Dorn, and D. Charters. *Intelligence In Peacekeeping*. Clementsport, NS: Canadian Peacekeeping Press, 1999.

Elbe, S. *Security And Global Health*. Cambridge: Polity, 2010.

Elbe, S., and K. Nakray. "Security And Global Health." *Sociological Research Online* 16, no. 3 (2011): 1. SAGE Publications. doi:10.1177/136078041101600303.

Eriksson, P. "Intelligence In Peacekeeping Operations." *International Journal Of Intelligence And Counterintelligence* 10, no. 1 (1997): 1–18. Informa UK Limited. doi:10.1080/08850609708435331.

Harris, A., and P. Dombrowski. "Military Collaboration With Humanitarian Organizations In Complex Emergencies." *Global Governance: A Review Of Multilateralism And International Organizations* 8, no. 2 (2002): 155–178. Brill. doi:10.1163/19426720-00802005.

Henwood, P. "Ebola In West Africa: From The Frontline." In *Ebola's Message: Public Health And Medicine In The Twenty-First Century*, edited by N. Evans, T. Smith, M. Majumder, S. Goldstein, and P. Henwood, 15–29. Cambridge: The MIT Press, 2016.

Joint and Coalition Operational Analysis. *Operation United Assistance: The DOD Response To Ebola In West Africa*. Virginia: JCOA, 2016.

Natsios, A. "Ngos And The UN System In Complex Humanitarian Emergencies: Conflict Or Cooperation?" *Third World Quarterly* 16, no. 3 (1995): 405–420. Informa UK Limited. doi:10.1080/01436599550035979.

Nguyen, V. "An Epidemic Of Suspicion — Ebola And Violence In The DRC." *New England Journal Of Medicine* 380, no. 14 (2019): 1298–1299. Massachusetts Medical Society. doi:10.1056/NEJMp1902682.

Rajagopalan, M. 2014. "China To Send Elite Army Unit To Help Fight Ebola In Liberia." *Reuters*. https://www.reuters.com/article/us-health-ebola-china/china-to-send-elite-army-unit-to-help-fight-ebola-in-liberia-idUSKBN0IK0N020141031

Sack, K., S. Fink, P. Belluck, and A. Nossiter. 2014. "How Ebola Roared Back." *New York Times*. https://www.nytimes.com/2014/12/30/health/how-ebola-roared-back.html

Sundnes, K. "Civilian-Military Cooperation And The Use Of Military Assets In Disaster And Humanitarian Relief Operations." *Prehospital And Disaster Medicine* 18, no. S1 (2003): S27–S28. Cambridge University Press (CUP). doi:10.1017/S1049023X00058179.

Zook, M., M. Graham, T. Shelton, and S. Gorman. "Volunteered Geographic Information And Crowdsourcing Disaster Relief: A Case Study Of The Haitian Earthquake." *World Medical & Health Policy* 2, no. 2 (2010): 6–32. Wiley. doi:10.2202/1948-4682.1069.

Influenza pandemic warning signals: Philadelphia in 1918 and 1977–1978

James M. Wilson, Garrett M. Scalaro and Jodie A. Powell

ABSTRACT

Global public health has struggled to provide timely warning of influenza pandemics. In this study, we review the signal pattern of local media reporting associated with the 1918 type A/H1N1 influenza pandemic and subsequent return of the A/H1N1 virus in 1977 and 1978 in Philadelphia. Open source local media reports are a critical source of warning intelligence for influenza pandemics. Documentation and analysis of pandemic influenza signal patterns is essential to capture lessons in effective warning intelligence for health security.

Introduction

A future 1918-like influenza pandemic represents a top global health security threat. The 1918 pandemic, which began in the final months of World War I, was associated with a novel type A/H1N1 influenza virus that emerged and spread globally without prior access to effective pharmaceutical countermeasures or a robust public health infrastructure. The virus is estimated to have killed 100 million worldwide.[1] In the United States, as many as 675,000 were killed, which was nearly six times the American casualties in World War I.[2] Recent popularized historical accounts emphasized tremendous acute socio-economic disruption and tragedy as community healthcare infrastructures were overwhelmed and some families lost multiple loved ones. In urban areas, reports of mortuaries overflowing with bodies due to lack of burial capacity astound us today just past the 100-year anniversary of the pandemic.[3]

From the perspective of the United States, the pandemic arrived in August 1918 in the context of the then-record breaking 1.5 million soldiers deploying to the warfront in Europe by oceanic ships.[4] These ships ferried soldiers to Europe and the military crews then returned, providing plenty of opportunity to bring the virus back to the United States. Returning infected soldiers sparked outbreaks in military camps outside of Boston and Philadelphia, followed by large epidemics in those cities and other northeastern cities with subsequent spread westward across the country.

Philadelphia, along with Boston and New York, was one of the first entry points to the United States of novel influenza type A/H1N1 virus in 1918, referred to as 'the Spanish flu'. The pandemic was recognized as a threat to the city beginning in July 1918 as the city's media coverage was primarily focused on World War I overseas in Europe.[5] The outbreak at Camp Dix, approximately 40 miles from Philadelphia, was sudden. Military physicians and nurses at the camp were abruptly overwhelmed with cases and caught by surprise with the intensity. City officials, underestimating the level of threat the pandemic represented, encouraged personal hygiene and disinfection but no social distancing measures. Cases were first publicly recognized in the city of Philadelphia in mid-September, with officials declaring they believed there were 75,000 estimated cases and 136 deaths. On October 4th, after inundation of the city with the disease, social distancing countermeasures were ordered by local officials.[6] Mortality across the city peaked the week of October 19th, and nearly all sectors of the city were effected with worker absenteeism.[7] The healthcare infrastructure was completely overwhelmed due to a combination of patient demand and infection of the healthcare workers themselves. Demand then cascaded to mortuary services, overwhelming them as well. At this point in US history, influenza was not a mandated reportable disease to public health officials, and there were no vaccines, antivirals, or antibiotics to mitigate impact.[8]

Public health officials and physicians noted unusual disease patterns, where young, previously healthy adults were predominantly effected. This was unusual because typical severe seasonal influenza illness affects infants and the elderly.[9] While the majority of patients exhibited self-limited illness lasting approximately 3 days, a minority developed secondary bacterial pneumonia and died in 7 to 10 days.[10] There continues to be academic debate whether this pandemic influenza virus itself was the cause of death or the secondary bacterial pneumonia.[11]

Due to the high percentage of population exposure to the virus, significant absenteeism rates were documented abruptly across multiple sectors of local, state, and national government and industry. The geotemporal intensity of disease transmission resulted in abrupt, unexpected socio-economic disruption that distracted national leadership from its priority at the time: the prosecution of World War I.[12]

The pandemic A/H1N1 influenza virus remained in global circulation until the next global pandemic involving type A/H2N2 in 1957. After the 1957 pandemic, A/H1N1 was displaced in circulation by A/H2N2 which was in turn displaced by the 1968 A/H3N2 pandemic influenza virus.[13] In December 1977, public health officials in the Soviet Union communicated to the United States they had isolated A/H1N1 after a twenty-year global absence. The virus was believed to be genetically similar to virus isolates that were in circulation prior to the 1957 pandemic, which raised questions about how this older virus was re-introduced to the world. In a rare example of diplomacy during the Cold War, the Soviet Union provided samples of the virus to the United States, which were submitted for vaccine production in late December 1977.[14] By this point, the virus was reported across 60 cities in the Soviet Union and Hong Kong, causing significant socio-economic disruption. Officials at the U.S. Centers for Disease Control (CDC) expressed concern and uncertainty regarding the potential impact of this reintroduced 1918 pandemic strain and publicly acknowledged the nation was unprepared due to the inherent delay to produce and distribute a vaccine in time.[15] This concern was validated a month later upon the arrival of A/USSR/90/77 in Cheyenne, Wyoming in January 1978.[16] Airmen who were stationed in England during A/H1N1's arrival there were believed to be infected and the subsequent source of introduction to Wyoming.[17]

Type A/H3N2 virus was in national circulation at the time and was not fully displaced by the reintroduced A/H1N1 that had effected the Soviet Union. This was surprising to CDC officials who had expected abrupt dominance of A/H1N1. This expectation was based on the observation that the 1957 pandemic strain of A/H2N2 had fully displaced A/H1N1 from global circulation, and the 1968 pandemic strain of A/H3N2 in turn displaced A/H2N2.[18] The A/H1N1 virus had, by January, advanced to Great Britain, Scandinavia, Taiwan, Singapore, Malaysia, and Japan.[19] As noted in the Soviet Union, young adults were the most effected, which was an epidemiological feature of the 1918 pandemic as well. Despite this epidemiological similarity with the 1918 pandemic, mortality not as high as observed in 1918. Mortality was the highest since the 1968 A/H3N2 pandemic, which was itself the mildest pandemic compared to those in 1918 and 1957.[20]

Philadelphia was aware of national media reports announcing the return of A/H1N1 virus in the Soviet Union after twenty years of absence in December 1977, followed by its arrival in the US (Wyoming) one month later in January.[21] High absenteeism was reported among high school and college students, with visiting hour restrictions at some of the nearby hospitals in New Jersey.[22] The city of Philadelphia did not feel the need to order school closures or other social distancing measures. The scale of socio-economic disruption was mild and not comparable to that observed during the 1918 pandemic.

Seven months after the Soviets recognized the virus in their country and six months after A/H1N1 was verified in Wyoming, the World Health Organization published concerns that the virus' reappearance was the result of a laboratory accident in China in May 1977.[23] This then placed the warning delay on the order of seven months before the first public warning in the United States. In 2015, an alternate theory was proposed: that the virus was accidentally reintroduced in the context of a live H1N1 vaccine clinical trial in China. The vaccine strain was not completely inactivated and therefore able to transmit across Asia.[24]

To date, global public health surveillance has struggled to provide timely warning for influenza pandemics. Open source media reports are a key source of warning intelligence for influenza pandemics.[25] Here we review the signal pattern of local media reporting associated with the 1918 influenza pandemic and subsequent return of the A/H1N1 virus in 1977 and 1978 in Philadelphia. This comparison enables review of an unprecedented signal of maximal impact (1918) with that of mildest impact (1977). These signal patterns are relevant to the modern challenges of global health security threat monitoring continues in the context of rapidly expanding social media and online media sources.

Materials and methods

A commercial online archival newspaper media provider, *Newspaper.com* was used for this study in conjunction with contemporary official reports.[26] Within *Newspaper.com*, we used the *Philadelphia Inquirer*, which had been present in Philadelphia as a leading newspaper since 1829 and was robustly represented in the *Newspaper.com* online digital archives. Keyword-based Boolean search functions were used within the archive, which used an optical character recognition algorithm. Other commercial online archival newspaper media providers were considered and provided similar results when keyword search queries were performed. One online newspaper archival provider was chosen to minimize potential variation between different queries.

To reproduce the warning signal timeline from the perspective of the Philadelphia reading public, days were numbered based on first publicly noted civilian cases within the city, beginning with Day 1. Negative day numbers were intended to highlight pre-event indicators of threat, and positive day numbers represent indicators of live crisis impact in the city. The events of 1918 and 1977–1978 were analyzed as separate case studies to enable comparison of the associated signal patterns.

Results

The 1918 influenza pandemic in Philadelphia

On 3 July 1918 (Day −78), the *Inquirer* reported German forces were experiencing significant impact on their force strength due to influenza, which was referred to three days later as a 'wildfire'.[27] On July 11th, the Kaiser and his family were reportedly infected, and the Kaiser was forced to retreat from the French front to recover.[28] On July 14th, impact on the civilian infrastructure in Germany was noted, where influenza was driving high patient demand in hospitals along with absenteeism significant enough to impact the industrial base.[29] The first article expressing concern that the epidemic might come to the United States was on July 22nd.[30] Five days later, there were reports that German industrial production had decreased by 50 per cent due to influenza.[31]

By August 11th, the crisis was now referred to as 'Spanish influenza', and the media made specific comparisons to the last pandemic of 1889- the 'Russian influenza'.[32] There was insinuation that the Germans somehow were responsible for starting the epidemic since it appeared to begin in Germany.[33] This was the start of a pattern of multiple articles blaming Germany that extended into September. At this point in history, the media did not use the term 'pandemic', but rather 'epidemic' to describe the crisis. There was no media report of preparedness activities occurring in Philadelphia in response to these reports, which was odd given their experience with the Russian influenza 29 years earlier.

On September 11th, a 'serious' outbreak of influenza was reported in Boston, which was believed to have started in late August.[34] There was no connection made between what Boston was seeing and the situation in Europe. This was followed six days later with report that the lead physician at Carney Hospital in South Boston died of influenza in the midst of tremendous patient demand. At this point, 'Spanish influenza' was reported in New York City.[35]

Camp Dix, which was located approximately 40 miles outside of Philadelphia, reported its first cases publicly on September 18th. All soldiers were ordered to gargle saltwater or tincture of iodine multiple times a day to prevent the epidemic from spreading as it had in Boston and other military camps.[36]

On September 19th (Day 1), the first civilian cases were reported among hospitals in Philadelphia.[37] Civilian and military officials were now collaborating to manage the apparent link between outbreaks in the military camps and spread to the civilian population. Civilian authorities had authorized the use of hospital beds in the city to assist with patient overflow from the military facilities. The day after the first 'few' cases were reported at Camp Dix, 1,500 cases were reported from the camp, along with several fatalities and initial indication of overwhelmed medical staff.[38] Local officials the same day declared, 'There was little fear that the disease would spread to any degree among citizens'. This was accompanied by a recommendation to cough or sneeze into handkerchiefs and to sterilize dining plates, cups, and utensils after use.[39] A US military officer was quoted as blaming German U-boats for deliberately introducing the epidemic to the US.[40]

On Day 2, medical officers at Camp Dix discounted the hypothesis that the epidemic was the result of a German bioweapon deployment. They also declared the outbreak was now under control in the encampment.[41] On Day 3, public health officials expressed concern they were unable to estimate the size of the epidemic in the city because influenza was not a reportable disease.[42] The next day was the first day of required influenza notifications from physicians to local health authorities. This was indicative of reactive disease surveillance, as influenza was not previously a reportable disease. Dr. A.A. Cairns, the chief medical officer of the Philadelphia Bureau of Health said, 'There is nothing alarming in the situation. I expect the disease will burn itself out in about two weeks. At least, that has been its history in other places.'[43]

Despite the optimism expressed by the military, Camp Dix was quarantined on Day 5.[44] Two days later, the camp sent an emergency request for assistance to the Red Cross in Philadelphia and New York.[45] On Days 7 and 8, civilian shipyards in Philadelphia responsible for building ships for the war effort reported significant absenteeism due to illness.[46] The military called a full halt nationwide to training new recruits on Day 8, which represented 142,000 men and threatened the United States' ability to support the war.[47]

The first official civilian case counts were reported on October 4th (Day 15), which was the result of mandated reporting on Day 3. Authorities estimated there were 75,000 cases and 189 fatalities. The Acting State Commissioner of Health ordered social distancing measures to be enacted immediately, which included the closure of all theaters, poolrooms, dance halls, and other places of public congregation for entertainment. He left the closure of churches and schools to local health authorities' discretion. Armories were ordered to be made available for hospital overload.[48] Philadelphia's authorities moved to order the closure of all schools and churches, as well as all Liberty Loan meetings. The Liberty Loan was a vital mechanism of supporting the war effort through financial contributions from citizens.[49] The police were ordered to enforce the new regulations, with no report of resistance. The same day, the public was asked to avoid unnecessary phone calls because 28 per cent of the telephone company's workforce was absent due to illness and could not keep up with the demand.[50]

October 5th was the start of a string of editorials and letters to the editor protesting 'fear-mongering' and the extreme social distancing measures ordered by authorities. On Day 19, the local medical association of physicians agreed with the concerns about overly aggressive official action they felt promoted the spread of fear.[51] Meanwhile, emergency calls for additional nursing staff from the Red Cross were published, fourth year medical students were called into service, and additional emergency ad hoc hospitals were created.[52]

On October 11th (Day 22), burial services were overwhelmed in the midst of thousands of fatalities. This prompted the mobilization of prisoners to assist with burying the dead. Nuns were called into service, and churches and schools were now used as auxiliary medical facilities. Hundreds of policemen were ill, and eighteen died.[53]

The epidemic was reported to be on the decline on October 14th (Day 25), where the lagging issue of burying the dead remained a challenge.[54] Two days later, this was reaffirmed.[55] Throughout the crisis, there were no indications of mass voluntary evacuations or civil unrest beyond the editorial exchanges protesting the social distancing measures ordered by authorities. On October 20th, there was a threat of possible martial law in Scranton, a town 125 miles from Philadelphia. This was because some liquor establishments kept their backdoors quietly open to serve the public.[56] In the waning days of the epidemic, there were more protests, culminating in an editorial praising the 'return to sanity' on October 29th (Day 40) as schools and churches were opened, followed the next day with the opening of public entertainment venues.[57]

The media reporting signal preceded official public health reporting. Newspaper mentions of 'influenza', 'pneumonia', or 'grippe' over time (Figure 1, blue line) preceded and mirrored the rise, peak, and fall of the forensically constructed mortality epidemic curve (orange line) that was not published until 1920.[58] The first week of recorded deaths was the week ending October 5th (Day 16) with 706 fatalities (Figure 1, orange line. The true beginning of mortality was not captured by the new reporting system. This conflicted with reports of less than 200 estimated fatalities reported by the Inquirer on October 4th, which likely reflected the challenges of ramping up surveillance during the crisis. Figure 2a displays the use of terminology over time, where the phrase 'Spanish influenza' (orange line) was unique and had not been used in prior seasons of influenza in Philadelphia. This

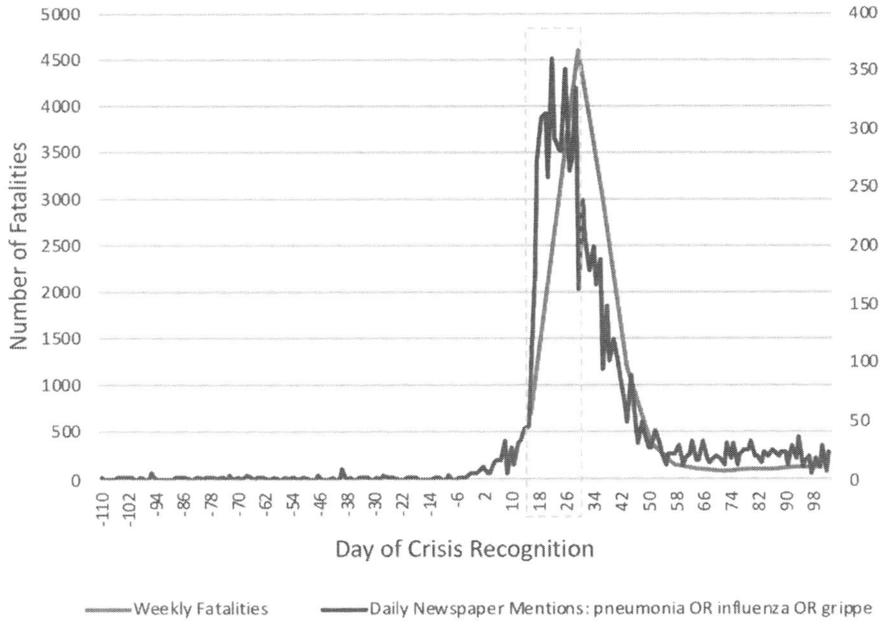

Figure 1. Weekly mortality due to pneumonia or influenza reported by public health officials versus local media reporting of the crisis in Philadelphia, 1918. Day 1 was September 19th, when the media reported civilian cases in the hospitals. The first week of public health-directed mortality reporting was the week ending October 5th (Day 16). This epidemic curve reflects the classic pattern of reactive surveillance undertaken when dealing with a previously unknown or non-notifiable disease. The dotted box indicates when social distancing measures were ordered by officials (Day 15 to 30).

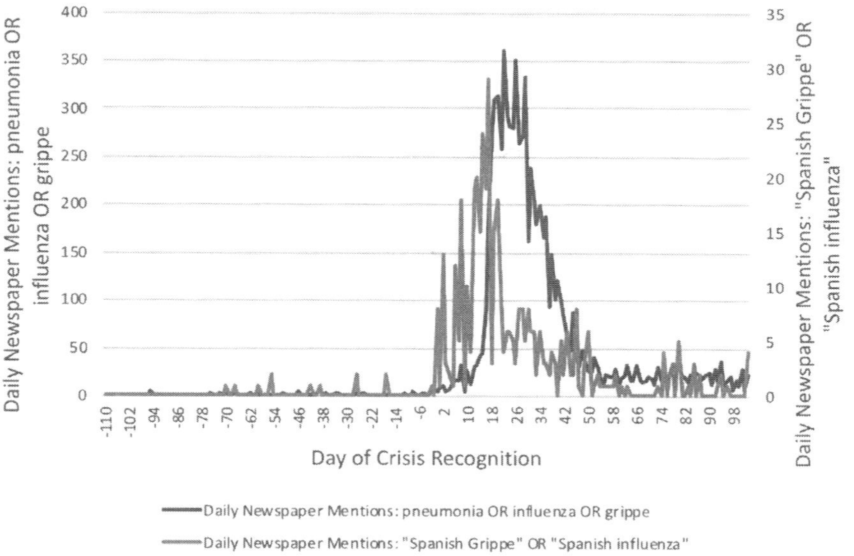

[a]

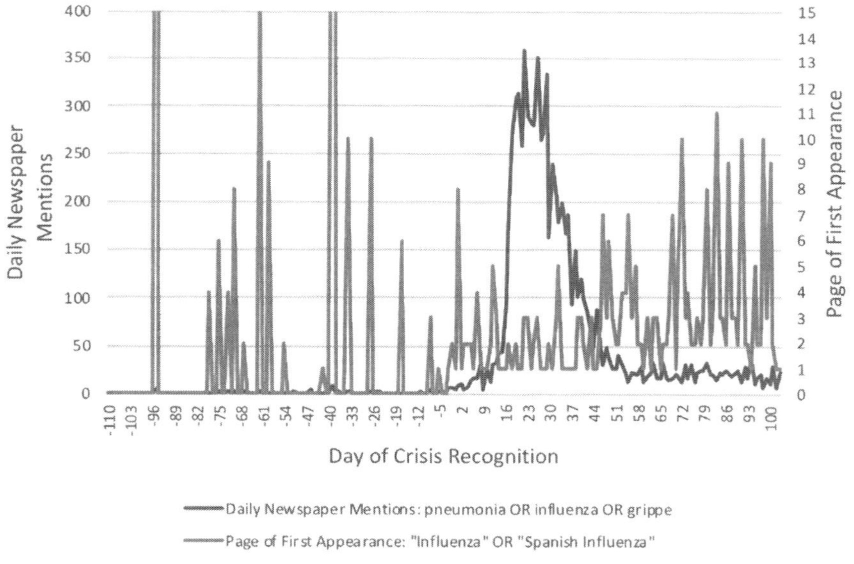

[b]

Figure 2. Terminology used by the *Philadelphia Inquirer* in 1918. 'Influenza', 'pneumonia', and 'grippe' were routine terms used for prior seasons of influenza. 'Spanish influenza' was a novel term used to denote the unique, non-routine situation [a]. Day 1 was September 19th. Prioritization of the threat was indicated by articles about influenza posted on the front page [b], displacing those related to World War I.

was an indicator of a non-routine situation. Physicians at the time understood the disease was 'influenza' but was unusual and came from a foreign location, Spain, where the first cases in Europe were later believed to have originated. This indicated early confusion regarding where the epidemic started: Germany or Spain. The term 'pneumonia' was used to denote the bacterial complication of influenza that often resulted in death. Prioritization of threat was indicated by the respective location within the newspaper of articles referencing the crisis, where articles focused on World War I were displaced (Figure 2b, orange line).

Some context was missing from the newspaper reports. On August 16th, an advisory was issued to marine quarantine stations on the East Coast to be vigilant for inbound ships from Europe with cases of influenza onboard.[59] This advisory was not publicly released nor published in the *Inquirer*. Weekly mortality peaked at 4,597 by October 19th (Day 30). This contrasted with official declaration of the epidemic peaking five days earlier on October 14th. This likely reflected a lag in mortality versus number of infected individuals reported to officials. In total, an estimated 15,785 died out of a city population of 1,761,371, which was 1 per cent of the population.[60]

The majority of illnesses were associated with mild cold-like symptoms lasting 3 days. Those patients who died were bed ridden for about a week and died between the seventh and tenth day.[61] Basic hygiene, infection control procedures, antibiotics, antivirals, or vaccines had not been developed yet at this point in history.[62]

From September 19th to October 14th (25 days) the city was impacted severely enough to warrant a description of 'disaster', defined as the entire chain of response overwhelmed in the face of a non-routine infectious disease.[63] The time period of first notice of civilian cases in the city to resolution with the lifting of social distancing measures on October 30th represented 41 days spent distracted from supporting the war effort and activities of daily living.

On 11 November 1918, the end of World War I was declared.[64] By December 2nd (Day 74) the Federal Reserve reported the economy had recovered. The Federal Reserve Bank of Philadelphia reported there were no fuel shortages, despite losses in coal output. Many merchants believed they would recover any revenue lost to the epidemic before the end of 1918.[65] This optimism was validated the following month with reports that coal output was still down, but retail trade in groceries and foodstuff was strong.[66]

An estimated 25 per cent of Philadelphia's physicians and nurses were enlisted in the military, which resulted in a medical infrastructure that was already strained by routine daily patient demand prior to the arrival of the pandemic.[67] Medication shortages were reported, along with price manipulation in the face of extreme demand. Healthcare providers required constant replacement due to illness or fatigue related to long, extended hours of work. A multitude of emergency hospitals were created out of not only churches and schools but municipal buildings, country clubs, private homes, theaters, garages, tents, and other ad hoc structures. There was significant mobilization of transportation to facilitate healthcare provider and patient transport along with medical supplies and food.[68] For example, a private automobile club donated the time and resources of 400 cars and 15 trucks converted to ambulances to support transport operations. Seventeen police vehicles and taxi services were also tasked to assist with transportation.[69] a surge in food preparation capacity was created to meet the demand of homebound families who were unable to prepare their own meals. A volunteer police force was required to enforce the quarantine and isolation of homes in the community, however little, if any, civil resistance was encountered. The need for volunteers to manage logistics for response and call centers was unprecedented.[70]

Explicit details of the status of mortuary services were superficial in the media reports. On 8 November 1918, the reality of the situation was described[71]:

> *It is doubtful whether the city of Philadelphia, at any time in its history, has been confronted with a more serious situation than that presented in connection with the care and burial of its dead during the recent epidemic. When the Philadelphia Council of National Defense turned its attention to this matter, conditions were appalling. The one morgue in the city with a maximum capacity for the care of thirty-six bodies, contained several hundred. These were piled three and four deep in the corridors and in almost every room, covered only by sheets which were often dirty and blood-stained. Most of these bodies were unembalmed with no ice near them and in temperature not even chilled. Their extremities were uncovered, and plainly visible. Some bodies were mortifying, and the stench was nauseating. In the rear of the building, the doors were open and bodies lying all over the floor, a spectacle for gaping curiosity seekers, including young children. It must be remembered that the morgue is located at Thirteenth and Wood Streets, in the very heart of the city.*

The accumulation of bodies was not only of the poor but also the wealthy in the city. Emergency funds were required to surge mortuary services. The guarantees of payment came directly from the city's treasury, backed by insurance companies.

The return of *A*/H1N1, 1977-1978

Philadelphia's local media began to discuss the reappearance of A/H1N1 in the Soviet Union on 17 December 1977, where CDC was quoted as saying the virus was 'not a particularly virulent virus'.[72] They noted the virus had caused 'moderate outbreaks ... throughout that nation'. On December 21st, there was report of school absenteeism due to influenza that was twice as high as typical for that time of year. The dominant circulating strain was believed to be A/H3N2 (not A/H1N1), which had been responsible for outbreaks in other states.[73] The following day, the Pennsylvania Health Secretary reported the current available influenza vaccine would not be effective for the A/H3N2 strain in circulation.[74]

On December 23rd, federal decisions to initiate vaccine production for what was now dubbed 'Russian flu' was reportedly stymied by the disastrous experience with the 1976 swine flu vaccination campaign.[75] In January 1976, 230 cases, 13 hospitalizations, and 1 fatality involving H1N1 swine flu were reported at Camp Dix, sparking fears of an imminent pandemic.[76] The 1976 national campaign received 137 USD million in funding and rolled out quickly in an effort to mitigate the potential impact of an influenza pandemic. Unfortunately, the vaccine was not completely safe, a key observation discovered after it was deployed to the public. Guillain-Barre syndrome (paralysis) was reported among recipients of the vaccine, with 55 fatalities. This stark reality was placed in context with the single fatality due to the actual virus. Fears of a pandemic were not realized, and there was no epidemic of swine influenza. The political fallout resulted in the dismissal of the CDC director.[77] In December 1977, the fact that more people died due to the emergency vaccination program than the actual virus threat caused tremendous hesitation among public health officials.

The following day, Leonid Brezhnev, the President of the Soviet Union, was reported to be recuperating from influenza, and the first cases of A/H3N2 were reported in the city of Philadelphia.[78] On December 27th, the state public health laboratory had ramped up testing to support influenza surveillance.[79] On New Year's Eve, New Jersey reported high patient demand at some of their hospitals' emergency departments; five days later the entire state was reporting similar impact. Pennsylvania officials indicated the situation represented normal, expected influenza activity.[80] There was no report of impact for the city of Philadelphia.

On January 17th, CDC officials visited with their counterparts in Moscow to discuss their experience with A/H1N1.[81] Ten days later, A/H1N1 was confirmed in Cheyenne, Wyoming, which was hypothesized to be the result of infected airmen at Warren Airbase. These airmen had visited England while A/H1N1 was spreading there and had returned to Warren Airbase ill.[82] On 9 February 1978, a question and answer column appeared in the newspaper, where the arrival of Russian flu was anticipated.[83] This was followed with satire the next day contrasting the disastrous 1976 swine influenza campaign with the lack of vaccine for the expected arrival of A/H1N1.[84]

Day 1 was February 11th, when probable A/H1N1 infections were reported across multiple colleges in Pennsylvania, where students were effected but not the professors. Based on the epidemiological data shared by the Soviet Union, this was compatible with A/H1N1 infection. No illnesses were reported from elementary and high schools because they were closed due to snow.[85] The next day, officials indicated they expected more influenza cases, but there was little they could do to slow down transmission.[86] On Day 3, New Jersey confirmed their first case of A/H1N1.[87] On Day 5, Camp Dix reported cases.[88] By Day 8, schools in New Jersey were reporting absenteeism as high as 40 per cent.[89] February 24th was the last day of substantive reporting, where 20 states were involved, including Washington, DC.[90] Throughout the entire thread of reporting, there was not a single article that spoke of cases specifically in the city of Philadelphia nor was there official reporting of case counts for Philadelphia. There was no report of school closures, healthcare infrastructure strain, public outcry, mass evacuations, or civil unrest.

Newspaper reporting patterns were similar to those observed with the 1918 pandemic, where use of an atypical moniker, 'Russian influenza', appeared ahead of A/H1N1's arrival in Philadelphia (Figure 3). The intensity of reporting, as measured by the number of keyword mentions, was nearly ten times less than that seen during the 1918 pandemic.

Context was missing in the *Philadelphia Inquirer*'s reporting. National level media reporting, beginning in October, quoted CDC as expecting a mild, routine influenza season for 1977–1978.[91] This expectation preceded the Soviets' disclosure. The Soviets had indicated transmission was 'widespread' in December and 'the flu has raised havoc with school attendance' with more than 60 cities effected by the epidemic since November.[92] In Moscow, mild social distancing measures were advised, where the government advised its citizens to stay home if ill.

In December, CDC examined the remaining stockpile of 1976 swine influenza vaccine in comparison to the Soviets' A/H1N1 virus samples. They reported publicly the vaccine would not be effective against the new virus.[93] They called for a response plan that included the manufacture of vaccine in January, however acknowledged it would take months to develop.[94] Thus, existing supplies of influenza vaccine were deemed ineffective against both the novel A/H1N1 that had appeared in Russia as well as the seasonal A/H3N2 strain that was already transmitting in the US. While this was reported in January, seasonal A/H3N2 was transmitting briskly throughout the country, where it 'has hit the Washington metropolitan area with such force that the emergency room staff at the Children's Hospital National Medical Center has been overwhelmed and has called for volunteer help from other hospital staffers'.[95] The overall impact of the season, by February, was attributed to seasonal A/H3N2, not the novel A/H1N1 virus.[96] The season was ultimately declared 'not the worst-but close', where the fatalities seen were concerning but not as high as that seen in 1976.[97]

By early March, A/H1N1 was found to be widespread in the nation, mainly effecting children in high school and young adults in college.[98] These patterns were expected based on the Soviets' initial information shared three months earlier. The following influenza season (1978–1979), A/H1N1 was in

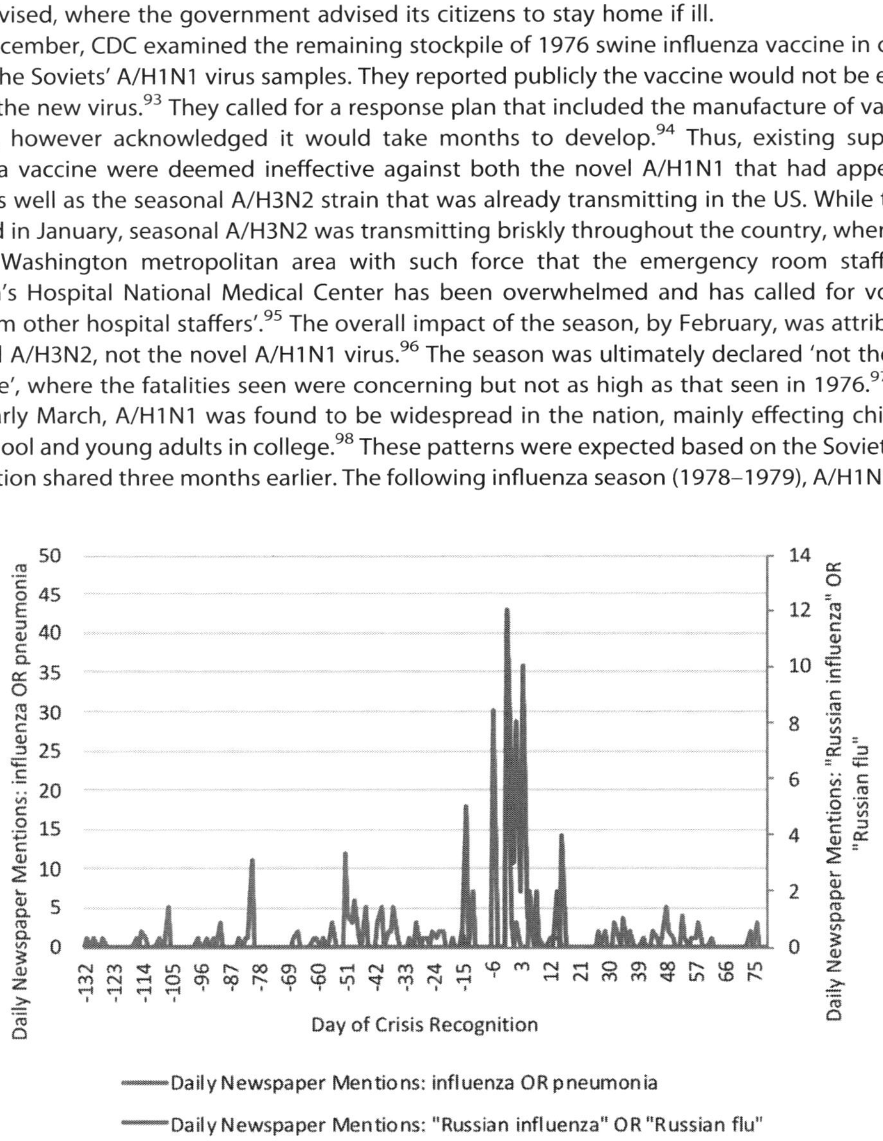

Figure 3. Terminology used by the *Philadelphia Inquirer* in 1977 and 1978. 'Influenza' and 'pneumonia' were routine terms used for prior seasons of influenza. 'Russian influenza' was a novel term used to denote the unique, non-routine situation. Day 1 was February 11th.

dominance, however the season was considered mild.[99] Thereafter to the present day, A/H1N1 has remained in global circulation.

Discussion

The 1918 influenza pandemic in Philadelphia

The cascade of reported indicators in 1918 Philadelphia represents a classic pandemic influenza warning signal. Reactive public health surveillance is indicative of a community's confrontation with an unfamiliar health security threat. Indications of unusual, non-routine activity were also revealed through unexpected epidemiological patterns. The routine influenza season in the US typically occurs in the winter (December-March), with a peak in February.[100] In 1918, the season began exceptionally early in the late summer and early fall months. Routine, seasonal influenza typically causes serious illness among the very young and elderly, however in 1918 serious illness was seen predominantly among the working age adults- a pattern that was echoed in mild form in 1977–1978. Typically, seasonal influenza affects a portion of the overall population that results in mild impact on worker absenteeism. In the case of 1918, there was significant, abrupt, and pervasive absenteeism across multiple government and commercial sectors that effected productivity. In routine seasonal influenza, mortality typically does not overwhelm mortuary services, however in 1918 the mortality was unprecedented in the city's generational memory.

The word 'pandemic' was not used by the newspaper articles in 1918. In 1918, routine words like 'influenza', 'grippe', 'pneumonia', and 'epidemic' were used. However, additional clues regarding the presence of a non-routine crisis included use of a novel phrase, 'Spanish influenza', as well as indicators of *extremis* experienced by responders in the face of overwhelming patient demand. Additionally, there was some debate in the media regarding the etiology- whether the Germans intentionally introduced influenza to the US by U-boats. At the same time, there were comparisons to the last influenza crisis, the 'Russian influenza' of 1889, which was referred to as a pandemic only decades later in modern times. Other studies have also shown declaration of a pandemic does not occur in the early stages of signal recognition.[101] This is representative of the inherent time delay in official public health detection, verification, reporting of cases, and assessment of health security crises.

Current literature and health security tabletop exercises[102] often focus on the dramatic disaster conditions associated with the peak of impact in 1918 Philadelphia. Disaster conditions were likely present for 25 days, with rapid economic recovery following nearly 75 days of crisis. Philadelphia's healthcare personnel did not have access to either a vaccine, anti-viral, or antibiotic yet exhibited tremendous community cohesion and maintained social order. This speaks to inherent community resiliency observed in other examples of health security crises.[103] We propose it is important to remember that pandemics represent significant, but short-lived periods of socio-economic disruption and political distraction where the involved communities are likely to recover, regardless of access to a specific medical countermeasure.

We hypothesize community orientation against a common threat during World War I may have promoted community support with official social distancing orders, despite complaints appearing in newspaper editorials. Pre-event orientation and social cohesion exhibited in the face of a common enemy may portend cooperation with disruptive, officially mandated countermeasures.[104]

Although the city had clear forewarning, there was little evidence of preparedness and hence behaved in a highly reactive manner. This was a curious observation given the city remembered the 1889 pandemic and referenced it in their media reporting. This may be due to inexperience and the relative infancy of organized public health in the United States. Modern day researchers have hypothesized social distancing measures were required earlier in the crisis to save more lives.[105] Under this hypothesis, Philadelphia waited too long to implement these critically important countermeasures, and excess lives were lost as a result. Some researchers have proposed an initial 'herald' wave was present in the United States in February, months before the crisis in Philadelphia.[106] If true, the signal was missed by public health authorities, and no warning was issued. Examination of internal communication records among public health authorities might clarify this observation.

The return of A/H1N1, 1977-1978

Unusual diplomacy was exhibited by the Soviet Union, where they communicated the return of A/H1N1 and shared epidemiological data and virus samples with the international community. This was critical information that informed the United States' preparedness posture and subsequent communications to the public. The anticipation of a relatively mild influenza season was validated by direct local experience and then validated years later with CDC's 1983 Influenza Surveillance Report.[107]

The geographic origin of A/H1N1 was not revealed until January 1978 when the Chinese disclosed to the World Health Organization that they experienced an epidemic of A/H1N1 in late May 1977.[108] Suspicions of etiology were not disclosed until June 1978- that the reappearance of the virus may have been the result of a laboratory accident in China.[109] This then represented a global warning failure, with a signal recognition delay of approximately seven months as far as the United States was concerned. This followed a similar pattern of warning failure associated with the emergence of the 1957 and 1968 influenza pandemics in China.[110] In 2015, a more probable theory of a clinical trial accident with live H1N1 vaccine was proposed.[111] This highlights the point that response cannot wait for the determination of attribution, which may be a time-delayed process.

Any anxiety regarding the return of A/H1N1 as the 'Russian influenza' was mitigated by

(1) information regarding the impact of A/H1N1 provided by the Soviet Union months before the virus' arrival;
(2) the disastrous vaccination campaign of the prior year involving H1N1 swine influenza at Camp Dix;
(3) effective communication by US public health officials in the national media that emphasized the mild impact and low mortality observed with A/H1N1.

The observed impact was also effected by the inability of A/H1N1 to displace the A/H3N2 virus, which had been in circulation and was responsible for school absenteeism and hospital demand before A/H1N1's arrival. Overall, the 1977–1978 influenza season was associated with the most excess deaths since the 1968 pandemic, which was considered the mildest of the influenza pandemics (Figure 4). The season was dominated by A/H3N2 viruses, which explained the majority of mortality.[112] This validated the Soviets' information that indicated the epidemic of A/H1N1 they experienced was mild.

Conclusions

Pandemic influenza signals appear in local media reporting typically ahead of reactive public health surveillance. These signals reflect local communities' awareness of non-routine infectious disease activity and associated impact on their healthcare infrastructure and activities of daily living. The sense of threat is reflected by the volume of reporting. The magnitude of impact is reflected in the expanded diversity of indicators over time. The cascade of indicators associated with pandemic influenza represents a key warning signal pattern:

(1) If the involved nation is not the first in the world to be effected, anticipation or forewarning of non-routine or novel influenza activity.
(2) Communication of novel, unexpected, or non-routine epidemiological patterns of influenza-like illness.

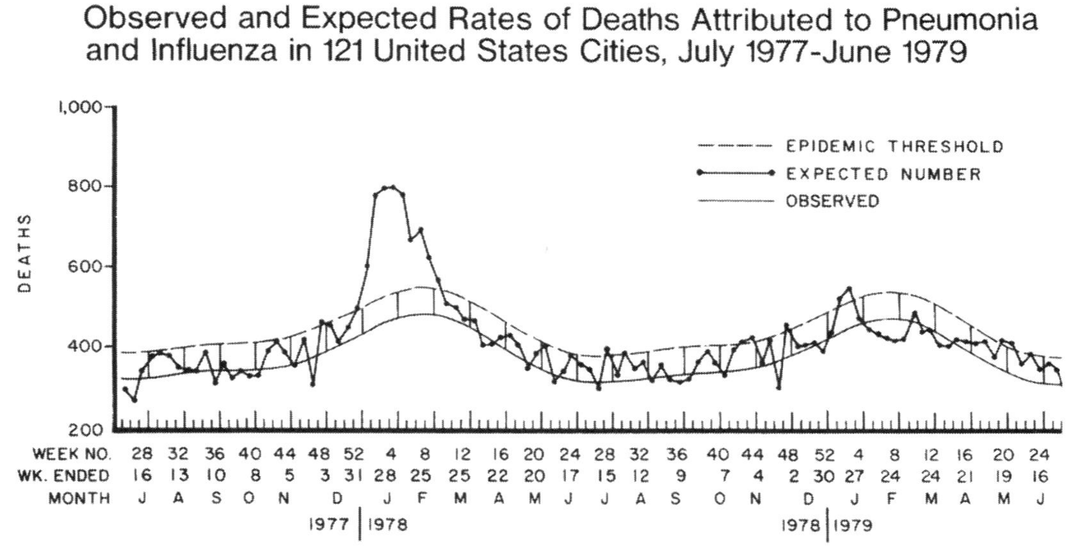

Figure 4. Forensic epidemiological analysis of the 1977–1978 influenza season by CDC, published in 1983.

(3) Abrupt and pervasive illness in the community evidenced by school absenteeism and closures; multi-sector worker absenteeism; and patient demand seen at the outpatient and emergency department levels of care.
(4) Reports of hospitalization and inpatient ward inundation as the less common clinical presentations of more seriously ill patients increases with pervasive community transmission. This is often coincident with report of healthcare worker illness and mortality.
(5) Impingement on mortuary services as fatality surge advances.

In the modern societal context, critical indicators include clustered, serious illness among healthcare providers- particularly in the acute care (hospital) setting. Within the acute care setting, we propose any report of intensive care unit personnel who are infected and admitted to the intensive care unit themselves should warrant immediate, prioritized attention for investigative verification. Multi-sector worker absenteeism is an uncommon indicator during routine influenza seasons and should be considered a critical indicator. The severity (mortality) of the involved influenza virus determines the depth of indicators reported, where milder seasons are associated with report of patient demand at the outpatient, emergency department, and inpatient levels of care. More serious seasons are associated with inundation of the intensive care units and long-term acute care facilities. Highest severity is seen with the collapse of intensive care units and mortuary services.

Because diagnostic systems and reporting processes are typically structured around routine, locally well-known diseases, public health reporting and response behavior is typically reactive unless forewarning and preparedness occurs. Conflicts among healthcare providers, public health officials, and other academic experts, along with claims of intentional release such as deployment of a biological weapon is indication of non-routine, unexpected, or unusual infectious disease activity.

Limitations in using local media for global pandemic monitoring include the potential to miss herald waves. It may be argued that even detection of herald waves may not prompt action if it cannot be shown that a novel virus is generating significant impact. In 1918, Philadelphia did not exhibit preparedness or proactive response- social distancing was implemented too late to fully reduce mortality. Other cities in the United States, having been forewarned, did implement social distancing earlier and thus saved lives.[113] The implementation of social distancing measures is a time-sensitive process that must be considered in the early stages of a pandemic. Avoidance of warning failures and delays is therefore critical. The events of 1976 offer caution in signal over-interpretation, however subsequent management of warning communications in 1977 represent an example of effective risk assessment. The events of 1977 also emphasize the importance of effective diplomacy, international information sharing, and appropriate analysis to drive effective risk communication with the public. Overall, these examples highlight the importance of capturing lessons involved in the detection, interpretation, and communication of pandemic warning signals and bridging that information to preparedness activities.

Influenza pandemics, particularly a 1918 scenario, represent archetypes of health security threats. An appropriate balance of communication regarding impacts is required for credible, effective warning communication to decision makers and the public. While the 1918 pandemic in Philadelphia was associated with an unprecedented level of morbidity, mortality, and socio-economic disruption, it remains a remarkable commentary on community resilience during a time when effective medical countermeasures were unavailable. Similar resilience has been observed for other health security crises and disasters.[114] Such balanced communication is important to avoid hyperbole that may erode the long-term credibility of a health security warning enterprise.

Notes

1. Johnson and Mueller, "Updating the Accounts," 105–15.
2. DeBruyne, *American War.*
3. Barry, *Great Influenza.*
4. Crosby, *America's Forgotten Pandemic*, 31.
5. Anonymous, "Fear New Epidemic," July 22.
6. Anonymous, "Theaters, Saloons", October 4.
7. Newman, *Reports on Public Health*, 288–89.
8. Crosby, *America's Forgotten Pandemic*, 3–32.
9. Ibid.
10. Jester et al., "Historical and Clinical," 32–37.
11. Morris, Cleary, and Clarke, "Secondary Bacterial Infections," 1041.
12. Crosby, *America's Forgotten Pandemic.*
13. Cox and Subbarao, "Global Epidemiology of Influenza," 407–21.
14. Schmeck, "U.S. Experts Meet," December 23.
15. Whitney, "Hundreds of Thousands," December 30.
16. Associated Press, "From Russia," January 27.
17. Barron, "Early victim," February 12.
18. Centers for Disease Control, *Influenza Surveillance Summary*.
19. See note 17 above.
20. See note 18 above.
21. Associated Press, "Hong Kong, Soviets", December 17; and Associated Press, "From Russia," January 27.
22. Shurkin, "Flu sweeps Pennsylvania," February 11.
23. Zakstelskaja et al., "Influenza in the USSR," 919–22.
24. Rozo and Gronvall, "The Reemergent 1977 H1N1," e01013-15.
25. Wilson, "Signal Recognition"; and Wilson, Iannarone, and Wang, "Media Reporting," S148-53.
26. Newspapers.com.
27. Anonymous, "Austrians Still Strong," July 3; and Anonymous, "Editorial Comment," July 6.
28. Anonymous, "All Highest, Kaiser," July 11.
29. Anonymous, "Spanish influenza," July 14.
30. Anonymous, "Fear New Epidemic May Reach Here," July 22.
31. Draper, "Crown Prince's Position," July 27.
32. Anonymous, "It's a Trying Malady," August 11.
33. Anonymous, "Editorial Comment," August 23.
34. Anonymous, "Influenza Grips Boston," September 11.
35. Anonymous, "Dr. Leen, Carney Hospital," September 17.
36. Anonymous, "Protect Camp Dix Men Against Influenza," September 17.
37. Anonymous, "Spanish Influenza Sends," September 19.
38. Anonymous, "1500 Cases Influenza Develops at Camp Dix," September 19.

39. Anonymous, "Krusen not Alarmed," September 19.
40. Anonymous, "U-Boats Freed Germs," September 19.
41. Anonymous, "Philadelphia Navy Yard," September 20.
42. Anonymous, "Spanish Influenza German," September 21.
43. Anonymous, "Spanish Influenza Epidemic Waning," September 23.
44. Anonymous, "Camp Dix Quarantined," September 24.
45. Anonymous, "Camp Dix Appeals," September 26.
46. Anonymous, "Influenza Outbreak," September 26; and Anonymous, "Spanish Influenza Invades Shipyards," September 27.
47. Anonymous, "Influenza Halts Call," September 17.
48. Anonymous, "Theaters, Saloons," October 4.
49. Treasury Department, *The Liberty Loan Legislation.*
50. Anonymous, "Telephone Service Faces," October 4.
51. Anonymous, "Spanish Influenza," October 5.
52. Anonymous, "More Nurses Needed," October 5.
53. Anonymous, "Fewer Influenza Cases Reported," October 11.
54. Anonymous, "Say Convalescents," October 14.
55. Anonymous, "Siege of Influenza," October 16.
56. Anonymous, "May Place Scranton," October 20.
57. Anonymous, "Denounce Stopping," October 23; and Anonymous, "Return of sanity to Philadelphia," October 29.
58. See note 7 above.
59. Anonymous, *Annual Report of the Surgeon General*, 175.
60. See note 7 above.
61. See note 10 above.
62. See note 4 above.
63. Quarantelli, *What is a Disaster?*.
64. Beckett, *The Great War*.
65. Federal Reserve Bank of Philadelphia. *Business Conditions*, 2 December 1918.
66. Federal Reserve Bank of Philadelphia. *Business Conditions*, 2 January 1919.
67. Yarnall, *Emergency Service*, 4.
68. Ibid., 5.
69. Ibid., 35.
70. Ibid., 35.
71. Ibid., 35.
72. Associated Press, "Hong Kong, Soviets", December 17.
73. Lloyd, "Flu reduces classes," December 21.
74. Inquirer Wire Services, "New a-Texas flu," December 22.
75. Associated Press, "Now it's Soviet flu," December 23.
76. Lessler et al., "Transmissibility of Swine flu," 755–62.
77. Sencer and Millar, "Reflections 1976 Swine," 29–33.
78. Associated Press, "Brezhnev: Stop Neutron Bomb," December 24.
79. Anonymous, "A State Laboratory," December 27.
80. Anonymous, "First Wave," December 31; and Associated Press, "All Counties," January 4.
81. Anonymous, "Soviet and American," January 17.
82. See note 16 above.
83. Anonymous, "Answers to Flu Questions," February 9.
84. Hoppe, "If you get Swine Flu," February 10.
85. See note 22 above.
86. Anonymous, "Another College Gets," February 12.
87. Anonymous, "New Jersey Reports," February 13.
88. Anonymous, "Five New Cases," February 15.
89. Anonymous, "Two More Cases," February 18.
90. Anonymous, "The Carter Administration," February 24.
91. Schmeck, "Scientists Expect Mild," October 6.
92. Schmeck, "U.S. Experts Meet," December 23; and Whitney, "Hundreds of thousands," December 30.
93. Colen, "U.S. fears," December 23.
94. Schmeck, "Soviet Flu," January 13.
95. Anonymous, "Death Toll From," February 4; and Colen, "Texas-type Flu," January 7.
96. Schmeck, "Major Flu Epidemics," February 11.
97. Colen, "U.S. Influenza Epidemic," February 11.
98. Associated Press, "Russian Flu Found Widespread," March 10.

99. See note 18 above.
100. Centers for Disease Control and Prevention. "The Influenza Season".
101. Wilson, "Signal Recognition"; and Wilson, Iannarone, and Wang, "Media Reporting," S148-53.
102. Dausey, Aledort, and Lurie, "Tabletop Exercises"; Barry, *Great Influenza.*
103. Wilson et al., "Reanalysis Anthrax Epidemic," e2686.
104. Wilson and Daniel, "Historical Reconstruction."
105. Markel et al., "Nonpharmaceutical Interventions," 644–54.
106. Olson et al., "Epidemiological Evidence," 11059-63; and Crosby, *America's Forgotten Pandemic*, 26.
107. See note 18 above.
108. World Health Organization, "Influenza," 22.
109. See note 23 above.
110. Wilson, Iannarone, and Wang, "Media Reporting," S148-53.
111. See note 24 above.
112. See note 18 above.
113. See note 105 above.
114. Wilson and Daniel, "Historical Reconstruction"; and Wilson et al., "Reanalysis Anthrax Epidemic," e2686.

Acknowledgements

The authors gratefully acknowledge the manuscript reviewers for their comments.

Disclosure statement

Dr. Wilson is employed by M2 Medical Intelligence.

Bibliography

Anonymous. 1918. "Austrians Still Strong". *The Philadelphia Inquirer*, July 3.
Anonymous. 1918. "Editorial Comment". *The Philadelphia Inquirer*, July 6.
Anonymous. 1918. "All Highest, Kaiser Himself, Has Grippe". *The Philadelphia Inquirer*, July 11.
Anonymous. 1918. "Spanish Influenza Is Due to Hunger". *The Philadelphia Inquirer*, July 14.
Anonymous. 1918. "Fear New Epidemic May Reach Here". *The Philadelphia Inquirer*, July 22.
Anonymous. 1918. "It's a Trying Malady". *The Philadelphia Inquirer*, August 11.
Anonymous. 1918. "Editorial Comment". *The Philadelphia Inquirer*, August 23.
Anonymous. 1918. "Influenza Grips Boston". *The Philadelphia Inquirer*, September 11.
Anonymous. 1918. "Dr. Leen, Carney Hospital, Dies Fighting Influenza". *The Philadelphia Inquirer*, September 17.
Anonymous. 1918. "Influenza Halts Call for 142,000 Men for Service". *The Philadelphia Inquirer*, September 17.
Anonymous. 1918. "Protect Camp Dix Men against Influenza". *The Philadelphia Inquirer*, September 17.
Anonymous. 1918. "1500 Cases Influenza Develops at Camp Dix". *The Philadelphia Inquirer*, September 19.
Anonymous. 1918. "Krusen Not Alarmed". *The Philadelphia Inquirer*, September 19.
Anonymous. 1918. "Spanish Influenza Sends 600 Sailors to Hospitals Here". *The Philadelphia Inquirer*, September 19.

Anonymous. 1918. "U-Boats Freed Germs, Says U.S. Officer". *The Philadelphia Inquirer*, September 19.
Anonymous. 1918. "Philadelphia Navy Yard Has 853 Cases—authorities Fighting Epidemic". *The Philadelphia Inquirer*, September 20.
Anonymous. 1918. "Spanish Influenza Is German Germ; Only La Grippe". *The Philadelphia Inquirer*, September 21.
Anonymous. 1918. "Spanish Influenza Epidemic Waning". *The Philadelphia Inquirer*, September 23.
Anonymous. 1918. "Camp Dix Quarantined; 11 Influenza Deaths". *The Philadelphia Inquirer*, September 24.
Anonymous. 1918. "Camp Dix Appeals for Doctors and Nurses". *The Philadelphia Inquirer*, September 26.
Anonymous. 1918. "Influenza Outbreak at Bristol Shipyard". *The Philadelphia Inquirer*, September 26.
Anonymous. 1918. "Spanish Influenza Invades Shipyards". *The Philadelphia Inquirer*, September 27.
Anonymous. 1918. "Telephone Service Faces a Crisis". *The Philadelphia Inquirer*, October 4.
Anonymous. 1918. "Theaters, Saloons in Pennsylvania Closed to Halt Influenza". *The Philadelphia Inquirer*, October 4.
Anonymous. 1918. "More Nurses Needed to Fight Influenza". *The Philadelphia Inquirer*, October 5.
Anonymous. 1918. "Spanish Influenza and the Fear of It". *The Philadelphia Inquirer*, October 5.
Anonymous. 1918. "Fewer Influenza Cases Reported". *The Philadelphia Inquirer*, October 11.
Anonymous. 1918. "Say Convalescents Break Health Rules". *The Philadelphia Inquirer*, October 14.
Anonymous. 1918. "Siege of Influenza at Breaking Point". *The Philadelphia Inquirer*, October 16.
Anonymous. 1918. "May Place Scranton under Martial Law". *The Philadelphia Inquirer*, October 20.
Anonymous. 1918. "Denounce Stopping of Liquor Selling by Pennsylvania Dealers". *The Philadelphia Inquirer*, October 23.
Anonymous. 1918. "Return of Sanity to Philadelphia". *The Philadelphia Inquirer*, October 29.
Anonymous. Annual Report of the Surgeon General of the Public Health Service of the United States for the Fiscal Year 1919. Washington: Government Printing Office, 1919.
Anonymous. 1977. "A State Laboratory in Chester County Is Prepared to Aid Physicians in Diagnosing Suspected Influenza Cases". *The Philadelphia Inquirer*, December 27.
Anonymous. 1977. "First Wave of Flu Outbreaks Hits; N.J. On List". *The Philadelphia Inquirer*, December 31.
Anonymous. 1978. "Soviet and American Scientists Begin Joint Meetings in Moscow to Control Influenza Epidemics". *The Philadelphia Inquirer*, January 17.
Anonymous. 1978. "Death Toll from Influenza Exceeds 1,000 in a Month". *The New York Times*, February 4.
Anonymous. 1978. "Answers to Flu Questions". *The Philadelphia Inquirer*, February 9.
Anonymous. 1978. "Another College Gets the Flu". *The Philadelphia Inquirer*, February 12.
Anonymous. 1978. "New Jersey Reports Its First Confirmed Case of Russian Flu". *The Philadelphia Inquirer*, February 13.
Anonymous. 1978. "Five New Cases of Russian Flu Confirmed in New Jersey". *The Philadelphia Inquirer*, February 15.
Anonymous. 1978. "Two More Cases of Russian Flu are Confirmed in New Jersey". *The Philadelphia Inquirer*, February 18.
Anonymous. 1978. "The Carter Administration Poses a Program of Flu Shots for the Elderly". *The Philadelphia Inquirer*, February 24.
Associated Press. 1977. "Hong Kong, Soviets Report New Flu Virus". *The Philadelphia Inquirer*, December 17.
Associated Press. 1977. "Now It's Soviet Flu, and Guess What's in the Works". *The Philadelphia Inquirer*, December 23.
Associated Press. 1977. "Brezhnev: Stop Neutron Bomb". *The Philadelphia Inquirer*, December 24.
Associated Press. 1978. "All Counties Reporting Flu Cases". *The Philadelphia Inquirer*, January 4.
Associated Press. 1978. "From Russia, with Coughing and Chills". *The Philadelphia Inquirer*, January 27.
Associated Press. 1978. "Russian Flu Found Widespread". *The New York Times*, March 10.
Barron, J. 1978. "Early Victim of Russian Flu Recalls, 'I Really Got Zapped'". *The Sunday Star-Tribune* (Wyoming), February 12.
Barry, J. M. *The Great Influenza: The Story of the Deadliest Pandemic in History*. New York City: Penguin Random House, 2004.
Beckett, I. F. W. *The Great War: 1914-1918*. New York: Routledge, 2007.
Centers for Disease Control. *Influenza Surveillance Summary: August 1977—March 1979*. Atlanta: Centers for Disease Control, 1983.
Centers for Disease Control and Prevention. "The Influenza Season".Accessed April 5, 2019. https://www.cdc.gov/flu/about/season/flu-season.htm
Colen, B. D. 1977. "U.S. Fears Chinese-Soviet Invasion- a New Flu Bug". *The Washington Post*, December 23.
Colen, B. D. 1978. "Texas-type Flu Sweeps across Area". *The Washington Post*, January 7.
Colen, B. D. 1978. "U.S. Influenza Epidemic Not the Worst- but Close". *The Washington Post*, February 11.
Cox, N. J., and K. Subbarao. "Global Epidemiology of Influenza: Past and Present." *Annual Reviews in Medicine* 51 (2000): 407–421. doi:10.1146/annurev.med.51.1.407.
Crosby, a. W. *America's Forgotten Pandemic: The Influenza of 1918*. Cambridge: Cambridge University Press, 1989.
Dausey, D. J., J. E. Aledort, and N. Lurie. *Tabletop Exercises for Pandemic Influenza Preparedness in Local Public Health Agencies*. Arlington: the RAND Corporation, 2006.
DeBruyne, N. F. *American War and Military Operations Casualties: Lists and Statistics*. Washington: Congressional Research Service, 2018.
Draper, a. a. 1918. "Crown Prince's Position Has Grown More Precarious". *The Philadelphia Inquirer*, July 27.
Federal Reserve Bank of Philadelphia. *Business Conditions in the Philadelphia Federal Reserve District (December 2, 1918)*. Philadelphia: Government Printing Office, 1918.

Federal Reserve Bank of Philadelphia. *Business Conditions in the Philadelphia Federal Reserve District*. 1919. Philadelphia: Government Printing Office, 2 January 1919.

Hoppe, a. 1978. "If You Get Swine Flu, You May Be in Luck". *The Philadelphia Inquirer*, February 10.

Inquirer Wire Services. 1977. "New a-Texas Flu Strain May Resist Current Vaccines, Health Chief Says". *The Philadelphia Inquirer*, December 22.

Jester, B., T. M. Uyeki, D. B. Jernigan, and T. M. Tumpey. "Historical and Clinical Aspects of the 1918 H1N1 Pandemic in the United States." *Virology* 527 (2019): 32–37. doi:10.1016/j.virol.2018.10.019.

Johnson, N. P., and J. Mueller. "Updating the Accounts: Global Mortality of the 1918-1920 "Spanish" Influenza Pandemic." *Bulletin of the History of Medicine* 76, no. 1 (2002): 105–115. doi:10.1353/bhm.2002.0022.

Lessler, J., D. a. Cummings, S. Fishman, a. Vora, and D. S. Burke. "Transmissibility of Swine Flu at Fort Dix, 1976." *Journal of the Royal Society Interface* 4, no. 15 (2007): 755–762. doi:10.1098/rsif.2007.0228.

Lloyd, L. 1977. "Flu Reduces Classes in 2 States". *The Philadelphia Inquirer*, December 21.

Markel, H., H. B. Lipman, J. a. Navarro, a. Sloan, J. R. Michalsen, a. M. Stern, and M. S. Cetron. "Nonpharmaceutical Interventions Implemented by US Cities during the 1918-1919 Influenza Pandemic." *JAMA* 298, no. 6 (2007): 644–654. doi:10.1001/jama.298.6.644.

Morris, D. E., D. W. Cleary, and S. C. Clarke. "Secondary Bacterial Infections Associated with Influenza Pandemics." *Frontiers in Microbiology* 8 (2017): 1041. doi:10.3389/fmicb.2017.01041.

Newman, G., ed. *Reports on Public Health and Medical Subjects (No. 4): Report on the Pandemic of Influenza, 1918-19*. London: Ministry of Health, 1920.

Newspapers.com. Accessed November 30, 2019. https://www.newspapers.com

Olson, D. R., L. Simonsen, P. J. Edelson, and S. S. Morse. "Epidemiological Evidence of an Early Wave of the 1918 Influenza Pandemic in New York City." *Proceedings of the National Academy of Sciences* 102, no. 31 (2005): 11059–11063. doi:10.1073/pnas.0408290102.

Quarantelli, H. L., ed. *What Is a Disaster? Perspectives on the Question*. New York: Routledge, 1998.

Rozo, M., and G. K. Gronvall. "The Reemergent 1977 H1N1 Strain and the Gain-of-function Debate." *MBio* 6, no. 4 (2015): e01013–15. doi:10.1128/mBio.01013-15.

Schmeck, H. M. 1977. "Scientists Expect Mild Winter Flu Season for U.S." *The New York Times*, October 6.

Schmeck, H. M. 1977. "U.S. Experts Meet on Flu Virus Widespread in Soviet Union". *The New York Times*, December 23.

Schmeck, H. M. 1978. "Major Flu Epidemics in U.S. Linked to Old Viruses, Not Russian Flu." *The New York Times*, February 11.

Schmeck, H. M. 1978. "Soviet Flu Prompts Call for Plan in U.S." *The New York Times*, January 13.

Sencer, D. J., and J. D. Millar. "Reflections on the 1976 Swine Flu Vaccination Program." *Journal of Emerging Infectious Diseases* 12, no. 1 (2006): 29–33. doi:10.3201/eid1201.051007.

Shurkin, J. N. 1978. "Flu Sweeps Pennsylvania, N.J. Colleges". *The Philadelphia Inquirer*, February 11.

The Treasury Department. *The Liberty Loan Legislation*. Washington: Government Printing Office, 1921.

Whitney, C. R. 1977. "Hundreds of Thousands are down with Flu in Soviet Union". *The New York Times*, December 30.

Wilson, J. M. "Signal Recognition during the Emergence of Pandemic Influenza Type A/H1N1: A Commercial Disease Intelligence Unit's Perspective." *Intelligence and National Security* (2016). doi:10.1080/02684527.2016.1253924.

Wilson, J. M., W. Brediger, T. P. Albright, and J. Smith-Gagen. "Reanalysis of the Anthrax Epidemic in Rhodesia, 1978-1984." *PeerJ* 4 (2016): e2686. doi:10.7717/peerj.2686.

Wilson, J. M., and M. Daniel. "Historical Reconstruction of the Community Response, and Related Epidemiology, of a Suspected Biological Weapon Attack in Ningbo, China (1940)." *Intelligence and National Security*(2019). doi:10.1080/02684527.2018.1536351.

Wilson, J. M., M. Iannarone, and C. Wang. "Media Reporting of the Emergence of the 1968 Influenza Pandemic in Hong Kong: Implications for Modern-day Situational Awareness." *Disaster Medicine and Public Health Preparedness* 3, no. 2 (2009): S148–53. doi:10.1097/DMP.0b013e3181abd603.

World Health Organization. "Influenza." *Weekly Epidemiological Record* 53, no. 3 (1978): 22.

Yarnall, C. *Emergency Service of the Pennsylvania Council of National Defense in the Influenza Crisis*. Philadelphia: Philadelphia Council of National Defense, 1918.

Zakstelskaja, L. J., M. a. Yakhno, V. a. Isacenko, E. V. Molibog, S. a. Hlustov, I. V. Antonova, N. V. Klitsunova, et al. "Influenza in the USSR in 1977: Recurrence of Influenza Virus a Subtype H1N1." *Bulletin of the World Health Organization* 56, no. 6 (1978): 919–922.

The 1999 West Nile virus warning signal revisited

James M. Wilson and Tracey McNamara

ABSTRACT

The 1999 unprecedented emergence of West Nile virus in the western hemisphere represented a health security warning intelligence failure. This paper reviews the timeline of warning signal recognition and associated missed opportunities to bridge strategic and tactical assessments. The complexity of signal evolution involving multiple public and private institutions and professional disciplines, coupled to inherent biases and shortfalls in interpretation, resulted in significant delays in warning communication and lost opportunity for preparedness and emergency response.

Introduction

The West Nile virus epidemic in the Americas that spread coast to coast from 1999 to 2002 produced 48,183 documented cases and 2,163 fatalities (4.5%) across the United States by 2017 and gained permanent ecological establishment.[1] The epidemic was the largest of its kind in the history of the western hemisphere.[2] West Nile disease is caused by a mosquito-borne virus that, in a minority of typically older patients, causes encephalitis (brain infection) and other neurological problems such as paralysis, and death. The virus is capable of infecting multiple species of animals, including birds, horses, and reptiles. The crisis represented a 'virgin soil' epidemic, where a pathogen exotic to the receiving geographic area was introduced to an ecosystem that did not have appreciable levels of herd immunity. Herd immunity refers to the number of host individuals, across multiple species, that have protective immunity thanks to prior exposure to the pathogen. The impact of morbidity and mortality due to a given infectious disease is mitigated by the level of herd immunity, where lack of herd immunity implies the potential for explosive transmission and higher severity of illness.[3]

The arrival of West Nile in the United States was initially recognized as an outbreak of bird die-offs and human encephalitis in New York City. The outbreak was eventually recognized as a prioritized warning signal through a complex, months-long, drawn-out pattern of siloed communications among disparate professional groups. Because of the unusual epidemiological and clinical presentation, discovery of a virus that did not morphologically match known endemic viruses, and recent social sensitization to the threat of biological terrorism, the situation was treated as a potential security threat.[4]

This case study reviews the sequence of warning intelligence failures that contributed to delayed recognition, threat assessment, and loss of potential opportunity to mitigate the impact of this introduced exotic pathogen.

Materials and methods

The authors utilized their own personal notes, government reports,[5] and the narrative timeline compiled by Drexler (2003) to reconstruct the sequence of awareness among the organizations involved with alert and verification of the initial New York City outbreak of West Nile virus. For the media signal analysis, keyword queries were used for a media source local to New York City, the *Daily News*, to extract the number of references in an online curated newspaper archive, *Newspapers.com*.[6] Days of the crisis were numbered based on the first day of the month of first awareness, June 1999. To reconstruct preceding events in Europe and the Middle East, a review of peer-reviewed academic literature was conducted in the National Library of Medicine's PubMed.[7] To evaluate air traffic data between the Middle East and the United States, data were analyzed from the US Department of Transportation Bureau of Transportation Statistics.[8]

Results

In the summer of 1996, an unusual epidemic of West Nile virus was reported in Romania, where officials from the US Centers for Disease Control and Prevention were invited to assist with the investigation.[9] It was believed to be the first documented large-scale epidemic in Europe involving human patients. Nearly 400 human patients were identified with 17 deaths and evidence of virus in local mosquito and bird populations. In the subsequent years, West Nile virus was found to have spread regionally, with additional human cases in the Czech Republic in 1997 and identification in horses in Italy and a large epidemic involving swans in Israel in 1998.[10] The swans in Israel were believed to have picked up the virus during their seasonal migration from West Nile-infected areas of Europe.[11] Overall, it appeared there was a new wave of virus transmission in Europe- an evolution of West Nile introduction to Europe since the 1960s from Africa, where it was previously endemic.

In June 1999, a private veterinary clinic in Bayside, Queens, New York City evaluated wild crows brought to the facility by local community citizens who were concerned the birds were acting strangely.[12] There was no indication the clinic was able to diagnose the disease or environmental exposure responsible. These cases of wildlife disease were not reported to local health authorities.

In early August, the New York State Department of Environmental Conservation (NYSDEC) received reports of bird die-offs involving crows in New York City parks. The NYSDEC was the state agency responsible for wildlife disease evaluation.[13] On August 9th (Day 69), dead wild crows were discovered outside the Queens Zoo property and reported to one of the authors (McNamara). McNamara served as the head veterinary pathologist for the parent organization for the Queens and Bronx Zoos as well as three additional zoos in the New York City area. McNamara, noting dead crows as well at the Bronx Zoo submitted samples to the NYSDEC. On August 12th, a report of no diagnosis was returned to the curator of the Queens Zoo. This caused consternation among the zoo's leadership due to the potential for an unknown disease to cause illness and death among both zoos' collections of exotic birds. Three days later, the first human patient was admitted to Flushing Hospital, Queens with undiagnosed, severe illness.[14]

On August 17th, the NYSDEC wildlife pathologist examines crow specimens however is unable to diagnose what killed them. On August 19th, McNamara was notified the Bronx Zoo samples also returned a result of no diagnosis. The NYSDEC wildlife pathologist was receiving many dead bird specimens, according to the local media the same day. On approximately August 20th, a Bayside, Queens local neighborhood newspaper reported crow die-offs, asking if '...a plague hit the Bayside area?'[15]

On August 23rd (Day 83), an infectious disease physician at Flushing Hospital notified local public health officials of two unusual cases of encephalitis and paralysis that were admitted to the intensive care unit. This included the patient admitted on August 12th.[16] Simultaneously, McNamara sent brain tissue samples from dead wild crows to the New York Department of Environmental Conservation. McNamara was not satisfied with the lack of diagnosis and began her own investigation. Her review of the samples in her laboratory indicated the presence of a possible viral encephalitis to explain the crow deaths.

Two more cases of encephalitis were admitted to the Flushing Hospital intensive care unit and two additional cases were admitted to another local hospital on August 27th. This was an unusual volume of encephalitis cases. The next day, local public health authorities arrived at Flushing

Hospital while a fifth case was admitted. On August 29th (Day 89), local public health officials notified the US Centers for Disease Control and Prevention as an emergency communication. Two days later, Saint Louis Encephalitis (SLE) virus was identified in samples from the Flushing Hospital patients at a local New York public health laboratory; these samples were shipped to the CDC arbovirus laboratory in Fort Collins, Colorado for verification.[17] SLE virus is a known, endemic mosquito-borne virus in the United States. Paralysis was not previously reported for endemic SLE infections in the United States. Prior seasons of SLE transmission in the United States began in the southern states with northward progression versus initial appearance in northern states. The southern warning signal did not precede this crisis.[18]

On September 3 (Day 94), New York City local public health were notified by CDC-Fort Collins of a confirmed diagnosis of SLE virus and initiated mosquito spraying. City officials communicated with the Federal Bureau of Investigation to report a possible act of biological terrorism. The next day (see Figure 1), local public health officials began speculation about a link between the bird die-offs and human cases. At this point, McNamara became aware of local news media attention on an unusual encephalitis outbreak involving human patients.[19]

McNamara called CDC-Fort Collins on September 9th (Day 100) with concerns the SLE diagnosis did not fit the epidemiological pattern she was seeing- a bird die-off. This was in the context of increased zoo employee anxiety about their risk of exposure to disease still killing the exotic bird population. SLE transmission did not cause bird die-offs based on prior experience with the virus in the US. Other viral avian diseases such as highly pathogenic avian influenza and Newcastle disease would have killed the zoo's chickens in the petting zoo area, and Eastern equine encephalitis would have killed the emus present in the park. These avian populations were spared, highlighting another epidemiological and clinical pattern that did not fit the initial SLE diagnosis. These birds would have served as sentinels for known causes of encephalitis in birds in the western hemisphere. The observation they were not dying indicated the possibility of a novel, previously unrecognized veterinary pathogen.

McNamara relayed concern that one of the Bronx veterinarians had accidentally stuck themselves with a needle while euthanizing a symptomatic flamingo. McNamara was advised that CDC did not process samples from animal species and did not share McNamara's concern that the epidemiological pattern did not make sense. McNamara proceeded to send samples to the National Veterinary Services Laboratory at the US Department of Agriculture in Ames, Iowa. Two days later, the National

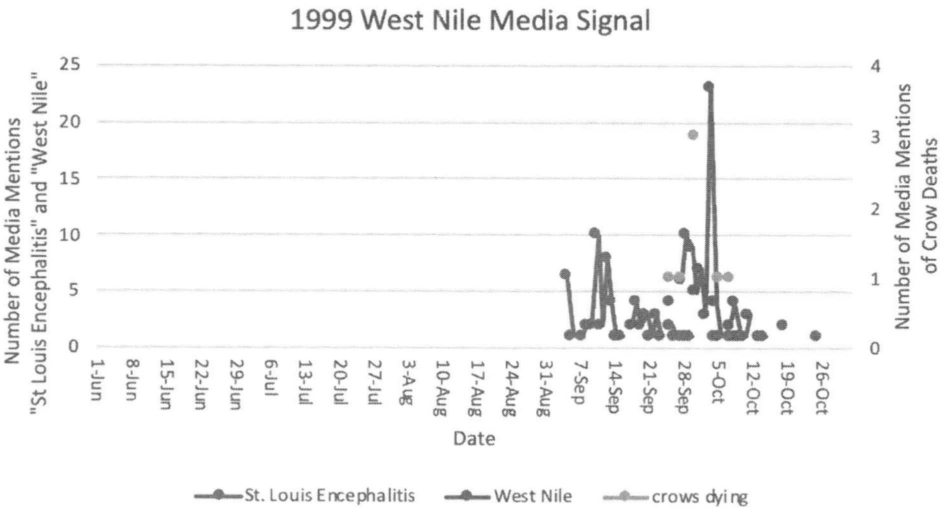

Figure 1. New York City media reporting signal for the 1999 West Nile virus outbreak.

Veterinary Services Laboratory called McNamara to report the avian samples were positive for a flavivirus, but no additional specific identification information was available. This was an unprecedented laboratory finding from the veterinary perspective- no flavivirus had been known to cause animal disease in the western hemisphere. The flavivirus family includes dengue, yellow fever, SLE, and West Nile virus species. McNamara notified CDC-Fort Collins, again emphasizing the pattern of transmission may not be SLE virus. The National Veterinary Services Laboratory forwards McNamara's samples to CDC for further testing.

In the third week of September, the Connecticut Agriculture Experimental Station identified flavivirus in both crow and mosquito samples, unbeknownst to McNamara. On September 21st, McNamara spoke with the U.S. Army Medical Research Institute for Infectious Diseases (USAMRIID) at Fort Detrick, Maryland and sent them samples. USAMRIID confirmed flavivirus in McNamara's samples and ruled out SLE virus on September 22nd (Day 113). That same day, CDC-Fort Collins identified flavivirus virus from McNamara's samples that were sent two weeks previously to the National Veterinary Services Laboratory. The last known West Nile-positive human patient was ill also on September 22nd. On the next day, an academic researcher, Ian Lipkin, identified flavivirus from New York City human brain samples and communicated that finding to the New York State Department of Health. CDC-Fort Collins retested human samples and revised their diagnosis to West Nile virus.[20]

On September 24th, Lipkin informed the NYSDEC the virus genetic sequences most closely matched Kunjin or West Nile virus. That same day, CDC notified the New York State Department of Health the bird samples were positive for West Nile, and Lipkin discovered positive West Nile virus genetic sequences in human samples. The next day (Day 115), the media reported the presence of West Nile in New York City's birds.[21]

The New York City media reporting signal began on September 4th (Day 95), with a report of an outbreak of St. Louis encephalitis (Figure 1). The transition in terminology to West Nile occurred on September 25th (Day 115), which was the day of first mention of crow die-offs in the media source used for this study. Human illness was reported before bird die-offs and to a more robust degree. The media signal was approximately three months from local community notation of the first indicators of crow deaths in June. The online newspaper archive used for this study, which reported on New York City writ large, did not make note of the local Queens community paper's report of an unusual outbreak of disease in crows in late August 23.[22]

Data from the Bureau of Transportation Statistics acquired in 2003 by one of the authors (Wilson) indicated the leading source of air traffic from the Middle East to New York City and Newark, New Jersey in 1999 was Israel, which seasonally peaked in August (Figure 2). There were, on average, 50,700 passengers that traveled between New York City and Israel in 1999.[23] The Bureau indicated to Wilson no public health official had asked for air traffic data – that this was the first time to their

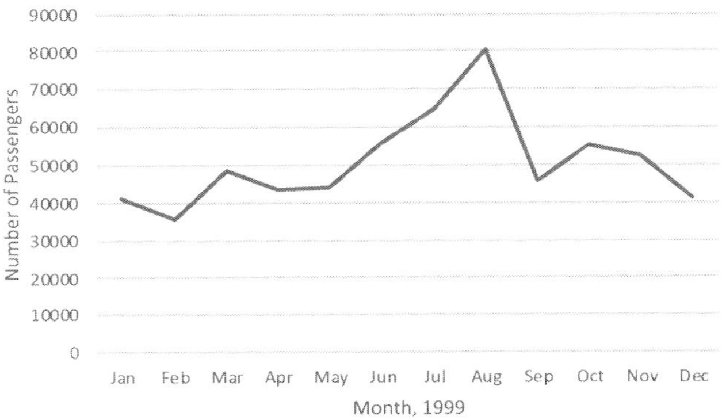

Figure 2. Bi-directional direct, non-stop air traffic between New York City and Israel, by month, in 1999.

recollection any public health official had asked for such data for any outbreak investigation. In 2001, the origin of the epidemic was reported to be Israel.[24] The mechanism of virus translocation to the United States, whether importation of infected mosquitoes or human passengers, was not proven.

Discussion

This case study highlights the challenges of integrating and maintaining a system of strategic health security warning intelligence with near-real time local warning communications. Unfortunately, reports of unusual West Nile activity in Europe did not result in a focus on preparedness in the United States. Connectivity between unusual West Nile activity in swans in Israel was not reported until years after the epidemic in New York City, and the air traffic connections between the United States and Israel were not known at the time. This information might have enabled focused warning communication to New York City and proactive preparedness activities such as mosquito spraying at the airports and education of veterinarians and healthcare clinicians. It is unknown whether proactive mosquito spraying at the airports would have stopped translocation of the virus to the western hemisphere. Israel did not have an established surveillance system for West Nile and thus was not a reportable human disease- this was created after the well-publicized New York epidemic. In 2001, Israel mandated reporting of West Nile infections in humans.[25]

Delays in unusual disease signal recognition result in delays in public health engagement, whether those signals appear in animals or in humans. It is arguable that, had McNamara not pushed for recognition of an animal signal that appeared at the same time as a human signal, the world would have drawn the conclusion that the New York epidemic was due to a routine mosquito-borne virus, Saint Louis encephalitis (SLE). McNamara did not know of the human signal until it was announced by the media on September 3rd, which highlights a missed potential opportunity of connecting the bird die-offs with human cases two weeks prior. There were important differences in threat assessment of a known, endemic disease (SLE) for which there was a given baseline of herd immunity versus an exotic disease (West Nile) where there was little to no herd immunity. Epidemics involving known, endemic disease implies routine public health response. Alternatively, virgin soil epidemics imply emergency response and potential for threat to national security. These situations suggest involvement of agencies involved with national defense or attribution investigation if there is suspicion of biological terrorism. Regardless of etiology, virgin soil epidemics are also often associated with greater socio-economic disruption to the involved communities than epidemics involving routine, locally familiar disease.

The critical role of the astute clinician-observer was highlighted in this case study with the involvement of the infectious disease physician at Flushing Hospital and McNamara at the Bronx Zoo. Had the local veterinarian in Bayside, Queens reported the apparent outbreak of unusual disease in crows in June, they too would have represented another astute observer. The presence of astute observers does not fully solve the challenge of recognition; however, the first known human case was missed, an unrecognized case that presented on August 2nd.[26] This highlights the value of experienced observers well trained in considering both routine and non-routine diseases among their patients. It also highlights the value of education and training in the recognition of rare diseases and pathogens of concern for potential use as potential biological weapons.

There were multiple community organizations, professional disciplines, and associated governmental agencies that exhibited siloed communication that interfered with timely recognition of the threat signal. These groups included: human health clinicians; community and exotic animal veterinarians; diagnostic laboratories including both veterinary and human health and spanning both military and civilian agencies; community special interest groups (i.e., in Queens that brought crows to the veterinary clinic); and public health authorities.

We estimated there were at least nine separate groups of people that together contributed to the final recognition and diagnosis of West Nile virus during this epidemic, of which two astute observers played key roles in initiating the warning sequence of communication. There was evidence of bias at

CDC when they believed SLE virus was initially responsible for the epidemic, and when questioned about their belief exhibited resistance to the presentation of competing hypotheses relating to discrepancies in epidemiological and clinical patterns of disease relating to both the avian and human cases.

There was evidence of bias in social sensitivity that ultimately prioritized public orientation to a threat signal and mount organized, emergency response. The driver for public health engagement was report of human versus animal disease. It is debatable whether public health would, or politically could, have engaged in response with report of a possible outbreak of disease in crows in June – unless a flavivirus unknown to the western hemisphere could have been diagnosed in June. This implies caution when considering research demonstrating the appearance of high threat infectious disease in animals preceding appearance in humans. Public perception and reaction to that perception may be focused on human disease as validation of threat, which highlights the challenges of integrating veterinary and human health disease surveillance to produce effective warning communication in health security.

There is caution in the use of open-source intelligence for warning signals related to health security threats. Warning signals associated with health security crises are often associated with significant delays in public communication. These delays are typically related to lack of local familiarity with the pathogen in question and therefore no prior investment in a specific, established public health surveillance system for the given pathogen.

Currently, the American system of biological threat warning does not include a robust wildlife diagnostic surveillance component. In addition, animal sentinels found in crowded urban centers like dogs, cats, and shelter animals and zoological collections do not fall under the jurisdiction of any federal agency and therefore are not currently under any formal surveillance. Should a similar warning signal appear in these sentinels, it is possible they would be missed. Even if this component existed, there remain significant communication defects between the veterinary and human health communities and the federal and private sectors.

As with other health security crises, there is often no available pharmaceutical countermeasure to mitigate impact. As of the date of this writing, there is no FDA-approved human vaccine for West Nile virus, nor is there an approved anti-viral. Education and mosquito control remain the mainstays of impact mitigation, which emphasizes the importance of early warning to prompt non-pharmaceutical countermeasures. Regardless of concerns about attribution, early warning coupled to proactive preparedness and response is crucial to mitigate the effects of health security threats.

Notes

1. Centers for Disease Control and Prevention, "West Nile Virus."
2. Centers for Disease Control and Prevention, "Provisional Surveillance Summary."
3. Crosby, "Virgin Soil Epidemics."
4. U.S. Government Accountability Office, "West Nile Virus Outbreak."
5. Ibid.
6. Newspapers.com.
7. PubMed.gov.
8. Bureau of Transportation Statistics, "Air Carriers."
9. Tsai et al., "West Nile Encephalitis."
10. Hubálek and Halouzka, "West Nile fever"; Hubálek, Halouzka, and Juricová, "West Nile fever"; and Giladi et al., "West Nile Encephalitis."
11. Malkinson et al., "Introduction of West Nile."
12. Drexler, *Secret Agents*, 32.
13. See note 5 above.
14. Ibid; and Drexler, *Secret Agents*, 20.
15. See note 5 above.
16. Drexler, *Secret Agents*, 20.
17. See note 5 above.
18. Drexler, *Secret Agents*, 56.

19. See note 5 above.
20. Ibid.
21. Ibid.
22. See note 7 above.
23. See note 9 above.
24. Giladi et al., "West Nile Encephalitis."
25. Ibid.
26. See note 5 above.

Acknowledgements

The authors gratefully acknowledge the manuscript reviewers for their comments.

Disclosure statement

Dr. Wilson is employed by M2 Medical Intelligence.

Bibliography

Bureau of Transportation Statistics. "Air Carriers: T-100 International Market." Accessed October 20, 2019. https://www.transtats.bts.gov/DL_SelectFields.asp

CDC. "Provisional Surveillance Summary of the West Nile Virus epidemic–United States, January–November 2002." *MMWR Morbidity Mortality Weekly Report* 51, no. 50 (2002): 1129–1133.

CDC. 2019. "West Nile Virus: Cumulative Maps & Data." Accessed October 20, 2019. https://www.cdc.gov/westnile/statsmaps/cumMapsData.html#three

Crosby, A. W. "Virgin Soil Epidemics as a Factor in the Aboriginal Depopulation in America." *The William and Mary Quarterly* 33, no. 2 (1976): 289–299. doi:10.2307/1922166.

Drexler, M. *Secret Agents: The Menace of Emerging Infections*. New York: Penguin Group, 2003.

Giladi, M., E. Metzkor-Cotter, D. A. Martin, Y. Siegman-Igra, A. D. Korczyn, R. Rosso, S. A. Berger, G. L. Campbell, and R. S. Lanciotti. "West Nile Encephalitis in Israel, 1999: The New York Connection." *Journal of Emerging Infectious Diseases* 7, no. 4 (2001): 659–661. doi:10.3201/eid0704.017410.

Hubálek, Z., and J. Halouzka. "West Nile Fever–a Reemerging Mosquito-borne Viral Disease in Europe." *Journal of Emerging Infectious Diseases* 5, no. 5 (1999): 643–650. doi:10.3201/eid0505.990505.

Hubálek, Z., J. Halouzka, and Z. Juricová. "West Nile Fever in Czechland." *Journal of Emerging Infectious Diseases* 5, no. 4 (1999): 594–595. doi:10.3201/eid0504.990430.

Lustig, Y., Z. Kaufman, E. Mendelson, L. Orshan, E. Anis, Y. Glazer, D. Cohen, T. Shohat, and R. Bassal. "Spatial Distribution of West Nile Virus in Humans and Mosquitoes in Israel, 2000-2014." *International Journal of Infectious Diseases* 64 (2017): 20–26. doi:10.1016/j.ijid.2017.08.011.

Malkinson, M., C. Banet, Y. Weisman, S. Pokamunski, R. King, M. T. Drouet, and V. Deubel. "Introduction of West Nile Virus in the Middle East by Migrating White Storks." *Journal of Emerging Infectious Diseases* 8, no. 4 (2002): 392–397. doi:10.3201/eid0804.010217.

Nash, D., F. Mostashari, A. Fine, J. Miller, D. O'Leary, K. Murray, A. Huang, et al. "West Nile Outbreak Response Working Group. 2001. The Outbreak of West Nile Virus Infection in the New York City Area in 1999." *New England Journal of Medicine* 344, no. 24 (1999): 1807–1814. doi:10.1056/NEJM200106143442401.

Newspapers.com. Accessed November 30, 2019. https://www.newspapers.com

PubMed.gov. Accessed November 30, 2019. https://www.ncbi.nlm.nih.gov/pubmed/

Tsai, T. F., F. Popovici, C. Cernescu, G. L. Campbell, and N. I. Nedelcu. "West Nile Encephalitis Epidemic in Southeastern Romania." *Lancet* 352, no. 9130 (1998): 767–771. doi:10.1016/S0140-6736(98)03538-7.

U.S. Government Accountability Office. "West Nile Virus Outbreak: Lessons for Public Health Preparedness." *GAO/HEHS-00-180*. Washington, DC, 2000.

Rapid validation of disease outbreak intelligence by small independent verification teams

Steven J. Hatfill

ABSTRACT

The requirement for rapid ground-truth verification is a major rate-limiting step in the early warning of global outbreaks of serious infectious disease. Until this problem is solved, the current and future systems for global disease surveillance will not be optimally functional. One solution is to create a well-funded team of military specialists capable of conducting a rapid on-site inspection and verification of any infectious disease outbreak posing a possible threat to international health security. There are multiple scenarios for the deployment of this team, including their entry into conflict areas to garner medical intelligence. This concept is not without precedent.

Background

With respect to intelligence collection, the presence of a severe contagious disease inside a country's borders may constitute a strategic issue with respect to its ripple effect on military and civilian activities and industrial production. The ability to discern if a given nation will have an extended disease crisis is a vital intelligence assessment. Consequently, many nations operate medical intelligence organizations which attempt to predict chronological patterns of infectious disease spread and estimate the impact on an infected country's demographics, supply and demand of drugs, future requirements for foreign aid, vaccination requirements for travel between countries, border control disease surveillance, and assessments on the infected country's military readiness. Hence, the rapid assessment of severe infectious disease outbreaks has applications for public health security and military defense.

However, the difficulties in this type of intelligence activity have been compounded in recent years by the appearance of an increasing number of new human pathogens that are new to medical science. In this respect, the term Emerging Infectious Disease (EID) refers to a previously unknown infectious disease that has suddenly appeared in a population, or one that is known, but it is suddenly increasing in its incidence or geographic range. Recent peer-reviewed research demonstrates a continuing increase in the number of EID that are jumping from wild animals into human populations worldwide with an average of one or two novel pathogen outbreaks every year.[1] There is also a plethora of previously unknown viral genetic sequences found in wild animals during general surveys.[2] This indicates there are still multiple, unrecognized, and potentially lethal species-crossing viruses in nature. Consequently, it is estimated that 10 to 40 new animal viruses will emerge into human populations over the next 20-years.[3] The pathogenic severity of these viruses are unknown but there is now a recognition that new EID outbreaks are a significant issue for national defense.[4]

In 2015, the U.S. Director of National Intelligence clearly expressed that natural infectious diseases were among the foremost global health security threats when he stated that, if a highly pathogenic avian influenza virus, like H7N9, were to become easily transmissible among humans, the outcome could be far more disruptive than the great influenza pandemic of 1918. It could lead to global economic losses, the unseating of governments, and the disturbance of geopolitical alliances.[5]

Introduction

The management of any communicable, lethal infectious disease involves the on-going collection of epidemic intelligence and the systematic rapid detection of new contagious disease outbreaks. Once surveillance measures have detected an outbreak, the basic public health response is to isolate the infected and contagious cases, identify other individuals that the first cases may have been in close contact with (case contact tracing) and isolate these contacts until it is confirmed that they have not contracted the infection.[6]

Early outbreak detection is also important for initiating other countermeasures such as vaccine and prophylactic drug dispersal (if available), animal culling programs (common in avian Influenza outbreaks), vector control (for insect transmitted diseases), and the mobilization of 'surge' medical resources if the local epidemic has the potential to expand into a larger geographic area.

These public health responses are labor-intensive, time-consuming and time-sensitive and the problem is made more difficult when special laboratories are needed to identify the pathogen involved. In addition, once a threshold number of infections have developed inside a high-density population area, it becomes a worst-case scenario with respect to outbreak control. Modern examples include the 2014 West Africa Ebola crisis.[7]

Therefore, it is essential to contain a lethal contagious disease outbreak before a human-adapted pathogen can gain access to the international air travel system. Even a single week of delay in recognizing an outbreak can have tremendous consequences for global heath.[8]

Realizing this risk, infectious disease scientists from around the world have worked in conjunction with the World Health Organization (WHO) to establish *the Global Outbreak Alert and Response Network* (GOARN). Established in 2000, this network is composed of numerous national health ministries, WHO regional and country offices, WHO collaborating centers, laboratories, academic institutions, nongovernmental organizations, and specific infectious disease centers in the United States, Canada, England, and Europe.[9]

To garner epidemic intelligence, the GOARN systematically gathers official reports and rumors of suspected outbreaks from a wide range of formal and informal sources. The GOARN also uses a specific data mining system to constantly scan the electronic global media and social media discussion groups. Developed by Health Canada this system is termed the *Global Public Health Intelligence Network* (GPHIN). It is a secure Internet-based multilingual early-warning tool that continuously searches global media sources such as news wires and web sites to identify information about disease outbreaks.[10]

During the first emergence of the 2003 Severe Acute Respiratory Syndrome (SARS) outbreak in Asia, the Canadian GPHIN picked up media reports of a respiratory disease outbreak in mainland China in November 2002. It sent this alert to the WHO that in turn, requested information from Chinese authorities on 5 and 11 of December. These two requests were ignored, and Chinese government officials did not inform the WHO of the outbreak until 28 February 2003. The international partners of GOARN were not notified until March 13.

This lack of openness caused delays in the efforts to control the SARS epidemic and it reemphasized the need for a rapid EID outbreak alert, verification, and management response system.[11]

In a response to this delayed verification, the WHO established a new set of formal International Health Regulations (IHR) in 2005. These rules are now binding on 196 countries and they require all signatory countries to conduct a program of national disease surveillance and to report any infectious disease event that may constitute a potential public health emergency of international concern.[12]

Yet, in spite of these multiple iterations of WHO cooperation with its signatories, and a plethora of new departments and reorganization attempts by many countries to address the threats posed by EID, the capability for global disease surveillance and rapid outbreak warning appears to be stagnating. This is evidenced by the multiple days of delay in the early detection of the 2009 H1N1 Influenza outbreak in Mexico,[13] the completely missed diagnosis of the first cluster of MERS-CoV virus cases in 2012 in Zarqa, Jordan,[14] the delayed recognition of the severity of the Ebola crisis in West Africa in 2014,[15] the mistrust by the international community over the cases of Bubonic Plague in China,[16] and the current distrust of Coronavirus infection and death rates in Wuhan, China.

The present WHO surveillance system appears to not be meeting the rapid surveillance requirements with respect to EID and an unverified contagious disease outbreak in a remote part of the world can still suddenly appear and begin to spread without early warning.[17] This is compounded by the fact that most local authorities remain unprepared for a major lethal infectious disease event that generates large numbers of patients and fatalities.[18]

To address this problem, the author performed a historical study of past EID outbreaks to identify any singular choke point(s) or major rate-limiting step(s) in the global pandemic surveillance and warning process. This was to assess how the alert process could be time-compressed to provide a more rapid public health response. In addition, the current theories and concepts of EID were re-examined to identify the major geographical regions at risk for new EID outbreaks and to formulate how the disease the surveillance and alert process could be improved in these areas.

Methods

The author used published peer-reviewed studies and Government Accountability Office (GAO) reports and testimony, to examine the repeated failure of the existing global disease surveillance systems to provide early timely warning of significant EID outbreaks over the last 25 years.[18] A timeline of events and actions were constructed for the 1999 West Nile virus outbreak in New York City; the 2003 emergence of the SARS virus outbreak in southern China; the A/H1N1 Influenza outbreak in 2009 in Mexico; the first 2012 cluster of cases of the MERS virus in Zarqa, Jordan; the failure to recognize the developing severity of the 2014 Ebola crisis in West Africa; the 2013–2015 Zika, Dengue, and Chikungunya virus pandemics and the still ongoing 2018 Ebola crisis in the Democratic Republic of the Congo,[19]

Results

The traditional WHO principles for global disease surveillance involve data collection, data collation, data analysis, and data dissemination to those who need the information for further action.[20] This system is dependent on the formal verification of an outbreak by examining the epidemiological data from affected countries operating under the IHR. While this process justifiably avoids the risk of false-positive alerts, this IHR requirement has resulted in previous missed windows for early outbreak detection by the WHO.

This is because in spite the IHR, every WHO signatory country is capable of non/under-reporting an infectious disease outbreak within their borders. The reasons for this may involve a concern over diagnostic uncertainty or a poor public health infrastructure in the affected country. Various political factors may be also be involved such as a fear of potential socioeconomic disruption or promoting fear in the population. Any of these factors may delay the alert of an evolving infectious disease outbreak for days to weeks.

Thus, the most important choke point appears to be obtaining laboratory and epidemiological data from the country affected by the outbreak, so the WHO can make a remote verification of an initial outbreak alert. This suggests the need for a more direct and rapid verification process for a suspected serious infectious disease outbreak, when first alerted by current and future global disease surveillance systems; one that is IHR independent.

In this respect, the data mining of the international media seems to provide a useful new tool for disease surveillance and early outbreak notification. However, this capability is offset by the requirement to still have real-world data supplied by the host country for outbreak verification. In addition, many parts of the world lack modern media connectivity that could hamper media collection and analysis. This is compounded by the fact that many of these regions are also the ones most likely to experience an outbreak of a previously unknown EID.

An examination of a database of 335 EID origins from 1940–2004, show a non-random pattern of emerging RNA viral diseases associated with '*biodiversity hotspots*'. A '*hotspot*' is a region defined as a threatened region containing 1,500 endemic species of vascular plants that has undergone at least a 70% recent loss of primary vegetation. There are 34 areas around the world that qualify under this definition, with nine other possible candidates.[21] These ecological regions are also home to 1.2 billion of the world's poorest people with a population that has doubled over the last 27 years.

The poverty and poor infrastructures in many of these 'hotspots' make it difficult to apply some of the newer big data-driven outbreak surveillance systems.[22] Even more problematic is the fact that some 90% of all the armed conflicts seen between the years of 1950 through to 2000, have occurred within a 'biological hotspot.'[23] Because of their remoteness and difficult terrain, these regions can often offer a tactical advantage to insurgent rebel groups. The infectious disease risk is derived from the fact that the guerilla rebels living in their self-constructed remote insurgent camps, have an increased probability of human-wild animal contact.,[24] In addition, the displaced civilian war refugees in a low-intensity conflict must also build camps, gather firewood and hunt for food. All these activities create additional stress on the native wildlife of these regions and it can place humans well inside the complex interplay of wild-type RNA viruses with their primary animal reservoirs and vectors in the conflict region.[25] This represents a worst-case scenario.

As seen in eastern border of the Democratic Republic of the Congo in 2018, the presence of armed rebels makes it dangerous to insert civilian medical and scientific teams to quickly verify that an outbreak is underway, monitor its progress, or implement epidemic countermeasures. The problem is further compounded if any of the responding medical personnel become infected themselves. In August of 2018 a physician was infected with the Ebola virus in the town of Oicha, which was almost entirely surrounded by Islamist ADF Ugandan rebels. This required the insertion of a rescue health team accompanied by armed security experts.[26]

As previously mentioned, a close study of past EID events indicates that the major rate-limiting step in the infectious disease outbreak warning process, is the requirement for rapid ground-truth verification. This indicates the need for a more direct, independent, epidemic intelligence verification method – one that does not rely on the WHO-IHR system and one that can perform a rapid, accurate and impartial 'boots on the ground' examination of any developing disease outbreak.

The fact that an EID verification may have to be undertaken inside a country embroiled in a low-intensity conflict suggests that one of these verification teams should be a small, specialized, armed military unit capable of conducting a conflict insertion into such a region to garner epidemiological data, collect biomedical samples, and evacuate any ill foreign nationals or military personnel under appropriate biological containment. This concept is not new and it was first formulated during the early stages of the U.S. conflict in Vietnam when medical infrastructures were still very basic and military aeromedical evacuation capabilities were very limited.

In late 1965, the U.S. Army Special Forces obtained funding from the Walter Reed Army Institute of Medical Research to establish a *Field Epidemiological Survey Team* (FEST) for early participation in the Vietnam war.[27]

The goal was to insert this armed team into geographical areas of South Vietnam that were about to receive large numbers of military personnel. Their mission was to assess these regions for their most prevalent tropical diseases, and to implement any countermeasures if they were available. All team members were Special Forces-qualified medical personnel with an attached entomologist, a veterinarian

Figure 1. U.S. army special forces-walter reed army institute of research field. Epidemiologic Survey Team (Airborne). Photo Credit; L. Dorogi. (DoD open source)

and several laboratory technicians. The unit underwent an additional fifteen-week pre-deployment training program and new equipment items were developed for remote area operations.

In 1966, the FEST was deployed to Vietnam with the 5th Special Forces Group (Airborne) to study malaria incidence among indigenous and U.S. forces during combat operations. Thereafter, it began to conduct increasingly important and diverse epidemiological studies.,[28] One critical study was the diagnosis and interventions involving Bubonic Plague outbreaks in Kontum Province, Dak To, and Nha Trang, where the FEST demonstrated the field effectiveness of streptomycin in two to three gram daily doses.[29] This was followed the rapid investigation of a possible pneumonic plague outbreak in IV Corps in its first non 'field' oriented study.[30]

Throughout 1966 and the first half of 1968, the FEST continued to investigate disease outbreaks, perform epidemiological surveys and collect biomedical samples for later research and validation, often under combat conditions (Figure 1).[31]

The FEST was deactivated in October 1968 as a result of an increased understanding of the tropical medical theater and a dramatically improved aeromedical evacuation capability. However, before it was disbanded the FEST proved *conclusively* that practical infectious disease epidemiology could be performed, and valuable medical intelligence collected in remote, hostile areas by a team that combined medical research skills with special operations military qualifications.[32]

A resurrection of this concept could have important applications with respect to the collection of epidemic intelligence and rapid outbreak verification inside a contested 'biodiversity hotspot' region involved in a low-intensity conflict.

Discussion

To improve early EID outbreak warning, the findings of this study suggest that multiple small, dedicated, national outbreak verification teams should be created that are either independent of the current WHO-IHR reporting system or that will work in conjunction with it in one of four primary scenarios. The activity of these teams could even be made as an extra provision of the IHR in a fashion similar to that of the current International Atomic Energy Agency (IAEA) Safeguard Inspectors which initiate on-site inspections to help ensure that that a signatory nation is living up to its international commitments not to use its nuclear program for nuclear-weapons purposes.[33]

The first scenario would involve the verification of an outbreak in a friendly, foreign country. At the first indications of a developing biological situation, a small team would operate through their own government and enter the affected country. There, the team would be dependent on the host country's cooperation and its internal diagnostic laboratory capability. However, they would stand ready to take biomedical samples and transport these to designated outside laboratories for analysis if required. This is already a common procedure under the current WHO-IHR surveillance system. However, the verification team would now also be used to investigate any early outbreak alerts discovered by WHO-independent advanced media data mining.

The second type of rapid verification deployment would involve the verification of a serious contagious disease outbreak in a rural or urban area inside a friendly poor-resource country with a limited health infrastructure. In this case, the verification team would use a commercial aircraft for transport. Biomedical samples would be collected and brought back to the high-containment laboratories of the dispatching country for disease assessment, full pathogen characterization and a search for effective drug treatments.

Alternatively, the verification team might fly by military transport aircraft accompanied by an advanced containerized laboratory with a small team of scientists and technicians. This has been done for years in the support of some nation's participation in Weapons of Mass Destruction (WMD) missions. The team and its containerized laboratory would be transported by military aircraft. After landing, the laboratory would remain on-board the aircraft at the closest international airport where the aircraft itself would serve as a forward operating base for the verification team if necessary.

For rapid pathogen isolation, the laboratory would be capable of various cell-line tissue culture, transmission electron microscopy, basic bacteriology, ELISA serology, and an RT-PCR Nucleic Acid Microarray system with a 22-hour time frame from pure culture to pathogen identification down to the viral family level.[34] For novel emerging disease agents, the laboratory would use random multiplex (RT)-PCR using 3′-locked random primers followed by rapid Ion Torrent genetic sequencing with a satellite-link to GenBank for nucleic acid sequence identification.[35]

The main mission of this verification team in a permissive poor-resource country, would be to land in the capital city, insert into the affected area, and confirm that an EID outbreak was underway. The team would collect clinical samples for analysis back at the mobile laboratory and later in external national laboratories. The team could also work with the local health authorities to construct an isolation treatment center to disrupt the epidemic cycle while the pathogen is being identified. The critical concept here, is the rapid deployment of these teams to provide a rapid verification of a suspected, still evolving outbreak.

The third scenario for team deployment would be for a suspected outbreak deep inside a denied territory such as North Korea. In this case, the verification team could be attached as a support unit to national intelligence authorities and forward-deploy to surrounding countries to await the appearance of any unusual outbreak in these locations. Alternatively, the teams could deploy to more remote but accessible permissive countries characterized with a concurrent a high volume of air or sea passenger traffic out of the denied territory.

The fourth and most difficult rapid verification deployment would occur when a suspected novel EID outbreak is occurring inside a conflict area. The recognition that EID pandemics have critical national security implications bring the national armed forces into this arena.

The fact that an EID outbreak may have to be verified inside a poor-resource country that is embroiled in a low-intensity conflict, indicates the need for a specialized *armed* military medical team able to conduct a conflict insert to garner epidemiological data, confirm the outbreak of an EID and secure biomedical samples for later detailed laboratory analysis. It is therefore reasonable to propose that this standing team should be composed of armed military special operations medical personnel with specialized epidemiological training suitable for this task.

One *implied mission* of this armed epidemiology team would be to work with the local population to teach basic contact tracing and isolation to disrupt the human epidemic cycle. This would also include teaching biologically-safe burial practices and possibly the establishment of a drop zone for the aerial delivery of additional supplies and equipment for expanded containment efforts. This would be in an attempt to contain the outbreak at its source.

Because many high-risk EID 'Hotspots' are also the working environment for conservationists, missionaries, non-government aid workers, representatives of outside government aid programs, and sometimes military special operations personnel, these groups run a low but definite risk of being in the middle of an EID outbreak that conceivably requires a medical evacuation. However, the presence of armed rebel groups could make it difficult to insert a civilian medical evacuation team. As previously mentioned, this may be a dangerous undertaking. This was most recently witnessed by the murder of DRC health workers fighting the current Ebola epidemic with seven murdered and more than 50 seriously hurt to date, according to an unofficial tally.[36]

Therefore, another *implied mission* for this team would be to rapidly insert into a remote conflict area to provide supportive medical care to infected foreign national personnel and initiate the biologically-secure transport of up to four casualties back for definitive health care and subsequent rapid evacuation to a dedicated infectious disease unit in their home country.

Such an evacuation could easily require a mix of local liaisons, ground vehicle transport, and rotary wing airlift before the final leg for aeromedical evacuation back to their country of origin. The risk for secondary infection of any attending medical personnel is high during this process if protective equipment, precautions, and isolation methods are not employed throughout the patient transport chain. Such transport might also delay starting antiviral therapies that may have only a narrow treatment window.

Following the first simultaneous 1976 outbreaks of Ebolavirus Disease in Sudan and Zaire and a recognition of the threat of EID to overseas U.S. personnel, the Department of Defense created the *Aeromedical Isolation and Special Medical Augmentation Response Team* (AIT-SMART).[37] Established in 1978, this rapid-response unit was combined with a USAF worldwide airlift capability and secure communications. This team was designed to safely evacuate highly contagious U.S. patients out of outbreak areas under high-level biological containment. At the same time, it provided critical care nursing for these isolated patients during their transport back to a specialized Medical Containment Suite (MCS) at the US Army Medical Research Institute for Infectious Diseases (USAMRIID) at Fort Detrick in Maryland.

Due to funding sequestrations under the Obama Administration, the AIT-SMART was decommissioned in 2010 along with the Fort Detrick Medical Containment Suite, and this unified capability was lost. In 2014, the U.S. was forced to contract private air carriers to evacuate several U.S. nationals out of West Africa under biocontainment.

In contrast, other nations have retained this aeromedical capability most particularly the British Royal Air Force. Since 1985, the U.K. Department of Health and Ministry of Defense has jointly operated a Deployable Air Isolator team (DAIT). Since 2012 has transported 11 high biological risk-patients out of outbreak areas back for definitive care in high-level isolation units in the United Kingdom.[38]

Summary

The rapid detection of new EID outbreaks is essential to initiate public health containment measures before a contagious disease can gain momentum and become pandemic. This threat is amplified with modern commercial air travel and the industry's projected continuing annual increase of 5–7.5% in air travel with an increase in the connectivity of most global regions. As global population numbers increase, EID outbreaks are projected to increase, it is essential to improve the verification response time for suspected outbreaks. While media data mining is a promising new tool for rapid detection, its functionality for early outbreak detection remains limited by the dependence of the GOARN on current WHO-IHR protocols.

This paper proposes the creation of small EID outbreak verification teams that are either independent of the current WHO-IHR reporting system or that will work in conjunction with it as special IHR inspectors in a fashion similar to the International Atomic Energy Agency (IAEA) Inspectors which initiate on-site inspections to help ensure that that a signatory nation is living up to its international nuclear commitments.

In addition, this paper outlines the need for a specialized, armed, military verification team to be created, based on the prototype FEST team previously described. Such a team would be trained to be capable of conducting an air, ground, or littoral conflict insertion into an outbreak area to verify an epidemic outbreak, apply on-site rapid point-of-care diagnostics to attempt pathogen identification, and teach initial epidemic control measures to the local population if practical.

Considering the possible need for future bio-contained aeromedical evacuation, it is reasonable to suggest that the proven concepts of the Fort Detrick AIT-SMART team and the Vietnam era FEST-team, be combined to form a specialized standing military *'Verification and Aeromedical Isolation Team'* (VAAI Team) with the additional capability for rapid diagnostic testing, providing time-sensitive antiviral drug therapy and performing the tactical evacuation of up to four personnel from an operational area to a definitive care facility under appropriate biological containment.

In addition to their primary special operations medical specialty, all team members would undergo a highly specialized three-phase 15-week core training program in epidemiology, rapid field point-of-care viral diagnostics, current antiviral pharmacology, biomedical sample collection, biologically-contained patient transport, and other techniques and procedures necessary to study a wide variety of infectious disease agents, animal reservoirs, and vectors. Two physicians, a veterinarian, and the team leader should be selected from the special operations community. On operations, the team should be self-sufficient for 14-days without resupply to remove them from any infection risk from the local money and food chain during their deployment to an outbreak area. The team may or may not be accompanied into the foreign country by a containerized laboratory and technicians who would remain at the closest secure foreign airfield.

When assessing the costs of training, maintaining, and deploying this proposed 12 to 14-man VAAI Team it is useful to compare the total projected 5-year cost of this effort, directly with the 750 USD million cost that was incurred by having to deploy the 101st Airborne Division (Air Assault) to execute *Operation United Assistance*. This was during the West Africa Ebola crisis in direct support to the USAID (United States Agency for International Development).[39]

This is in addition to the USAID's own expenditure of more than 2.3 USD billion dollars against this infectious disease outbreak.[40] It does not include the cost of screening for cases of Ebolavirus disease at U.S. airports and the panicked incident management of the small number of cases of Ebolavirus disease that eventually appeared in the United States.

The early deployment of a VAAI Team at the very beginning of the 2014 West Africa Ebola outbreak, would have provided significant ongoing medical intelligence to USAID. It could have made a significant impact on this event before it required the expensive deployment of over 3,000 U.S. military personnel to build, train, and staff a large number of Ebola treatment Centers in Liberia.

This proposed team and its unique capabilities would be of major assistance to improving the national biological security of all countries. Along with this effort, funding should be provided to outside researchers for the further development of accurate, ruggedized, rapid Point-of-Care diagnostics for known emerging disease agents.

Mobile labs, FEST deployments and biologically-secure patient transport to communicable disease treatment centers, are concepts which have evolved and then disappeared over time due to a lack of funding or lack of use, only to be needed again in the future.

The almost exponential increase in global infectious disease outbreaks together with the now rising number of outbreaks of new EID since the mid-1990s, have combined with an increasing global population and an increasing level of high-density urbanization. When this is added to the increased interconnectivity caused by global travel, it suggests that it is time for renewed efforts in global disease surveillance verification and rapid response to new EID threats.

Notes

1. Jones, Patel, and Levy, "Global Trends in Emerging Infectious Diseases," 990; and Smith et al.,"Global Rise in Infectious Disease Outbreaks", 3.
2. Turmelle and Olival, "Viral Richness in Bats," 522.

3. Parrish et al., "Cross-Species Virus Transmission," 457; and 5. Woolhouse, "Human Viruses," 2864.
4. National Intelligence Estimate (NIE 99-17D).
5. Clapper, "Statement for the Record," 10.
6. Kang et al.,"Contact Tracing for Imported Case," 1646.
7. Bell et al., "Overview, Control Strategies, and Lessons Learned".
8. Hui et al., "Severe Acute Respiratory Syndrome vs. MERS".
9. Mackenzie J.S., "The Global Outbreak Alert and Response Network".
10. Dion et al. "Big Data and the Global Public Health Intelligence Network".
11. Heyman et al., "Global Surveillance, National Surveillance, and SARS".
12. World Health Organization Revision of the International Health Regulations. 2003.
13. Wilson, "Signal Recognition During the Emergence of Pandemic A/H1N1," 8".
14. Zumla et al. "Middle East Respiratory Syndrome".
15. Funk et al., "A Case Study of Ebola in the Western Area".
16. Yeung, "Two People Got the Plague in China."
17. Kim et al., "Middle East Respiratory Syndrome Coronavirus Outbreak".
18. Hatfill et al., *Three Seconds Until Midnight*, 321.
19. HHS OIG (OEI). "Pandemic Influenza Preparedness: Medical Surge", 12; HEHS-00-180 "West Nile Virus Outbreak"; Roth et al., "Concurrent Outbreaks of Dengue."; and Timeline of the Ebola Outbreak Response in Democratic Republic of the Congo, 2018.
20. Grein et al., "Rumors of Disease in the Global Village," 97.
21. Myers et. al., "Biodiversity Hotspots for Conservation Priorities," 853.
22. Brownstein et al., "Digital Disease Detection," 2153.
23. Hanson et al., "Warfare in Biodiversity Hotspots," 578.
24. Toph et al., "Global Hotspots and Correlates of Emerging Zoonotic Diseases," 1124; and Draulens et al., "The Impact of War on Forest Areas in the DRC," 2.
25. Taylor et al., "Risk Factors for Human Disease Emergence," 983.
26. Soucheray, "Doctor Infected With Ebola in DRC Conflict Zone," 1.
27. Dorogi, "Special Forces-Field Epidemiologic Survey Team (Airborne)," 54.
28. Colwell et al., "Histopathology of Liver Diseases," 300; and Colwell et al., "Big Spleen Syndrome," 120.
29. Legters et al., "Clinical and Epidemiological Notes on an Outbreak of Plague," 372.
30. Legters et al., "Epidemiological Notes on an Outbreak of Pneumonia," 445.
31. Roger et al., "A Prospective Study of Malaria among Indigenous Forces," 115; and Boone et al., "Report of a Survey for Schistosomiasis in the Mekong Delta," 316.
32. Foreword; "U.S. Army Medical Research Team Vietnam and Institute Pasteur,"2; and Hembree et al., "Distribution and Prevalence of Bancroftian Filariasis," 309.
33. IAEA Safeguards Overview: Comprehensive Safeguards Agreements.
34. Eunice et al., "Microarray Assay to Screen for Viral Pathogens," 2536.
35. Clem et al., "Random Multiplex (RT)-PCR with 3′-Locked Random Primers", 2.
36. WHO Disease outbreak news: Update Ebola Virus Disease".
37. Christopher and Eitzen, "Air Evac Under Biosafety Containment," 241.
38. Nicol et al., "Aeromedical Transfer of Patients with Viral Hemorrhagic Fever".5.
39. Operation united assistance. "The DoD Response to West Africa."
40. USAID, "West Africa Ebola Outbreak Fact Sheet #3, 2016.

Disclosure statement

No potential conflict of interest was reported by the author.

Funding

This work was financially supported by the Asymmetrical Biodiversity Studies and Observation Group, NPF.

Bibliography

Allen, T., K. A. Murray, P. Allen, K. A. Murray, C. Zambrana-Torrelio, S.S. Morse, et al. "Global Hotspots and Correlates of Emerging Zoonotic Diseases." *Nature Communications* 8, (2017): 1124. doi:10.1038/s41467-017-00923-8.

Bell, B. P., I. K. Damon, D. B. Jernigan, T. A. Kenyon, S. T. Nichol, J. P. O'Connor, J. W. Tappero, et al. "Overview, Control Strategies, and Lessons Learned in the CDC Response to the 2014–2016 Ebola Epidemic." *MMWR Supplements* 65, no. 3 (2016): 4–11. doi:10.15585/mmwr.su6503a2.

Boone, S. C., D. M. Robertson, and R. F. Proctor. "Report of a Survey for Areas Endemic for Schistosomiasis in the Mekong River Delta, IV Corps Tactical Zone". *U.S. Army Medical Research Team (WRAIR) Vietnam and Institute Pasteur of Vietnam*. Annual Progress Report (1 September 1966-31 August 1967), 316–345, 1967.

Brownstein, J. S., C. C. Freifeld, and L. C. Madoff. "Digital Disease Detection — Harnessing the Web for Public Health Surveillance." *New England Journal of Medicine* 360, no. 21 (2009): 2153–2157. doi:10.1056/NEJMp0900702.

Chen, E. C., S. A. Miller, J. L. DeRisi, and C.Y.Chiu. "Using a Pan-Viral Microarray Assay (Virochip) to Screen Clinical Samples for Viral Pathogens." *Journal of Visualized Experiments : JoVE* 50, (2011): 2536. Published online Apr 27 (2011). doi:10.3791/2536.

Christopher, G. W., and E. M. Eitzen Jr. "Air Evacuation Under Biosafety Containment." *Journal of Emerging Infectious Diseases* 5, no. 2 (1999): 241–246. Mar-Apr. doi:10.3201/eid0502.990208.

Clapper, J. "Statement for the Record, Worldwide Threat Assessment of the U.S.Intelligence Community." *Senate Armed Services Committee*, 2015. https://www.dni.gov/files/documents/Unclassified_2015_ATA_SFR_-_SASC_FINAL.pdf

Clem, A. L., J. Sims, S. Telang, J. W. Eaton, and J. Chesney. "Virus Detection and Identification Using Random Multiplex (RT)-PCR with 3′-locked Random Primers." *Virol Journal* 4 (2007): 6. doi:10.1186/1743-422X-4-65.

Colwell, E. J., B. Dunn, and L. J. Legters. "Histopathology of Liver Diseases among Residents of Mekong River Dela. T U.S. Army Medical Research Team (WRAIR) Vietnam and Institute Pasteur of Vietnam." *Annual Progress Report (1 September 1966-31 August 1967)*, 300–315, 1967.

Colwell, E. J., and L. J. Legters. ""Big Spleen Syndrome" Studies of Etiology at Selected Sites in I and IV Corps Tactical Zone, U.S. Army Medical Research Team (WRAIR) Vietnam and Institute Pasteur of Vietnam." *Annual Progress Report (1 September 1966-31 August 1967)*, 120–137, 1967.

Dion, M., P. Abdel Malik, and A. Mawudeku. "Big Data and the Global Public Health Intelligence Network (GPHIN)." *Canadian Communicable Disease Reports* 41, no. 9 (2015): 209–214. eCollection PMID:29769954. doi:10.14745/ccdr.v41i09a02.

Dorogi, L. T. "The United States Army Special Forces-Walter Reed Army Institute of Research Field Epidemiologic Survey Team (Airborne)." *Journal of Spec Ops Medicine* 9, no. 2 (2009): 54–71.

Draulens, D., E. van Krunkelsven . "The Impact of War on Forest Areas in the Democratic Republic of the Congo." *Cambridge Journals* 36, no. 1 (2000): 35–40. Tervuren, Belgium. doi: 10.1017/S0030605302000066.

"Foreword; U.S. Army Medical Research Team (WRAIR) Vietnam and Institute Pasteur." *Annual Progress Report (1 July 1968-30 June 1969)*, 1969.

Funk, S., A. Camacho, A. J. Kucharski, R. Lowe, R. M. Eggo, and W. J. Edmunds. "Assessing the Performance of Real-time Epidemic Forecasts: A Case Study of Ebola in the Western Area Region of Sierra Leone, 2014-15." *PLOS Computational Biology* 15, no. 2 (2019): e1006785. doi:10.1371/journal.pcbi.1006785.

Grein, T. W., K. B. Kamara, G. Rodier, A.J. Plant, P. Bovier, M.J. Ryan, T. Ohyama, and D.L. Heymann. "Rumors of Disease in the Global Village: Outbreak Verification." *Journal of Emerging Infectious Disease* 6, no. 2 (2000): 97–102. doi:10.3201/eid0602.000201.

Hanson, T., T. M. Brooks, A. da Fonseca, M. Hoffmann, J. F. Lamoreux, G. Machlis, C. G. Mittermeier, et al. "Warfare in Biodiversity Hotspots." *Conservation Biology* 23, no. 3 (2009): 578–587. doi:10.1111/j.1523-1739.2009.01166.x.

Hart, T., and R. Mwinyihali. *Armed Conflict and Biodiversity in Sub-Saharan Africa: The Case of the Democratic Republic of Congo*. Washington, DC: Biodiversity Support Program/WWF, 2001.

Hatfill, S., R. Coullahan, and J. Walsh. *Three Seconds Until Midnight*. USA: Amazon, 2019.

HEHS-00-180: West Nile Virus Outbreak: Lessons for Public Health Preparedness, 2000. https://www.gao.gov/products/HEHS-00-180

Hembree, S. C., G. Rodier. "Distribution and Prevalence of Bancroftian Filariasis in US Army Special Forces Camps in the Republic of Vietnam." *Military Medicine* 139, no. 4 (1974): 309–312. doi:10.1093/milmed/139.4.309.

Heyman, D. L., and G. Rodier. "Global Surveillance, National Surveillance, and SARS." *Journal of Emerging Infectious Diseases* 10, no. 2 (2003): 173–175. doi:10.3201/eid1002.031038.

HHS Office of Inspector General, Office of Evaluation and Inspections (OEI). "State and Local Pandemic Influenza Preparedness: Medical Surge." *OEI-02-08-00210*, 2009. https://oig.hhs.gov/oei/reports/oei-02-08-00210.pdf

Hui, D., Z. A. Memish, and A. Zumla. "Severe Acute Respiratory Syndrome Vs. The Middle East Respiratory Syndrome." *Current Opinion in Pulmonary Medicine* 20, no. 3, (2014): 233–241. doi:10.1097/MCP.0000000000000046.

IAEA Safeguards Overview: Comprehensive Safeguards Agreements and Additional Protocols, 2019. https://www.iaea.org/publications/factsheets/iaea-safeguards-overview

Jones, K., N. Patel, M. A., Levy, A. Storeygard, D. Balk, J. L. Gittleman, and P. Daszak. "Global Trends in Emerging Infectious Diseases." *Nature* 451, no. 7181 (2008): 990–993. doi:10.1038/nature06536.

Kang, M., T. Song, H. Zhong, J. Hou, J. Wang, J. Li, J. Wu, et al. "Contact Tracing for Imported Case of Middle East Respiratory Syndrome, China, 2015." *Journal of Emerging Infectious Diseases* 22, no. 9 (2016): 1644–1646. doi:10.3201/eid2209.152116.

Kim, K. H., T. E. Tandi, J. W. Choi, J. M. Moon, M. S. Kim. "Middle East Respiratory Syndrome Coronavirus (Mers-cov) Outbreak in South Korea-2015: Epidemiology, Characteristics and Public Health Implications." *The Journal of Hospital Infection* 95, no. 2 (2017): 207–213. doi:10.1016/j.jhin.2016.10.008.

Legters, L. J., and A. J. Cottingham Jr. "Clinical and Epidemiological Notes on an Outbreak of Plague at Dak to Special Forces Camp, II Corps Tactical Zone." *U.S. Army Medical Research Team (WRAIR) Vietnam and Institute Pasteur of Vietnam, Annual Progress Report (1 September 1966-31 August)*, 371–432, 1967.

Legters, L. J., D. H. Hunter, R. F. Proctor, and F. G. Conrad, Clinical and Epidemiological Notes on an Outbreak of Pneumonia in Rach Gia, Kien Giang Province, IV Corps Tactical Zone, April-May 1967, *U.S. Army Medical Research Team (WRAIR) Vietnam and Institute Pasteur of Vietnam, Annual Progress Report* (1 September 1966-31 August), (1967), pp. 444–462.

Mackenzie, J. S., P. Drury, R. R. Arthur, M. J. Ryan, T. Grein, R. Slattery, S. Suri, et al. "The Global Outbreak Alert and Response Network." *Global Public Health* 9, no. 9 (2014): 1023–1039. Sep 4. PMID: 25186571. doi: 10.1080/17441692.2014.951870.

Myers, N., R. A. Mittermeier, C. G. Mittermeier, G. A. B. da Fonseca, J. Kent . "Biodiversity Hotspots for Conservation Priorities." *Nature* 403, no. 6772 (2000): 853. 858. doi:10.1038/35002501.

National Intelligence Estimate (NIE 99-17D). *The Global Infectious Disease Threat and Its Implications for the United States.* McLean, VA: National Intelligence Council, 2000.

Nicol, E., S. Mepham, J. Naylor, I. Mollan, M. Adam, J. d'Arcy, P. Gillen, E. Vincent, B. Mollan, D. Mulvaney, A. Green, and M. Jacobs. "Aeromedical Transfer of Patients with Viral Hemorrhagic Fever." *Journal of Emerging Infectious Diseases* 25, no. 1–January (2019). https://wwwnc.cdc.gov/eid/article/25/1/18-0662_article

Operation United Assistance. "The DOD Response to Ebola in West Africa." *Joint and Coalition Operational Analysis, Joint Staff J-7*, 2016.

Parrish, C. R., E. C. Holmes, D. M. Morens, E. C. Park, D. S. Burke, C. H. Calisher, C. A. Laughlin, P. Daszak P. et al. "Cross-Species Virus Transmission and the Emergence of New Epidemic Diseases." *Microbiology and Molecular Biology Reviews* (2008). doi:10.1128/MMBR.00004-08.

Roger, R. N., E. H. Fife, and C. R. Webb. "A Prospective Study of Malaria among Indigenous Forces in Vietnam with Observations on Incidence, Chemoprophylaxis, and Immunology." *U.S. Army Medical Research Team (WRAIR) Vietnam and Institute Pasteur of Vietnam, Annual Progress Report (1 Sept. 1967-30 June1968)*, 115–116, 1968.

Roth, A., A. Mercier, C. Lepers, D. Hoy, S. Duituturaga, E. Benyon, L. Guillaumot, et al. "Concurrent Outbreaks of Dengue, Chikungunya and Zika Virus Infections – An Unprecedented Epidemic Wave of Mosquito-borne Viruses in the Pacific 2012–2014." *Eurosurveillance* 19, no. 41 (2014): 20929. 1560-7917. PMID 25345518. doi:10.2807/1560-7917.ES2014.19.41.20929.

Smith, K. F., M. Goldberg, S. Rosenthal, L. Carlson, J. Chen, C. Chen and S. Ramachandran. "Global Rise in Infectious Disease Outbreaks." *Journal of the Royal Society Interface* 11, (2014): 21140950. doi:10.1098/rsif.2014.0950.

Soucheray, S. "Doctor Infected with Ebola in DRC Conflict Zone." *CIDRAP News*, August 24, 2018. http://www.cidrap.umn.edu/news-perspective/2018/08/doctor-infected-ebola-drc-conflict-zone

Taylor, L. H., S. M. Latham, and M. E. J. Woolhouse. "Risk Factors for Human Disease Emergence." *Royal Society Philosophical Transactions Biological Sciences* 356, no. 1411 (2001): 983–989. doi:10.1098/rstb.2001.0888.

"Timeline of the Ebola Outbreak Response in the Democratic Republic of the Congo." 2018. https://www.who.int/ebola/drc-2018/timeline/en/

Trujillo, C. M., D. R. Levinson, and S. A. Linick "Quarterly Progress Report on U.S. Government Activities, International Ebola Preparedness and Response", 2015. https://oig.usaid.gov/sites/default/files/2018-06/ebola_response_09302015.pdf

Turmelle, A. S., and K. J. Olival. "Viral Richness in Bats." *Ecohealth* 6, no. 4 (2009): 522–539. doi:10.1007/s10393-009-0263-8.

US Agency for International Development (USAID). "West Africa Ebola Outbreak Fact Sheet."*#3,2016, 6 November*, 2015. http://www.usaid.gov/sites/default/files/documents/1866/westafricafs0311062015.pdf.

WHO Disease outbreak news: Update Ebola virus disease – Democratic Republic of the Congo 7 November, 2019. https://www.who.int/csr/don/07-november-2019-ebola-drc/en/

Wilson, J. M. "Signal Recognition during the Emergence of Pandemic Influenza Type A/H1N1: A Commercial Disease Intelligence Unit's Perspective." *Intelligence and National Security* (2016). doi:10.1080/02684527.2016.1253924.

Withers, M. R., G. C. Christopher, S. J. Hatfill, and J. J. Gutierrez-Nunez. "Aeromedical Evacuation of Patients with Contagious Infections." In *Aeromedical Evacuation; Management of Acute and Stabilized Patients*, edited by W. Hurd and J. Jernigan, pp.147–160. 2nd ed. Myrtle Beach, SC: Springer Press, 2019.

Woolhouse, M., F. Scott, Z. Hudson, R. Howey, and M. Chase-Topping. "Chase-Topping M "Human Viruses: Discovery and Emergence"." *Philosophical Transactions of the Royal Society B: Biological Sciences* 367, no. 1604 (2012): 2864–2871. doi:10.1098/rstb.2011.0354.

World Health Organization Revision of the international Health Regulations. World Health Assembly Resolution WHA56.28. Geneva: World Health Organization, 2003. http://www.who.int/gb/EB_WHA/PDF/WHA56/ea56r28.pdf

Yeung, J. "Two People Got the Plague in China. Why Is It Still a Thing?". *CNN.* 14 November, (2019).

Zumla, A., D. Shui, and S. Perlman. "Middle East Respiratory Syndrome." *The Lancet* 386, no. 9997 (2015): 995–1007. doi:10.1016/S0140-6736(15)60454-8.

Threat potential of pharmaceutical based agents

D. J. Heslop and P. G. Blain

ABSTRACT

The potential use of 'pharmaceuticals' has been identified by civilian law enforcement agencies, and counter-terrorism responders, as a threat that fills the gap between physical restraint and lethal weapons. This rise in availability of synthetic opiates reassessment of the overall public health threat from pharmaceutical based agents. The large quantities of illicitly synthetized novel opioids create a significant risk of accidental exposures or, potentially, a major deliberate release, and represents a global health security concern. Here we present a health security risk assessment of PBAs and approaches to threat prevention or mitigation, gaps in research, and medical countermeasure considerations.

Introduction

The medical aspects of the use of '*Drugs as Weapons*' was first discussed in a Report from the British Medical Association Board of Science in 2007.[1] At that time, pharmaceutical based agents (PBAs) were being mainly considered by civilian law enforcement agencies, and counter-terrorism responders, to meet a capability needed in the force gap between physical restraint and lethal weapons.[2] The Chemical Weapons Convention (CWC) permits deployment of incapacitating pharmaceutical agents for law enforcement, including domestic riot control purposes and civilian security, but does not allow for their use as a method of warfare. Developments in neuroscience and toxicology, and the wider use of PBAs as incapacitating chemical agents (ICAs), pose a challenge to the CWC constraint .[3]

The current public health crisis in North America from opioid drug misuse, with an increasing proportion of deaths due to illegally manufactured fentanyl and fentanyl analogues, has resulted in a reassessment of the overall public health threat from pharmaceutical based agents .[4] The large quantities of illicitly synthetized novel opioids, that are being distributed globally, create a significant risk of accidental exposures or, potentially, a major deliberate release. The supply, distribution, and potency of these novel fentanyl analogues has become a global health security concern and the logistics for emergency preparedness, resilience, response and recovery are recognized to be major problems for emergency first responders and health care services .[5]

A health security risk assessment of PBAs and approaches to threat prevention or mitigation will be discussed. The logistical problems affecting adequate incident preparedness, and the optimum first responder clinical management of exposed individuals, will be presented alongside lessons learned from clinical experience. The need for rapidly accessible and adequate doses of medical countermeasures, that can be administered speedily to exposed individuals, will be considered, and research and development needs for potent and long-acting antidotes discussed.

Pharmaceutical based agents

The classification of chemical and biological (CB) agents, with the potential for use as a weapon into specific categories, has traditionally been divided according to clinical toxidrome or membership of broad categories defined by functional activity. For example, hazardous substances are often divided into the widely used Chemical, Biological, Radiological, Nuclear and Explosive (CBRNe) categorisation reflecting a predominantly physicochemical and functional classification .[6] In reality, the full range of chemical and biological agent threats can be best described as a CBRN Threat Spectrum (Figure 1, with permission) with toxic industrial chemicals and genetically modified pathogens occupying the extremes of the spectrum.

Recent advances in synthetic biology, and their supporting and enabling technologies, are allowing the emergence of biological agents that fall between or across these historical boundaries and norms. An example of these are the biological toxins that share characteristics of both chemical agents in relation to behaviour within an environment and non-transmissibility, but are proteinaceous biologicals derived from organisms. Advances in genetics are now also extending the spectrum of CBRN agents into novel infectious agents, conferring new properties and capacities on classical agents or creating entirely new pathogenic agents from previously non-pathogenic sources.[7] In the natural world moderately pathogenic agents, such as the common cold or influenza, are good examples of how incapacitation outside of traditional incapacitant categorisations can have a functional impact on human activities by reducing task effectiveness and increasing burdens on health systems without necessarily causing mortality.

Incapacitating agents encapsulate a broad range of chemicals that are intended to produce, or predominantly cause, an incapacitating effect. For substances selected and fielded for use as incapacitants there are no universally accepted criteria for what constitutes incapacitation.[8] Nevertheless, for practical purposes, incapacitation is an effect that impedes the ability of an individual to make decisions, undertake actions, or to perform to an acceptable or desirable standard. The infliction of permanent injury or death on the exposed human is usually not an intended outcome but, inevitably, may be a side effect of exposure at high dose or occur in certain exposure scenarios. Incapacitants selected for use usually attempt to minimise the likelihood of unintended permanent injury or death. They may be classified as less-lethal technologies because of their inherent properties, method of deployment and rules of engagement. It must always be noted that unexpected or accidental exposure to incapacitants at high dose can result in irreversible injury or death.

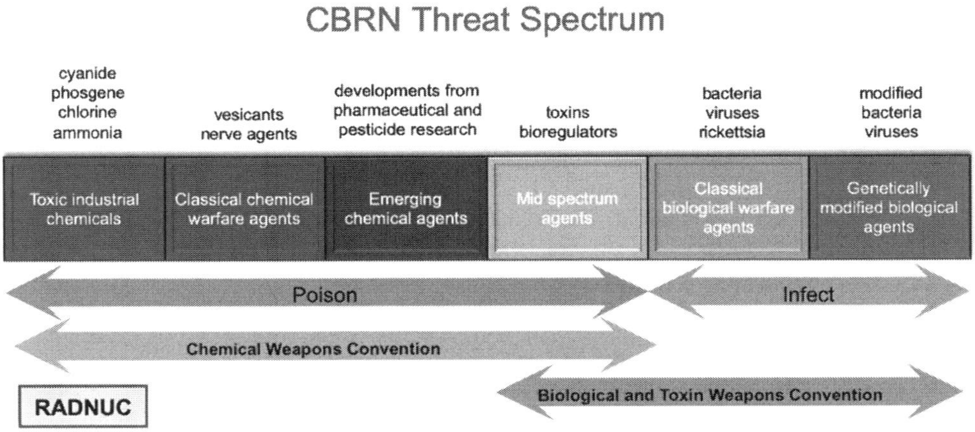

Figure 1. CBRN Threat Spectrum – adapted from an original concept of Graham Pearson, former Director, Dstl Porton Down, UK (with permission).

The ideal attributes of a '*functional*' incapacitant include being capable of directed deployment and targeted delivery, produce rapid total incapacitation, or disruption of a specific capability, in an individual or small group and cause predictable effects with little variation in extent or nature. It must also not compromise the survival or safety of an unattended incapacitated individual and is reversible over time, or by specific treatment, without any residual adverse effects.[9]

Pharmaceutical Based Agents (PBAs) are a subset of incapacitating agents and mostly comprise chemicals that have been designed for medical pharmaceutical use but which in overdose, or certain exposure contexts, can cause either incapacitation, permanent injury or death. These compounds fall into the mid-sections of the chemical and biological threat agents' spectrum (as above), sometimes possessing characteristics of both traditional chemical and biological agents.

PBAs with the potential for use as incapacitants can be divided into broad groups as outlined in Table 1.

Incapacitating PBAs are primarily intended to reduce conscious awareness but may also affect cognition sufficient to significantly degrade an individual's capability to make rational decisions in sensitive or decisive situations. This outcome would severely degrade a leader's capabilities and, with broader deployment, the coordination and effectiveness of a military unit .[10]

The properties of a PBA that would limit medical safety acceptance include narrow safety margins (ratio: lethal dose/effective dose), severity of side effects, lack of an effective antidote for use by medical responders, a wide natural variation in human susceptibility, due to genetics, age, illness, and the likelihood of collateral effects causing harm or death such as airway obstruction or a physical accident. Their use must also be in compliance with operational policy and rules of engagement. Of the many potential chemicals and drugs, the candidate compounds with the optimum profile for use as incapacitants are the opioids.

Opiate and opioid drugs

There is a difference between opiates and opioids. Opiates are chemical substances extracted from opium found in the exudate of the unripe seed capsule of *Papaver somniferum* (the Poppy plant). The exudate contains several types of alkaloids such as morphine and codeine. An opioid is a compound with morphine-like activity. Natural opium alkaloids include morphine and codeine, semi-synthetic opiates include diacetylmorphine (i.e. heroin, which was first synthesized in the UK in 1874 by CR Wright), oxycodone (derived from thebaine) and pholcodeine. Purely synthetic opioids include pethidine (meperidine), methadone, dextropropoxyphene, tramadol, fentanyl and the range of fentanyl derivatives including alfentanil, sufentanil, remifentanil and carfentanil .[11]

Opioid crisis in North America

Between 1996 and 2001 pharmaceutical companies extensively promoted OxyContin (oxycodone), and other opioids, as specific and highly effective treatments for chronic pain relief, but downrated the risk of drug addiction. In six years, the number of prescriptions for opioids rose from 700 K per year to 6 M per year. By 2002 prescription opioids were attributed in the cause of death in over 5 K patients per year. In 2012 the opioid market was worth 11 USDBn but by 2015 opioid associated overdose deaths exceeded 1,000 per week. Notably, at this time some 60% of these deaths were from opioids (fentanyls) obtained 'on the street' rather than by prescription (Figure 2) .[12]

The US is estimated to consume nearly 80% of the global production of opioid pills, despite constituting just 5% of the world population. There are now >150 overdose deaths per day in the US (>60 K per year) and fentanyl, and fentanyl analogues, have become much more widely available due to illicit importation from China via Mexico (Figure 3).[13] Many street drugs are now cut with fentanyls as these are cheaper and more potent than heroin and so provide higher profits to the drug dealers.

Table 1. Selected potential pharmaceutical based agents and threat summary.

Drug Type	Examples	Conventional Clinical Use	Principal Mechanism of Action	Used	Notes
Opiates and opioids	Fentanyl and derivatives	Analgesia Anaesthesia	Agonists: peripheral and central μ and other receptors	Incapacitating agent used in civilian security operations	Respiratory depression and asphyxia by mechanical obstruction
Psychodelics	Lysergic acid diethylamide (LSD)	Nil	Agonists: serotonin and dopamine receptors	Historical assessment and trials	Hallucination and cognitive degradation
Anticholinergics	3-Quinuclidinyl benzilate (BZ)	Nil	Antagonist: muscarinic cholinergic receptors	Balkan War	Cognitive degradation
GABA Modulators	Muscimol Baclofen Alcohol Propofol	Sedation Anaesthesia Anxiolysis	GABA agonists. GABA positive allosteric modulators	nil known	
Neuroleptic anaesthetics	Ketamine	Analgesia Anaesthesia	Antagonist: NMDA type glutamate receptors	nil known	Less respiratory depression. Sensory distortion and risk of psychiatric problems
α_2-adrenoceptor agonists	Dexmedetomidine	Sedation	Agonist: pre-junctional α_{2A}-adrenoceptors in locus coeruleus	nil known	No respiratory depression
Benzodiazepines	Lorazepam Temazepam Diazepam	Sedation Anxiolysis Anaesthesia	Agonists: regulatory site on GABA-A receptors	nil known	Cardiovascular and respiratory depression

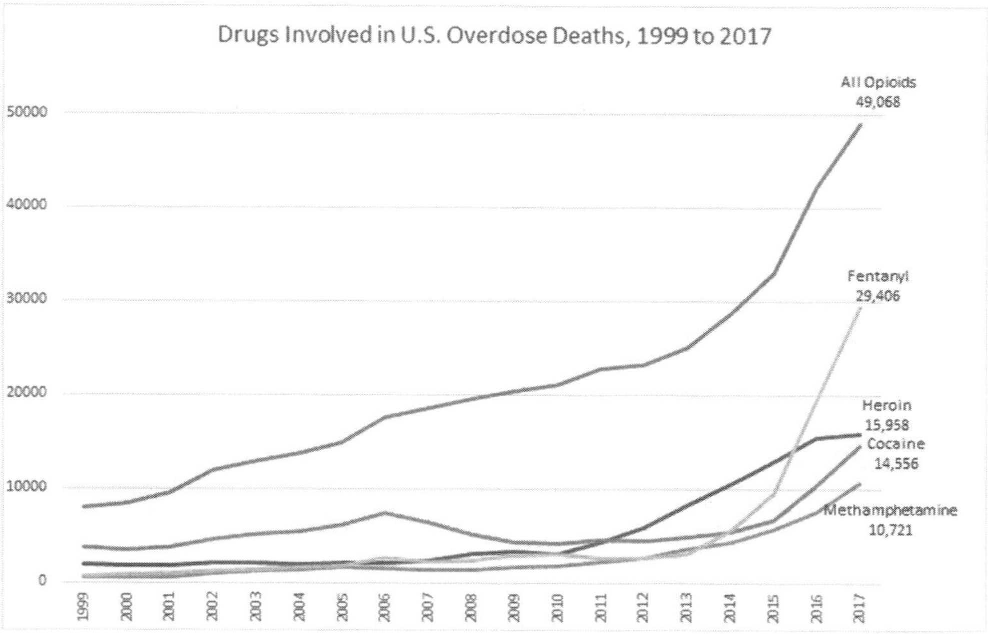

Figure 2. Overdose death rates (from National Institute of Drug Abuse).

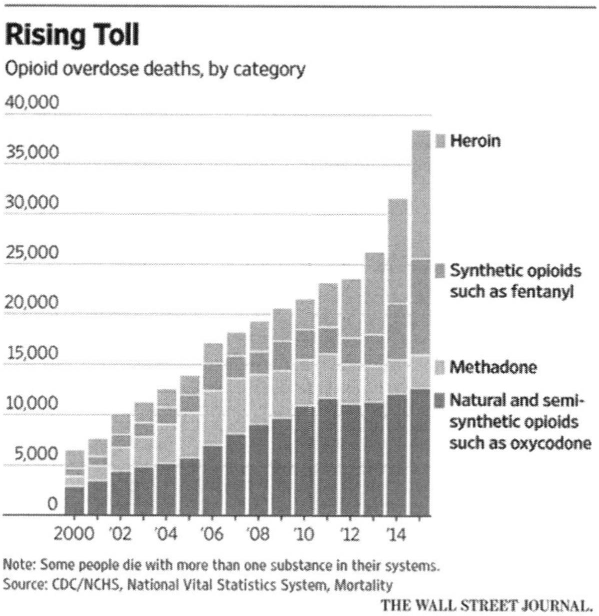

Figure 3. Opiate related deaths by opiate and opioid category.

Fentanyls

Fentanyl is an opioid drug that was synthesized from pethidine in the 1960s by Janssen Pharmaceuticals. It is widely used as a safe short-acting intravenous (IV) analgesic/anaesthetic with an efficacy potency of 100 times that of morphine. In clinical practice it has a crucial role in anesthetics and pain relief and is among the pharmacologically 'cleanest' opioids with few cardio-vascular adverse effects and without causing histamine release.

The drug's high lipid solubility means it enters the brain rapidly and produces peak analgesia in under 5 min after IV injection. The duration of action is short and starts wearing off after 30–40 min due to redistribution and elimination. Variants of the fentanyl molecule (analogues) are less commonly used in clinical practice and include remifentanil and sufentanil[14] (Figure 4). Certain formulations of fentanyl enable administration as transdermal patches, intranasal spray or buccal 'lozenges' for longer term pain relief. Fentanyl is available only by medical prescription or for use by clinicians in hospitals .[15]

Carfentanil

Carfentanil (carfentanyl) is a fentanyl analogue estimated to be some 10,000 times as potent as morphine (100 times fentanyl) (Table 2) and effective in humans at a 1 µg dose (a dot). The lethal dose is between 2–20 µg (a grain of salt). Carfentanil is intended for large animal use only as its extreme potency makes it highly dangerous to humans. Consequently, carfentanil is only available to veterinarians for tranquilizing very large animals (dose µg/ton weight) and marketed under the trade name Wildnil. The extreme potency makes carfentanil totally inappropriate for use in humans.[16] However, carfentanil, synthesized in China, is now widely available in the illicit drug market .[17]

Pharmacology of opioids

Opioids interact, as ligands, with specific neuronal receptors that are distributed widely in the brain, spinal cord, peripheral nervous system, and gastrointestinal tract. These 'opioid' receptors are a

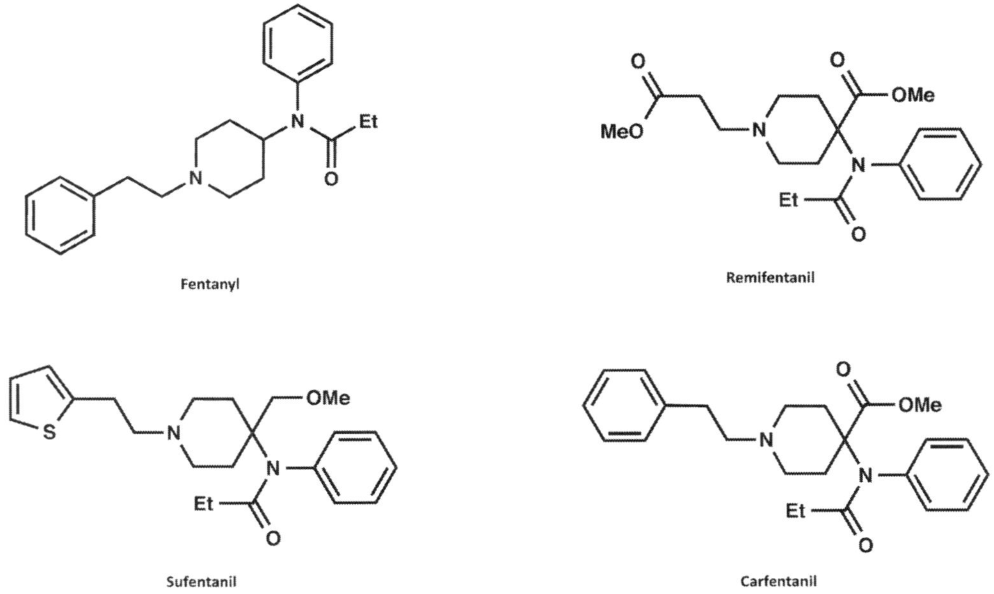

Figure 4. Comparative molecular structures of fentanyl and major analogues.

Table 2. Relative potency of various opiates and opioids.

Relative Potency of Opioid Drugs			
Drug	Relative Potency	Lipid Solubility (Octanol-to-Water Ratio	Therapeutic Index (LD_{50} or Lowest ED_{50}
Meperidine	0.5	40	5
Morphine	1	1.4	70
Methadone	4	120	12
Alfentanil	75	150	1080
Remifentanil	220	18	33,000
Fentanyl	300	800	277
Sufentanil	4500	1800	25,211
Carfentanil	10,000	N/A	10,594

ED_{50}=median effective dose; LD_{50}=median lethal dose; N/A=data not available.
Adaptive from Alavattam S. Sleep-Inducing Compounds. Final Report. Office of Counterproliferation, BCWAD, DIA. 2015

group of inhibitory G protein-coupled receptors for endogenous neuropeptide agonists such as endorphins, enkephalins and endomorphins. An agonist is a chemical that binds to a receptor and activates the receptor to produce a biological response. A receptor antagonist is a receptor ligand or drug that blocks or reduces a biological response by binding to and inhibiting a receptor, so an antagonist blocks the action of the agonist. Such drugs are sometimes called blockers e.g. α blockers, β blockers, and calcium channel blockers.[18]

Opiates and opioids are receptor agonists and their principal effects arise from their activity on μ receptors. Activation of the μ_1 receptor reduces conscious awareness whereas activation of the μ_2 receptor reduces respiratory drive. It is the latter that compromises the safe use of these drugs. The precise roles and actions of the other receptors affected by opioids, κ and δ receptors, are not as well understood (Tables 3 & 4).

Naloxone (μ, κ, δ receptors antagonist)

Naloxone (Figure 5) is a non-selective competitive opioid receptor antagonist that antagonizes all opiate and opioid effects, but to a varying degree. Respiratory depression is reversed but sedation less completely. Naloxone has a short duration of action (some 20 to 30 min) and may need to be administered as repeated bolus doses or an infusion, as many opioids act for longer. Naloxone is used as an acute antidote for opiate and opioid poisoning and also as a diagnostic test for opioid

Table 3. Effects of receptor binding of opiates and opioids at μ receptors.

Opiates and Opioids	Effects at μ receptors
Heroin, Morphine, Fentanyl, Remifentanil, Carfentanil	Agonists
Buprenorphine	Partial Agonist
Naloxone, Naltrexone, Nalmefene	Antagonist

Table 4. Clinical and physiological effects of agonists at opiate receptors.

Opioid Receptors	Effects of an Agonist
Mu_1 (μ_1)	analgesia, euphoria, anaesthesia
Mu_2 (μ_2)	constipation, respiratory depression
Kappa (k)	spinal analgesia, dysphoria
Delta (∂)	unknown

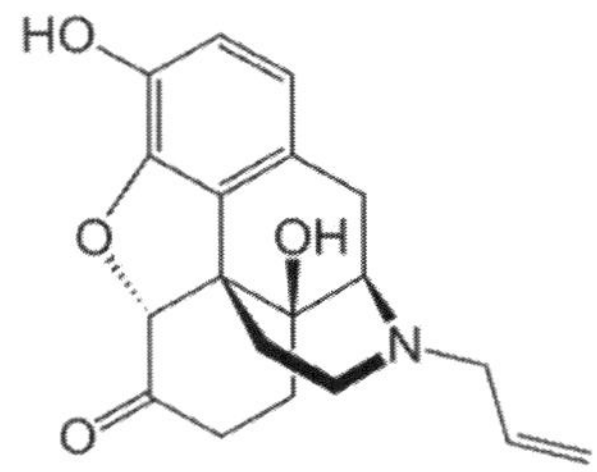

Figure 5. Naloxone molecule.

addiction. It is available for emergency clinical use as 400 μg and 2 mg pre-filled syringes. A nasal spray (2 mg naloxone) is increasingly available for use by law enforcement officers and first responders .[19]

Synthesis of fentanyls

The synthetic routes of fentanyl and fentanyl analogues require several steps (Figure 6)[20] and a proficiency in synthetic chemistry.

The increased interest by several Nation States in fentanyls as potential human incapacitants for law enforcement and civilian use had encouraged the development of novel synthetic pathways, including the 'one pot' synthesis route (Figure 7).[21]

Global fentanyl 'trade'

China is currently the main global source of illicit fentanyls and fentanyl analogues. The country has vast chemical and pharmaceutical industries that are weakly regulated and poorly monitored. The drugs are then shipped to the US and Canada, often via Mexico.

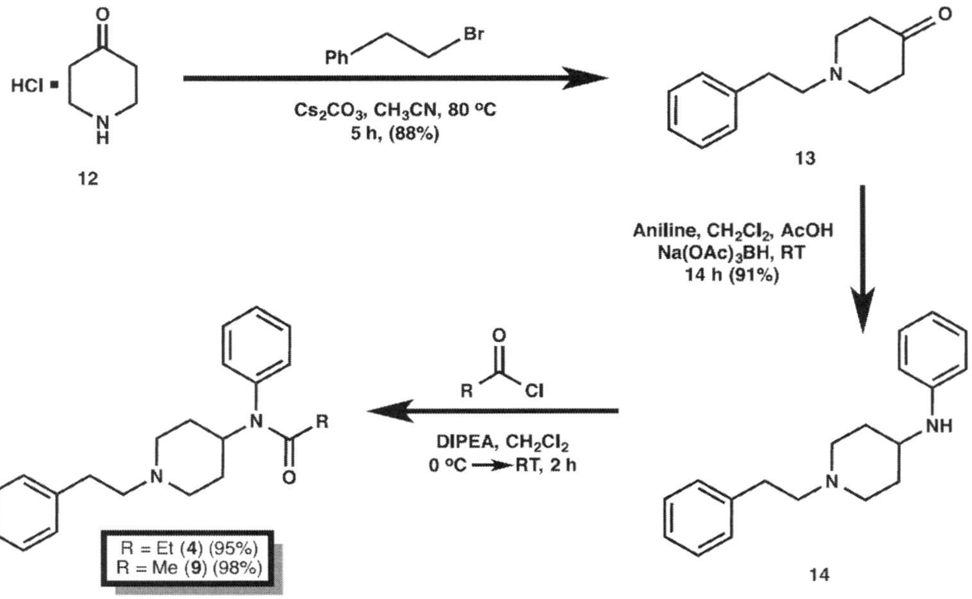

Figure 6. Synthesis of fentanyl and related compounds.

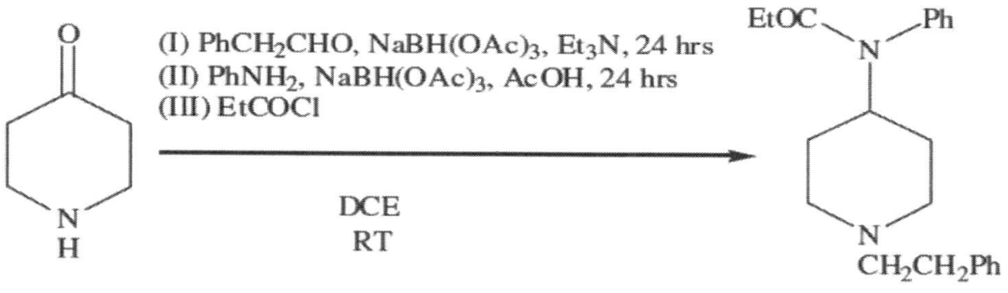

1

2

40 %

Fentanyl, N-(1-phenethyl-4-piperidyl) propionanilide, was prepared by performing three successive one pot reactions at room temparature.

Figure 7. One pot synthesis technique for fentanyl.

By adding different chemical groups, the synthetic chemists create new, unregulated variants (Figure 8),[22] some of which are even more potent than the original fentanyl molecule and some are more resistant to antidotes such as naloxone. More than 30 new fentanyl analogues have been identified.

The opium poppy is no longer the starting point for these new compounds which simply require a synthetic chemistry laboratory for manufacture.

Other countries have an undeclared state interest in fentanyls since, if used for domestic law enforcement as chemical incapacitants, these compounds are currently outside of the Chemical Weapons Convention .[23]

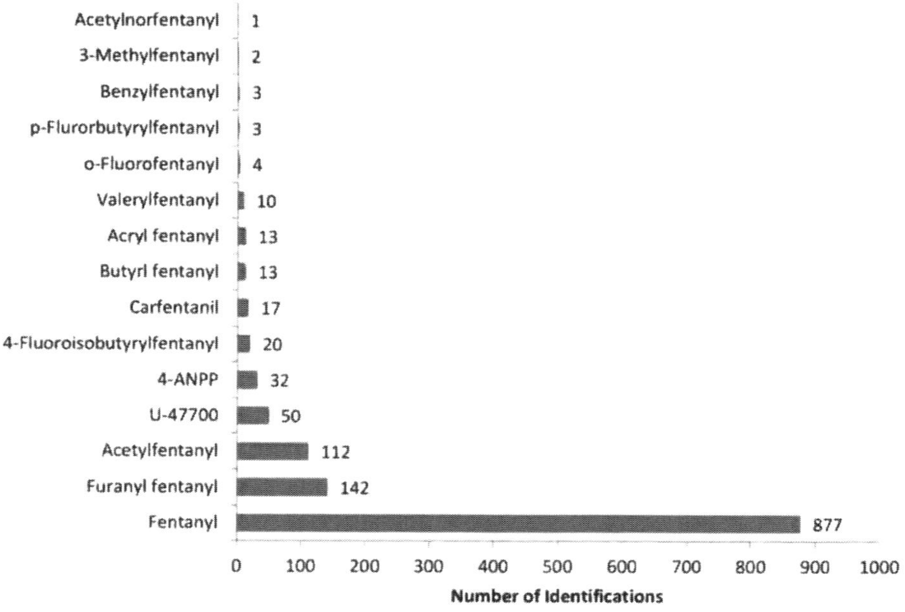

Figure 8. Synthetic opioids seized and identified in 2016.

A broad range of fentanyl analogues, including carfentanil, are available on the illicit drug market. Reported seizures of 25–42 Kg and more, in powder form, are proving to be a major problem in the US and Canada, and increasingly in other countries. These seizures pose a range of serious risks to Individuals potentially exposed to the powder, particularly during entry to drug packaging premises. Law enforcement personnel require adequate protection and countermeasures when engaged in such operations. The potential malicious use as a chemical weapon requires appropriate physical protection of first responders and availability of rapid acting medical treatments of exposure.

Opioids were used in a civilian context in the Moscow Theatre hostage rescue operation, but by military personnel using a novel combination and deployment of fentanyls.

Dubrovka Theatre siege in Moscow

In October 2002, 50 armed Chechen rebels entered the Dubrovka Theatre and took around 900 people hostages. The hostages consisted of men, women and children of many nationalities, who had been watching a production of 'Nord Ost'. Chechen women, the so-called 'black widows', were positioned around the auditorium and were equipped with explosives.

Fifty-seven hours into the siege, an elite army troop started an assault. In the auditorium, one survivor recalled seeing a grey mist descending on to the hostages. As this mist entered the auditorium, the Chechen gunmen fled but the women remained in the auditorium with the hostages and were rendered unconscious by the gas, along with everyone else. The Chechen men were shot by the soldiers. First responder rescuers had access to antidotes to treat the hostages affected by the incapacitant gas, but these drugs were outside, and it was reported there were not enough medical personnel to administer the injections. This oversight led to the death of some hostages, some of whom had either stopped breathing, or mechanically obstructed their airway. At least 129 civilians died during the storming of the theatre and of those rescued, 245 were hospitalised, eight in a serious condition. In total more than 750 hostages were rescued alive .[24]

The foreign nationals were from 14 countries including Germany, Austria, Switzerland, the Netherlands, Australia, Great Britain and the United States. Following pressure from Western Governments, whose citizens were among the hundreds of hostages affected by the gas, to identify the incapacitating agent(s) used, Russian Health Minister, Yuri Shevchenko, stated that *'a fentanyl-based substance was used to neutralise the terrorists.'* Clothing from British members of the audience was obtained and analysed at Dstl in the UK. Traces of carfentanil and remifentanil were identified.[25]

Many lessons were identified from this deployment of fentanyls as an incapacitant. One obvious difficulty was targeting with a safe but effective dose and controlling the duration of exposure especially with the rapidity of effect by the inhalation route of exposure. In the auditorium there would be steep concentration gradients in the aerosols depending on location and so a significant difficulty controlling the level and duration of exposure. Added to this was the inability of drowsy/unconscious victims to flee exposure and thus limit the dose received. The deployment was totally indiscriminate and significantly compromised the safety of those exposed, who varied from children through to the old, and healthy to those with pre-existing morbidities.

Population health security

Fentanyl analogues are now synthesized so cheaply by rogue chemists that large amounts (tens of kilograms) are appearing on the illicit drug market in US, Canada, Australasia, Turkey and Europe. These compounds are added to other drugs, such as heroin, but their higher, and unpredictable, potency is resulting in significant increases in accidental overdose deaths of drug users. These synthesized compounds include carfentanil, as well as other novel analogues such as butyrylfentanyl and acetylthiofentanyl, and many others of unknown potency and toxicity. Large amounts are available in a micro-powder form that would easily aerosolize.

The lessons from the Moscow Theatre use emphasize the potential issues of exposure to potent fentanyls as the effective incapacitating dose is close to a lethal dose. The effect of inhalation exposure to a highly potent fentanyl analogue is so rapid, and insufficient antidote treatments would be available for a large number of casualties. In addition, the cause would not be immediately obvious, unless prior identity is declared, and clinical signs may be mistaken for nerve agent poisoning .[26]

The lethal dose for carfentanil is between 2 µg and 20 µg (grains of salt) and, while fanciful, it has been calculated that 2 g could kill between 100 K and 1 M people. Obviously, this would only be even feasible under very specific conditions and if widely dispersed as a fine powder that was inhalable. The potential threat from these potent drugs has led US Department of Homeland Security to consider designating fentanyl analogues a Weapon of Mass Destruction .[27]

The properties of these opioids have led some to suggest they are optimum for deliberate mass effect (or assassination) and several scenarios for use have been proposed. These include mass gathering such as at a sports stadium, shopping mall and parades with many dispersion options suggested including low power explosive or aerial spraying from a drone. In reality, it is much more likely that an exposure incident following a drug courier car crash or accidental release at a drug house, would release large amounts of a powdered fentanyl analogue. Nevertheless, whatever scenario occurred there is a need for effective, rapid and safe antidotes to reverse the lethal effects of a potent opioid or similar Pharmaceutical Based Agent.

Treatments and countermeasures

Treating exposure to incapacitants in general involves two management strategies operating in parallel. The first strategy is a generic approach to exposure to any potentially hazardous agent and operates with either knowledge of the nature of the exposure or without it. The second strategy is the medical approach to the casualty, with use of specific medical treatments and algorithms to support survival and address injuries specific for the hazardous material in question .[28]

First and foremost, the ideal management of exposure to incapacitating agents requires either detection of the agent, or recognition that an exposure or event may have occurred in an individual. Without this information, only generic trauma and medical management can be implemented with the continual re-evaluation of the casualty for the signs and symptoms typical of various exposures to facilitate diagnosis as early as possible.

Antidotes

There are a limited number of specific antidotes to exposure to certain incapacitants, the most notable being antidotes for the management of opiate or opioid overdose, and for organophosphate nerve agents. The primary focus of medical treatment of incapacitants is to resuscitate, stabilise and support a casualty until the incapacitant is metabolised, excreted or otherwise removed from the casualty, resulting in recovery.

The main drug countermeasure for opioid poisoning is immediate administration in the hot zone of high dose (5–10 mg) naloxone, the specific antidote.[29] However, at the moment medical services would be unable to adequately respond to high numbers of opioid casualties as the success of a response is constrained by speed of toxic effect onset and insufficient supply and doses (currently 2 mg) of the antidote, naloxone, available at an incident site.

Decontamination

Decontamination, along with the continued administration of medical countermeasures, is one of the most important interventions in the warm zone of an incident. Effective decontamination, conducted through the application of a validated and accepted process, minimises further exposure to a casualty. In the absence of decontamination, the likelihood of successful medical management of exposure to any agent is significantly reduced. The recently published Primary Response Incident Site Management (PRISM) guidelines published by Biological Advanced Research Development Agency (BARDA) outline current evidence for the best practice approach to decontamination.[30] Removal of contaminated clothing either by self-disrobing or through removal by cutting of clothing by operators has been shown to reduce contaminant load by approximately 90%. Followed by a dry decontamination step, this can be again reduced by 90%, resulting in a 99% reduction in contaminant load with two basic steps and prior to detailed or mass wet decontamination procedures that again can reduce contamination by another 90% to 99.9% estimated reduction[31] . Additional decontamination,[32] specifically targeted towards the hazardous material in question, can then be performed involving the use of inactivating agents (e.g. sodium hypochlorite, reactive skin decontamination lotion (RSDL),[33] and amphoteric acid-base neutralisers,[34] and antidote compounds used outside of therapy), physical removal,[35] adsorbents, wound irrigation and debridement,[36] and others approaches appropriate for mass casualty settings.[37] The contamination of a release site will be persistent and require extensive clean-up.

Detection and recognition

Understanding which incapacitant an individual may be exposed to is a fundamental requirement for reducing risks. Current technologies are not well suited to providing rapid detection capabilities in the field or near patient. Accurate assessment techniques utilising Gas Chromatography Mass Spectroscopy (GC-MS) can provide sufficiently accurate detection capacity within hours of receipt of a sample, but not as readily in the field where decisions regarding missions and clinical treatment are being made. Other techniques such as Raman spectroscopy, now available for field use, can provide more rapid but not definitive information potentially able to guide treatment approaches when coupled with clinical syndromic diagnosis. Historically, first responders have relied on colorimetric field assays for use in the field where an unknown substance is present. Such approaches are fraught with the potential for exposure to sufficient quantities of the hazard to result in casualties. In the absence of casualties exhibiting clinical signs and with symptoms of exposure, reliance on intelligence led data collection and emerging detection techniques (e.g. electrochemical and variations on spectroscopy) are most able to provide rapid information on the presence of incapacitants, in a field setting, to guide decision making.

Risk management

The risk management of potential incapacitant exposure can be described in terms of the internationally accepted standards on risk appreciation and management.[38] Broadly this involves the use of the hierarchy of risk controls,[39] to identify measures to reduce the risk that at-risk individuals become exposed. For first responders, it is not possible to eliminate or substitute the potential risk of exposure in situations where the presence of an incapacitant may be unexpected or a surprise. Additionally, there are situations where the need to conduct activities in an environment known or likely to contain incapacitant must be balanced against the need to protect individuals. In such cases other risk controls are required and are outlined below.

Administrative and logistic risk controls

The preparedness and training of individuals at risk of exposure in a hazardous environment is an important component of risk management. Skills and capacity to identify self and colleague deterioration following exposure, the physico-chemical characteristics of various threat agents, hazard identification, and the proper handling and operation of safety equipment and PPE is essential to ensure risk controls operate as intended. The provision of sufficient numbers of antidotes for use by at risk personnel in the field (e.g. naloxone injectors/atomisers, decontamination options) to individuals, and the provision of initial and currency training, is also important.

Personal protective equipment

The PPE requirements for incapacitants vary between agents and are summarised in Table 5 .[40]

Discussion

There is already a major public health crisis in North America due to the initially unstated addictive properties of the opioids widely promoted as the ideal treatment for chronic pain. Progressive tolerance and the addiction need led to increased demand for higher doses that were eventually not met by prescription provision. Many patients turned to sourcing their opioids from the illicit drug market where the drug was often of unknown quality, potency or even identity. Overdoses increased and so did deaths. Coupled with deaths from illicit drug users overdosing from heroin cut with potent fentanyls, the annual death rate soared. It could be argued that one threat potential from these PBAs has already been realised?

The possibility of an accidental release of a large amount of opioid powder is a realistic risk given the many kilograms amounts being transported by drug dealers. The Mexican government recently seized approximately 25.75 tons (23,368 kilograms or 51,517 pounds) of powdered fentanyl that originated in Shanghai China.[41]

There is a similar threat to law enforcers entering drug formulating premises. The likelihood of a deliberate release of an opioid, intended to cause mass casualties, is a low risk but high impact event that would result in high mortality. First responder protocols and resources currently do not consider the management of large numbers of opioid poisoned casualties requiring high dose antidote rapidly to reverse respiratory depression. Risk management is hampered by inadequate/slow detection techniques for decision makers. This is leading to delays in response, delays in forensics, and knock on practical effects in law enforcement and so on.

Incapacitation might be as effective as more conventional means in producing desired solutions in hostage release etc., but without the risk of lethal outcomes. Consequently, incapacitating agents have a lower threshold for use than highly toxic/lethal agents as the potential for harm is reduced. However, this perception is risking increased use of incapacitants, especially in the current climate where use of CW is becoming normalised. The operational attraction of incapacitation has the

Table 5. PPE requirements for potential exposure to potent opiates or opioid compounds.

Personal protective equipment recommendations for protection against fentanyl

Personal Protective Equipment	Pre-Hospital Patient Care			Law Enforcement Routine Duties			Investigations and Evidence Collection			Special Operations and Decontamination		
Exposure Level	Minimal	Moderate	High	Minimal	Moderate	High	Minimal	Moderate	High	Minimal	Moderate	High
Respiratory Protection												
Disposable N100, R100, or P100 FFR[1]		✓	Not recommended		✓	Not recommended		✓			✓	
Elastomeric APR[2]								●	✓		●	✓
PAPR[3]									●		●	●
SCBA[4]									■			■
Face and Eye Protection												
Safety goggles/glasses[5]		✓			✓			✓	✓		✓	✓
Hand Protection												
Nitrile gloves[6]	✓	✓		✓	✓		✓	✓		✓	✓	
Nitrile gloves, double or use of thicker gloves		●			●			●	●		●	✓
Dermal Protection												
Wrist/arm protection[7]		✓			✓			✓			✓	
Particulate hazards protective ensemble (i.e., NFPA 1999 Single or Multi-Use or NFPA 1994 Class 4 Ensemble)									✓			✓
Chemical hazards protective ensemble (i.e., NFPA 1994 Class 3 Ensemble or Higher)									●			●

potential to encourage the development of new incapacitants with a broader range of actions and thereby a greater probability of actually causing harm. Less lethal does not mean non-lethal.

Mitigation and response

PBAs are well placed to increased representation in the range of incapacitants. The barriers for non-state actors are reducing with rapid dissemination of dual use technologies, all in one system, and lower entry costs for development. The substances are ubiquitous now in society.

The most obvious mitigation policy would be to prevent synthesized fentanyls reaching the illicit drug market. This will take time so adequate training in the recognition of exposure and treatment needs is required. There is also an urgent need to provide ample supplies of high dose antidote (possibly as auto-injectors containing 5–10 mg naloxone) to law enforcers, emergency responders and at-risk individuals. The antidote needs to be accessible near the casualties, not in a remote stockpile, so a more widely distributed stockpile is needed.

In the longer term a programme to develop effective longer acting antidotes, or variations on existing drugs such as naltrexone and nalmefene, is necessary. The ideal would be receptor and receptor subtype specific antidotes that would, for example, rapidly reverse respiratory depression by antagonizing the μ_2 receptor subtype.

Conclusions

Highly potent, and potentially lethal, fentanyl analogues are now widely available in the illicit drug market in the US, Canada, Australasia, Turkey and Europe. This class of drugs poses the major threat potential of PBAs. Recognized (carfentanil) and unknown novel analogues are being synthesized and imported in large amounts (e.g. >25 Kg) often in fine powder form. Law enforcement officers on drug raids need to be protected from exposure and effects and able to immediately treat themselves and colleagues, if affected. Emergency planners and responders also need to factor the threat of accidental exposure, or deliberate use, into their major emergency preparedness, resilience, response and recovery plans and their training programmes.

Notes

1. BMA, *The Use of Drugs as Weapons*, 5.
2. Ibid., 1–2.
3. Ibid., 7–8.
4. Morrison, *Fentanyl Opens a Grave New Health Security Threat.*
5. DEA, *DEA Intelligence Brief.*
6. Banks, *Medical Management of Chemical Casualties Handbook.*
7. Gryphon Scientific LLC, *Risk & Benefit Analysis of Gain of Function Research*, 1–8; and National Science Advisory Board for Biosecurity, *Recommendations for the Evaluation and Oversight of Proposed Gain-of-Function Research*, 4–7.
8. Blain, "Human Incapacitants."
9. Ibid., 661.
10. Banks, *Medical Management of Chemical Casualties Handbook (Fifth Edition)*. Chapter 12.
11. See note 9 above.
12. See note 4 above.
13. Arce, *Major Fentanyl Shipment from China Seized in Mexico.*
14. Valdez et al., "An Efficient, Optimized Synthesis of Fentanyl and Related Analogs," 2.
15. See note 9 above.
16. Ibid.
17. See note 5 above.
18. Chauhan et al., "Chemical Warfare Agents."
19. See note 11 above.
20. Valdez et al., "An Efficient, Optimized Synthesis of Fentanyl and Related Analogs," 3–4.

21. Gupta and Pande, "A Convenient One Pot Synthesis of Fentanyl."
22. See note 5 above.
23. BMA, *The Use of Drugs as Weapons*, 1–2.
24. Banks, *Medical Management of Chemical Casualties Handbook (Fifth Edition)*. Chapter 12,, 419.
25. Riches et al., "Analysis of Clothing and Urine from Moscow Theatre Siege Casualties Reveals Carfentanil and Remifentanil Use."
26. See note 19 above.
27. Turner, *Homeland Security is Reportedly Considering Labeling Fentanyl as a Weapon of Mass Destruction*.
28. Borden Institute (U.S.) and U.S. Army Medical Research Institute of Chemical Defense, *Field Management of Chemical and Biological Casualties Handbook*.
29. See note 11 above.
30. Chilcott and Amlôt, *Primary Response Incident Scene Management (PRISM) Guidance for Chemical Incidents Vols 1–3*.
31. Ibid.
32. Amlot et al., "Comparative Analysis of Showering Protocols for Mass-casualty Decontamination"; Carter et al., "Emergency Responders' Experiences of and Expectations Regarding Decontamination"; Chilcott et al., "The United Kingdom's Initial opeRational Response and Specialist Operational Response to CBRN and HazMat Incidents"; Egan and Amlôt, "Modelling Mass Casualty Decontamination Systems Informed by Field Exercise Data"; Monteith and Pearce, "Self-care Decontamination within a Chemical Exposure Mass-casualty Incident"; and Singh et al., "Decontamination of Chemical Warfare Agents."
33. Kumar et al., "Chemical, biological, radiological, and nuclear decontamination."
34. Ibid.
35. Capoun and Krykorkova, "Comparison of Selected Methods for Individual Decontamination of Chemical Warfare Agents."
36. Banks, *Medical Management of Chemical Casualties Handbook*; and Borden Institute (U.S.) and U.S. Army Medical Research Institute of Chemical Defense, *Field Management of Chemical and Biological Casualties Handbook*.
37. Chilcott, "Managing Mass Casualties and Decontamination"; Krieger et al., "Understanding Public Responses to Chemical, Biological, Radiological and Nuclear Incidents-Driving Factors, Emerging Themes and Research Gaps"; Lake and Divarco, *Guidelines for Mass Casualty Decontamination During an Hazmat/Weapon of Mass Destruction Incident: Volumes I and II*; SBECOM, *Updated Guidelines for Mass Casualty Decontamination During a HAZMAT/ Weapon of Mass Destruction Incident, Volumes I and II*; Singh et al., "Decontamination of Chemical Warfare Agents"; and US Department of Homeland Security and US Department of Health and Human Services, *Patient Decontamination in a Mass Chemical Exposure Incident*.
38. International Standards Organization (ISO), *Risk Management: Principles and Guidelines*.
39. Rasmussen, "Risk Management in a Dynamic Society"; and CDC, *Hierarchy of Risk Controls*.
40. Centers for Disease Control, *Fentanyl – Preventing Occupational Exposure to Emergency Responders*.
41. See note 14 above.

Disclosure statement

No potential conflict of interest was reported by the authors.

ORCID

D. J. Heslop http://orcid.org/0000-0002-1978-770X
P. G. Blain http://orcid.org/0000-0001-7960-0479

Bibliography

Amlot, R., J. Larner, H. Matar, D. Jones, H. Carter, E. Turner, S. Price, and R. Chilcott. "Comparative Analysis of Showering Protocols for Mass-casualty Decontamination." *Prehospital and Disaster Medicine* 25, no. 5 (2010): 435. doi:10.1017/S1049023X00008529.

Arce, R. "Major Fentanyl Shipment from China Seized in Mexico." Breitbart. Accessed 22 November 2019. https://www.breitbart.com/border/2019/08/25/25-tons-of-fentanyl-from-china-seized-in-mexico/

Banks, D. *Medical Management of Chemical Casualties Handbook*. Fifth ed. Fort Sam Houston, Texas: Borden Institute, 2014.

Biomedical Advanced Research Development Authority (BARDA). *Primary Response Incident Scene Management (PRISM) Guidance for Chemical Incidents Vols 1-3*. Washington DC, US Department of Health and Human Services, 2015.

Blain, P. "Human Incapacitants." Chap. 57. In *Clinical Neurotoxicology: Syndromes, Substances, Environments*, edited by M. Dobbs, 660–673. Elsevier, Philadelphia, USA, 2009.

BMA. *The Use of Drugs as Weapons: The Concerns and Responsibilities of Healthcare Professionals*. BMA Board of Science, London, UK, 2007.

Borden Institute (U.S.) and U.S. Army Medical Research Institute of Chemical Defense. *Field Management of Chemical and Biological Casualties Handbook*. Fifth ed. Fort Sam Houston, Texas: Borden Institute, 2016.

Calder, A., and S. Bland. "Chemical, Biological, Radiological and Nuclear Considerations in a Major Incident." *Surgery (United Kingdom)* 33, no. 9 (2015). doi:10.1016/j.mpsur.2015.07.006.

Capoun, T., and J. Krykorkova. "Comparison of Selected Methods for Individual Decontamination of Chemical Warfare Agents." *Toxics* 2, no. 2 (2014): 307–326. doi:10.3390/toxics2020307.

Carter, H., J. Drury, G. Rubin, R. Williams, and R. Amlôt. "Emergency Responders' Experiences of and Expectations regarding Decontamination." *International Journal of Emergency Services* 3, no. 2 (2014): 179–192. doi:10.1108/IJES-08-2013-0022.

CDC. "Hierarchy of Risk Controls." CDC. Accessed 22 November 2019. https://www.cdc.gov/niosh/topics/hierarchy/default.html

Centers for Disease Control. "Fentanyl - Preventing Occupational Exposure to Emergency Responders." CDC. Accessed 22 November 2019. https://www.cdc.gov/niosh/topics/fentanyl/risk.html

Chauhan, S., R. D'Cruz, S. Faruqi, K. K. Singh, S. Varma, M. Singh, and V. Karthik. "Chemical Warfare Agents." *Environmental Toxicology and Pharmacology* 26, no. 2 (2008): 113. doi:10.1016/j.etap.2008.03.003.

Chilcott, R. "Managing Mass Casualties and Decontamination." *Environment International* 72 (2014): 37–45. doi:10.1016/j.envint.2014.02.006.

Chilcott, R., J. Larner, and H. Matar. "The United Kingdom's Initial Operational Response and Specialist Operational Response to CBRN and HazMat Incidents: A Primer on Decontamination Protocols for Healthcare Professionals." *Emergency Medicine Journal* 36, no. 8 (2019): 117. doi:10.1136/emermed-2019-208798.

DEA. *DEA Intelligence Brief: Fentanyl Remains the Most Significant Synthetic Opioid Threat and Poses the Greatest Threat to the Opioid User Market in the United States*. United States Department of Justice, Washington, DC, 2018.

Egan, J., and R. Amlôt. "Modelling Mass Casualty Decontamination Systems Informed by Field Exercise Data." *International Journal of Environmental Research and Public Health* 9, no. 10 (2012): 3685. doi:10.3390/ijerph9103685.

Gupta, K., and A. Pande. "A Convenient One Pot Synthesis of Fentanyl." *Journal of Chemical Research* 2005, no. 7 (2005): 452. doi:10.3184/030823405774309078.

Holdsworth, D., S. Bland, and D. O'Reilly. "CBRN Response and the Future." *Journal of the Royal Army Medical Corps* 158, no. 1 (2012): 58. doi:10.1136/jramc-158-01-15.

International Standards Organization (ISO). 2009. "Risk Management: Principles and Guidelines." Chap. Geneva, Switzerland.

Krieger, K., R. Amlot, and M. Rogers. "Understanding Public Responses to Chemical, Biological, Radiological and Nuclear incidents-Driving Factors, Emerging Themes and Research Gaps." *Environment International* 72 (2014): 66–74. doi:10.1016/j.envint.2014.04.017.

Kumar, V., R. Goel, R. Chawla, M. Silambarasan, and R. Sharma. "Chemical, Biological, Radiological, and Nuclear Decontamination: Recent Trends and Future Perspective." *Journal of Pharmacy and Bioallied Sciences* 2, no. 3 (2010): 220–238. doi:10.4103/0975-7406.68505.

Monteith, R., and L. Pearce. "Self-care Decontamination within a Chemical Exposure Mass-casualty Incident." *Prehospital and Disaster Medicine* 30, no. 3 (2015): 288–296. doi:10.1017/S1049023X15004677.

Morrison, J. "Fentanyl Opens a Grave New Health Security Threat: Synthetic Opioids." Centre for International and Strategic Studies.

NSABB. *Recommendations for the Evaluation and Oversight of Proposed Gain-of-function Research*. National Institutes of Health, Washington, DC, 2016.

OPEM. *Strategies for First Receiver Decontamination*. Commonwealth of Massachusetts, Boston, MA, 2014.

Rasmussen, J. "Risk Management in A Dynamic Society: A Modelling Problem." *Safety Science* 27, no. 2–3 (1997): 183–213. doi:10.1016/S0925-7535(97)00052-0.

Riches, J., R. Read, R. Black, N. Cooper, and C. Timperley. "Analysis of Clothing and Urine from Moscow Theatre Siege Casualties Reveals Carfentanil and Remifentanil Use." *Journal of Analytical Toxicology* 36, no. 9 (2012): 647–656. doi:10.1093/jat/bks078.

Scottish Government. *Guidance for Health Facilities on Surface Decontamination of Self-Presenting Persons Potentially Exposed to Hazardous Chemical, Biological or Radiological Substances*. NHS Scotland, Edinburgh, Scotland, 2013.

Singh, B., G. Prasad, K. Pandey, R. Danikhel, and R. Vijayaraghavan. "Decontamination of Chemical Warfare Agents." *Defence Science Journal* 60, no. 4 (2010): 428. doi:10.14429/dsj.60.487.

Turner, A. "Homeland Security Is Reportedly considering Labeling Fentanyl as a Weapon of Mass Destruction." *CNBC*. Washington DC: CNBC, 2019.

U.S. Army Chemical Biological, Radiological and Nuclear School. *Updated Guidelines for Mass Casualty Decontamination during a HAZMAT/Weapon of Mass Destruction Incident, Volumes I and II*. US Army, Fort Leonard Wood, MO, USA, 2013.

US Department of Homeland Security. *Patient Decontamination in a Mass Chemical Exposure Incident: National Planning Guidance for Communities*. US Department of Homeland Security, Washington, DC, 2014.

US RDECOM & ECBC. *Guidelines for Mass Casualty Decontamination during an Hazmat/Weapon of Mass Destruction Incident: Volumes I and II*. U.S. Army Chemical Biological, Radiological and Nuclear School, Washington, DC, 2013.

Valdez, C., R. Leif, and B. Mayer. "An Efficient, Optimized Synthesis of Fentanyl and Related Analogs." *PLoS ONE* 9, no. 9 (2014): e108250. doi:10.1371/journal.pone.0108250.

OPEN ACCESS

Towards understanding cybersecurity capability in Australian healthcare organisations: a systematic review of recent trends, threats and mitigation

K. L. Offner, E. Sitnikova, K. Joiner and C. R. MacIntyre

ABSTRACT

Cybersecurity threats in the Health sector are increasing globally due to the rising value of sensitive health information and availability of digitalised personal health records. This systematic review compares international and Australian health system cybersecurity landscapes in relation to the introduction of universal electronic health records. It examines recent trends in healthcare cybersecurity breaches that can disrupt essential services if patient safety and privacy are compromised. Often health systems and health mangers are ill-equipped to mitigate such threats. Recommendations are provided to proactively mature the cybersecurity culture within healthcare organisations, thus increasing their resilience to cyber threat.

Introduction

Healthcare is a ubiquitous need and affects every person in society. The healthcare sector is responsible for collecting and storing highly sensitive and confidential data whilst simultaneously being required to share it amongst medical staff, patients and other organisations. HealthCare Systems (HCS) are compelled to evolve with advances in technology. The transition of healthcare from hospital centred, specialist focused approaches to distributed, patient centred care has been facilitated through health record digitalisation[1] and is widely recognised as both inevitable and essential.[2] Breaches of HCS cybersecurity that expose personal information or data will negatively impact both patients and the healthcare institution, with potentially life-threatening consequences.[3] The cybersecurity risk to healthcare, including ransomware attacks, hacking of personal medical devices and theft of personal medical data, is continuously rising.[4] Stolen health records are worth more than records from any other industry,[5] due to the high value of personal information.[6] Sold on the darkweb, they can fund criminal activity and enable identity theft, blackmail, extortion and even murder.[7] In 2015, the US Office of Personnel Management (OPM) and Anthem Health, which provides healthcare for Federal employees, were both hacked within months of each other, apparently by the same perpetrator.[8] This means the hackers can link personnel records with sensitive health data for federal employees and enable targeted harm to high-value individuals.[9] Despite a global increase in cyberattacks on health entities the healthcare sector has significantly trailed other sectors in the ability to secure its critical data.[10] Cybersecurity in healthcare is identified as an emerging health security challenge, but there is low awareness in the health sector of the risk.[11] A healthcare cybersecurity capability approach is required to address increasing cyberthreats. The recent introduction of a universal electronic medical record My Health Record (MHR) in Australia provides an opportunity to examine healthcare cybersecurity capability.

Health cybersecurity capability is the capacity of the organisation or sector to produce an outcome, such as proactive cyber-awareness and defence.[12] Healthcare institutions have traditionally been focussed on patient care and not cybersecurity and pursued the electronic health record as a holy grail of optimal patient care. Yet healthcare lags behind other sectors in both securing data and developing comprehensive employee cybersecurity training programs.[13] As patient information grows in both volume and value, health managers are required to develop cybersecurity capability across organisations. Cybersecurity capability development includes updating existing information technology but also recognising the need for, and proactively acquiring, new technology, cybersecurity talent and comprehensive organisation training.[14]

The paradigm shift to digitalised healthcare requires information technologies to store vast amounts of electronic patient information across diverse operating systems.[15] The integration of new technologies with outdated, legacy or unsupported operating systems compromises interoperability and increases cybersecurity vulnerability.[16] The 2017 global WannaCry ransomware attack[17] provides a stark example of this. Widespread use of obsolete Windows XP software[18] in combination with ignored cybersecurity warnings to undertake system upgrades enabled the malware to spread across the National Health Service (NHS) in the UK. WannaCry severely affected NHS" ability to provide patient care for a week between 12–17 May 2017, spread to 200,000 computers in over 100 countries, and is the largest malware cyberattack to date.[19] WannaCry had not specifically targeted the healthcare sector,[20] but was able to spread to 80 out of 236 NHS trusts and 603 primary care organisations across England[21] due to poor cyber-hygiene and a lack of appreciation amongst healthcare executive management of the business risk impact of cyber breaches.[22] Ambulances had to be diverted, diagnostic equipment was infected, pathology and radiology unable to function, patient records were inaccessible and nearly 7000 medical appointments were cancelled.[23]

Healthcare has the reputation of 'low security maturity',[24] and lacks sophisticated data security tools compared to other industries.[25] This is due to budgetary constraints,[26] lack of cybersecurity training and awareness among health managers, the heterogenous healthcare information infrastructure, and innumerable wireless connected devices.[27] Current healthcare cyber-defence is often reactive and undertaken after malicious attack.[28] The retrospective nature of healthcare cybersecurity,[29] along with sector reliance upon perimeter defence (antivirus, firewalls) for protection[30] compounds cyber risk. Such measures are unlikely to protect against sophisticated and persistent attacks[31] or mitigate insider threats.[32] Other significant barriers to healthcare cybersecurity are lack of appropriate cybersecurity professionals working in health,[33] constantly emerging and evolving malware threats,[34] and complex network infrastructure.[35]

Aims

- To compare the international and Australian health system cybersecurity landscape in relation to introduction of the universal MHR in Australia.
- To examine recent trends in healthcare cybersecurity breaches in Australia and worldwide.

Methods

A systematic review of the relevant literature and background information regarding global cybersecurity in health systems and digital medical records was conducted using the PRISMA criteria. Ten databases in total were searched: Medline/PubMed; Embase; Emcare; CINAHL; Psycinfo; Web of Science; Scopus; Compendex; IEEE; and Google Scholar Advanced Search to obtain grey literature. The key concepts utilised were e-health records AND cybersecurity. The keywords used in the search are listed below:

- Electronic health records/OR medical record, computerised/OR digital health record* OR electronic medical record*

- Cyber security/OR data security/OR medical identity theft/OR terrorism/OR Malware/OR Ransomware OR Cyber adj4 (crime OR attack OR security OR threat OR terror)

The Google Scholar Advanced Search utilised 'healthcare AND cybersecurity' to obtain grey literature such as conference proceeding books, conference papers and thesis dissertations. Due to the emergent nature of electronic health records, the current social and political debate around privacy and security and the recent changes to MHR implementation, the decision was made to include media reports. The Factiva database was utilised to search relevant media articles. Key concepts were health data breach AND MHR. The search process is illustrated below in Figure 1.

Study eligibility

Articles were considered for inclusion if they were:

- English language publications,
- Published between 2014–2019 in a peer reviewed or scholarly journal,
- Full-text version of the manuscript, conference paper or prospective thesis/paper,
- Strategy, Guideline, Report or Policy review documents which provide relevant subject insight or recommendation

Study selection

Studies were selected if they discussed an issue related to cybersecurity in healthcare either in the title or the abstract. Studies were excluded if their content was not specific to cybersecurity within healthcare, or if they were focused solely on presenting a technical algorithmic solution without discussion of the general cybersecurity landscape. Two independent reviewers checked titles and abstracts as collated on a shared EndNote library.

Information synthesis

The findings of the included studies were synthesised narratively into themes which included:

(1) Theme 1 – emerging trends in cybersecurity risk,
(2) Theme 2 – cybersecurity capability countermeasures and mitigation strategies,
(3) Theme 3 – current cybersecurity issues within Australia.

An analysis of Australian healthcare cybersecurity capability is presented in the discussion session.

We also reviewed the accreditation requirements of the two peak bodies in health management in Australia, the Australian College of Health Systems Management Australia and the Royal Australasian College of Medical Educators, for health cybersecurity as a curriculum requirement.

Results

We identified 316 relevant records. Of the 316 records, 100 outlined cyberattacks on HCS. The common cyberattack types identified in the review are defined and categorised in Table 1 below. Mitigation strategies were presented in 131 of the records. An additional 29 records outlined cyber risk or cyberattack type, but also presented a specific countermeasure to potentially mitigate the threat discussed. A total of 27 records presented findings relevant to the Australian context. A summary of findings is presented in tables 2 and 3.

Ten systematic reviews were identified as part of the search, 5 of which were published since 2018. There were 32 Reports included as relevant to this review. These included official

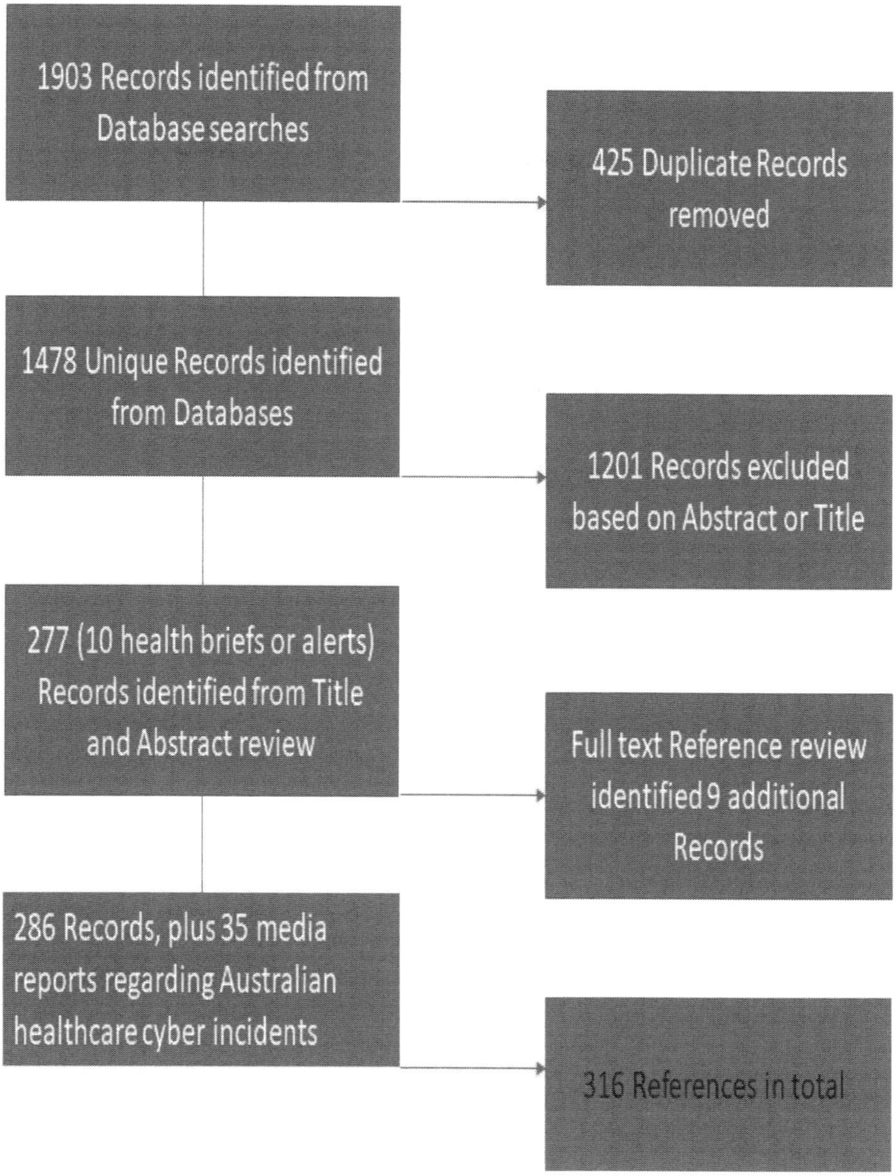

Figure 1. Flow chart of literature search screening process.

Government responses to data breaches (n = 3), Australian Government publications (n = 9), cybersecurity industry benchmark reports (n = 9), the Royal Australian College of General Practitioners cybersecurity position paper (n = 1), and finally a joint academic and consumer group report. Grey literature was identified and included to address publication bias. A total of 15 Conference Proceeding papers and 4 dissertation thesis papers were identified. The results are summarised in Table 1–4. Table 1 shows HCS Cybersecurity Attack and Threat Categories, Table 2 shows a summary of findings under Theme 1 (Cybersecurity Threat and Risk Landscape), Table 3b shows a summary of findings under Theme 2 (Cybersecurity Capability, Countermeasures and

Table 1. HCS cybersecurity attack and threat categories.

Attack Type	Definition and Examples	Threat Category
Hacking	The use of a computer to gain unauthorized access to data in a system to enable theft or destruction.[a] Mimikatz steals credentials from accessed server domains to enable network compromise. Used with other tools in NotPetya[b]	*Accessibility & Integrity* via system and network infiltration and *Confidentiality* of credentials.
Distributed Denial of Service (DDoS)/Denial of Service (DoS)	DDoS/DoS attacks are main threats to the availability of physical and network systems. Creates traffic jamming that disrupts communication through interference or collision, overflowing the buffer memory of network cards, and broadcasting spoofed network packets.[c] Network flooding with useless data traffic exhausts network resources making it unavailable to the authentic users.[d] Able to be spread by mobile applications and can be refined to also exfiltrate information.	System *Accessibility*
Malware	Computer code created with malicious intent, often spread through phishing. Can disrupt entire organisation or lie dormant until initiated. Masqueraded as legitimate upgrades and used in the 2015 Anthem Health Insurance attack.[e]	*Accessibility* through DoS, or attack to vendor supply chains; *Integrity* of data through encryption; *Confidentiality* via data breach/theft
Ransomware	Encrypts files on compromised computers for cryptocurrency ransom.[f] Potentially life threatening as decryption key may not be provided after payment.[g] Able to avoid detection and only encrypt specific information[h] or can spread across entire network.[i] New ransomware code is developed at a rate of 100,000 a day.[j] In 2019 it compiled over 70% of malware incidents.[k] Spread via inadvertent download of code through infected websites or most commonly in healthcare, in phishing emails.[l]	*Integrity, Accessibility and Confidentiality* of physical and network systems and data
Phishing	Indiscriminate scam emails that contain malware allowing attackers entry into the system by installing a virus, or to trick users to reveal credentials.[m] Can create a 'beachhead' to launch other attacks – often to install malware.[n] Increasingly sophisticated and role targeted, often employing follow up messages or calls to encourage opening infected links.[o] Used to deploy Remote Access Tools such as JBiFrost.[p]	*Accessibility* & *Integrity* via email compromise & computer intrusion to enable administrative control. Due poor cyber-hygiene practices of end users
Spear phishing	Carefully targeted emails to small groups or individuals using personalised information to 'verify' the message & link.[q]	*Confidentiality* of targeted credentials
Command and Control Obfuscators	Can both disguise the actor's communication within an infected network to evade detection and re-direct network traffic to alternate hosts/ports. Has been used to exploit Windows vulnerabilities.[r]	Network and web server compromise affecting *Accessibility, Integrity and Condentiality*
Lateral Movement Frameworks	Continued penetration tools that escalates privileges, collects credentials and enables information download. Able to move across a network and operate from memory making detection difficult. Can be used to initiate inter-organisation phishing exercises.	As Above
Sinkhole	Internet of Things (IoT) and/or medical device compromise at network level that diverts all network traffic to a compromised sensor node. As it is an active attack can escalate to DoS.[s]	*Confidentiality, Accessibility and Integrity*
Wormhole	Uses packet or relay connections to form a tunnel between two attackers to route data. Can potentially affect any device with connection to a wireless sensor network.[t]	As Above
Sybil	Sensor nodes are provided with multiple identities creating redundant or false information from medical or monitoring devices.[u]	Integrity of vital patient information

(*Continued*)

Table 1. (Continued).

Attack Type	Definition and Examples	Threat Category
Hello Flood	Attackers with high powered transmitters can create a signal that appears to be in proximity to the device to mimic a parent node for eavesdropping or to broadcast data to the entire network.[v]	Confidentiality
Cryptojacking or Crypto Mining Malware (CMM)	Malware introduced to draw huge organisational computing power and network resources to covertly mine digital currency.[w] CMM detections increased 459% between 2017 to 2018.[x]	
Orange Worm malware	Installs backdoor software that lies dormant within systems to target healthcare supply chains such as pharmaceuticals, IT companies and medical device vendors, potentially to enable economic espionage by nation-states.[y]	Accessibility of supply

Key: Orange = System Threat; Blue = User-based Threat; Green = Mobile or medical connected device Threat
[a]Carter, "Considerations for Genomic Data Privacy and Security when Working in the Cloud."
[b]Australian Cyber Security Centre (ACSC), Joint report on publicly available hacking tools.
[c]Almohri et al., On Threat Modeling and Mitigation of Medical Cyber-Physical Systems.
[d]Ahanger & Aljumah, "Internet of things: A comprehensive study of security issues and defense mechanisms."
[e]Institute for Critical Infrastructure Technology (ICIT), Industry Brief: Hacking Healthcare.
[f]Wirth, "Cyberinsights. The Times They Are a-Changin': Part One."
[g]Boddy et al., "An investigation into healthcare-data patterns."
[h]Lee, Moon & Park. CloudRPS: a cloud analysis based enhanced ransomware prevention system.
[i]Sittig & Singh. "A Socio-technical Approach to Preventing, Mitigating, and Recovering from Ransomware Attacks."
[j]Spence et al., "Ransomware in Healthcare Facilities: A Harbinger of the future?"
[k]Verizon, 2019 Data Breach Investigations Report.
[l]Lee, Moon & Park. CloudRPS: a cloud analysis based enhanced ransomware prevention system.
[m]Institute for Critical Infrastructure Technology (ICIT), Industry Brief: Hacking Healthcare.
n Wright, Aaron & Bates. "The Big Phish: Cyberattacks Against U.S. Healthcare Systems."
o Wirth, "Cyberinsights. The Times They Are a-Changin': Part One."
p Australian Cyber Security Centre (ACSC), Joint report on publicly available hacking tools.
q Wright, Aaron & Bates. "The Big Phish: Cyberattacks Against U.S. Healthcare Systems."
r Australian Cyber Security Centre (ACSC), Joint report on publicly available hacking tools.
s Ahanger & Aljumah, "Internet of things: A comprehensive study of security issues and defense mechanisms."
t Ibid.
u Ibid.
v Ibid.
w BDO USA Healthcare, Brace for the Breach - Cyberthreat Insights 2019.
x Verizon, 2019 Data Breach Investigations Report.
y BDO USA Healthcare, Brace for the Breach - Cyberthreat Insights 2019.

Table 2. Summary of findings – Theme 1 Cybersecurity Threat and Risk Landscape.

Population: Digitalised/electronic health records, personal health information and data
Setting: Healthcare Systems (HCS)
Intervention: International cybersecurity risks and threats (n = 100)
Comparison: Australian cybersecurity risks and threats (n = 19)

Outcomes (sub-themes)	International Records	Australian Records	Comments
Medical Cyber Physical Streams (MCPS) and/or Medical Internet of Things (MIoT)	40	5	Lack of interoperability combined with the vulnerability caused by MCPS intrinsic attributes are recognised as the most significant emerging cybersecurity threat in international records Australia (TGA) and US (FDA) greater MCPS regulation than UK/Europe
Breaches of privacy, confidentiality and/or consent for data use	24	8	Australian records remain predominantly concerned with threats to data protection, privacy and confidentiality. Issues of consent are discussed concurrently with data protection in Australian records.
Cloud Computing	11	1	Recognised in international records as a potential attack vector to data in storage and transit
Malware	10	1	Lack of Australian records outlining malware specific threats. Australian malware information accessed through Australian Government publications (Office of Australian Information Commissioner or Australian Cyber Security Centre).
Health Apps	8	3	Information security issues and lack of regulation of health apps are addressed in recent records, especially when endorsed for use in mental health and dementia
Insider threat	7	1	Paucity of records discussing this despite cybersecurity industry recognition it is the leading cause of data breach worldwide.

Table 3. Summary of findings Theme 2 – Cybersecurity Capability, Countermeasures and Mitigation strategies.

Population: Digitalised/electronic health records, personal health information and data
Setting: Healthcare Systems (HCS)
Intervention: International cybersecurity capability, protective countermeasures or mitigation (n = 131)
Comparison: Australian cybersecurity capability, protective countermeasures or mitigation (n = 15)

Outcomes (sub-themes)	International Records	Australian Records	Comments
Cryptographic architecture or	**51**	11	International and Australian focus on technological solutions rather than holistic capability building approaches,
technological solutions	22	1	education, or recognition of insider threat.
Risk assessment and governance	16	1	A comparison of risk assessment frameworks is presented in Table 4.
Regulation and/or legislation	16	0	A comparison of regulatory and legislative protection is presented in Table 4.
Holistic approach/Proactive	12	0	The importance of developing a proactive culture that engages all employees is presented in recent international records
cybersecurity culture	9	1	The need for practical, scenario-based education and simulation is emphasised, especially to address inadvertent insider
Education and/or simulation	5	0	threat
Capability and cyber maturity			System and organisational maturity to detect, identify, plan and manage data and infrastructure protection.
Cyber-hygiene			Digital security practices such as strong passwords, 2 factor authentication, encryption of shared patient information and data etc.

Table 4. International regulatory frameworks for data privacy and security.

Country	Framework/Regulation	Remit
European Union	General Data Protection Regulation (GDPR) 2018 is designed to harmonise data **privacy** laws across Europe to protect against privacy and data breaches.	Applies to all personal data held by an organisation. Breaches reported to the Information Commissioner's Office with fines for non-compliance up to €20 m.
United Kingdom	Data Protection Bill 2017	
United States	Health Insurance Accountability and Portability Act (HIPAA) 1996 and Omnibus 2013	Privacy and security rules. Mandatory end-to-end encryption of data that is in motion and at rest. Mandatory education of staff,[a] risk assessment[b] and breach notification. Non-compliance can lead to substantial fines of millions of dollars.
United States	The National Institute of Standards and Technology (NIST Framework)	Guidelines on security and privacy in public and cloud computing. Framework for Improving Critical Infrastructure Cybersecurity, 2018 includes five capability categories: identify, protect, detect, respond, and recover. Not specific to healthcare.[c]
United States	Food and Drug Administration (FDA).	Oversight of medical devices process, regulatory decision making, post-market surveillance, and product development life cycle.[d]
Canada	Canadian Personal Health Information Protection Act (PHIPA) 2005 update.	Includes health technology and allows data deidentification for health systems planning, delivery, and design. Audits undertaken by Privacy Commissioner.
	Personal Information Protection and Electronic Documents Act (PIPEDA) of 2005.	Outlines the role of health records and technology: organisations can conduct data linkages if patient privacy is protected during re-identification. Consent required.[e]
Australia	My Health Records Act and Privacy Act (the My Health Records Rules and Regulation), Australian Privacy Act 1988, and the Data Privacy Amendment, Notifiable Data Breaches Act 2017	Covers the collection, use and disclosure of the personal health information, as well as penalties. Expanded upon in the next section.
		No clear distinction made between those who control or own personal information and those who process personal information.[f]
Global	International Organization for Standardization (ISO)	Used by Australian Digital Health Agency (ADHA). Comprehensive but complex and expensive to implement.[g]

[a] Upendra et al., "Operationalizing Medical Device Cybersecurity at a Tertiary Care Medical Center."
[b] Abouzakhar and Angelopoulou, Internet of Things Security: A Review of Risks and Threats to Healthcare Sector.
[c] Akinsanya, Papadaki & Sun. Current Cybersecurity Maturity Models: How Effective in Healthcare Cloud?
[d] Schwartz et al., "The evolving state of medical device cybersecurity."
[e] Thakkar & Gordon, "Privacy and Policy Implications for Big Data and Health Information Technology for Patients: A Historical and Legal Analysis".
[f] Flaumenhaft & Ben-Assuli. "Personal health records, global policy and regulation review."
[g] Akinsanya, Papadaki & Sun. Current Cybersecurity Maturity Models: How Effective in Healthcare Cloud?

Mitigation Strategies) and Table 4 shows the identified international regulatory and legislative frameworks for data privacy and security.

Theme 1 – Emerging trends in cybersecurity risk

Cyber-attacks can occur at any connection of the network and at any endpoint. Interoperability of software, operating platforms, medical device interfaces and information exchange networks is an essential requirement of a digitalised health system and is crucial to cybersecurity risk management.[36] The emergence of medical cyber physical streams, wireless connectivity and the advent of medical applications in healthcare have exponentially increased attack surfaces and vectors.[37] Protecting every entry point to the health system is now impossible.[38]

Medical cyber physical systems

This term encapsulates Medical Internet of Things (MIoT) and medical devices, both implantable and wearable. Medical Cyber-Physical Systems (MCPS) are increasingly used in hospitals to provide high-quality healthcare and have emerged as promising platforms for monitoring and controlling multiple aspects of patient health.[39] It is estimated there will be 20 billion connected devices by 2020, and 50 billion by 2028.[40] The intrinsic features of MCPS increase their inherent security risks.[41] These features make MCPS myriad, mobile, heterogenous and increasingly ubiquitous.[42] They are often left unattended (as in implantable devices) to record intimate physiological data and are constrained in size, power and memory function which provides them only basic security capability.[43] MCPS features make them vulnerable to compromise[44] meaning their connection to and reliance upon the healthcare network significantly increases the cybersecurity risk to the entire healthcare system.[45] MCPS have become considerable potential attack vectors[46] to enable intrusion by malicious actors, installation of malware and alteration of treatment delivery.[47] Cybersecurity measures such as vulnerability scans or patch management are often not available[48] or only possible by manufacturers.[49] There exists an international lack of clarity on post-sale ownership, software update and security regulation of MCPS.[50] Manufacturers may be reluctant to provide documentation detailing device cybersecurity vulnerabilities[51] or patching and upgrade policies[52] as this is viewed as proprietary information. The absence of healthcare standards[53] to promote MCPS interoperability[54] increases incompatibility[55] between different healthcare systems and medical devices[56] and creates a healthcare vendor market that pushes patient devices to market before cybersecurity issues are addressed.[57] The cybersecurity vulnerability of medical devices and the lack of vendor and regulatory oversight has been recognised as a strategic priority by the Australian Therapeutic Goods Administration.[58]

Data confidentiality, privacy and consent

Privacy of confidential patient data and issues concerning the use of personal information was the next sub-theme identified. Risk to personal information can be categorised as cybersecurity threats to healthcare confidentiality, accessibility and integrity.[59] Confidentiality is compromised through loss of personal health records or data, as well loss of consumer confidence.[60] Accessibility to health records, software platforms, operating systems and hardware is affected through denial of service (DoS) malware or ransomware attacks.[61] Integrity of health data is exposed if it is corrupted, deleted or altered; or if wireless communication to essential devices or monitors are compromised.[62]

Healthcare is both a vulnerable and attractive target for cyberattack due to its economic size[63] and broad attack surface.[64] An increased focus by the health sector on cybersecurity is warranted considering the criticality of the health sector and the type of user information stored within health information systems.[65] Health information and medical data are highly valuable assets to patients, healthcare providers and identity thieves alike.[66] Estimates place health data as between ten[67] and twenty times[68] more lucrative than credit card or banking details. Credit card or banking details can be changed if stolen. Uniquely identifiable health history or data cannot.[69]

Cloud computing

Cloud computing was identified as a cybersecurity risk to data and information both during transfer and storage. The huge volume of health information produced has made centralised storage, encryption, deployment and maintenance of data prohibitive at the individual organisation level.[70] The advent of cloud computing allowed storage, processing and analysis of data to be outsourced to a remote server.[71] Cloud models share the cost of data accessibility and management, as well as sharing the cybersecurity risks – the scalability and efficiency of cloud computing means any potential breach exposes data to a far wider audience.[72] There are two attack vectors possible with cloud storage – attacks to data at rest which modifies or replaces information; and attacks to data in motion occurring during transfer to or from geographically distributed cloud servers. Encryption technology is essential to ensure the security of patient health information and data stored on cloud platforms.[73] A compromised host operating system could enable attackers to access hypervisor processes and services (such as a virtual machine monitor, a computer software, firmware or hardware that creates and runs virtual machines) and, potentially, any client application.

Malware

Records under this sub-theme discussed malware generally or applied examples such as the WannaCry attacks in the UK. Malware attack types and threat categorisation is outlined in detail in Table 1.

Health application ('app') security

The combined ubiquity of use and paucity of security provisions of Health apps are recognised as an increasing cybersecurity risk to the confidentiality of personal data and to the integrity of interconnected HCS infrastructure. Health apps can generate, store, and process huge volumes of identifiable health data.[74] The ubiquity, simplicity, low cost and improved encryption of WhatsApp, makes it attractive for telemedicine services[75] in resource constrained settings[76] and to facilitate professional networks and team communication.[77] Use of WhatsApp is now so commonplace amongst clinicians that urgent guidelines are required to ensure that clinicians do not inadvertently breach patient privacy or confidentiality.[78]

Mental health apps are promoted by health services as a discreet, accessible and affordable alternative to face-to-face therapy.[79] However, little research exists examining the safety and security of apps in medical practice, or of the proliferation of apps endorsed for mental health and dementia. A recent Australian study found that over half of government endorsed apps did not have a privacy policy to inform users how personal information would be collected, retained or shared with others.[80] Patient confidentiality and safety[81] or the security of communications,[82] are often not considered by app developers who are largely unregulated in terms of content, authorship or trustworthiness.[83] The author of a cross-sectional survey investigating the privacy and information security of health apps in wearable devices[84] identified a lack of awareness among respondents (n = 106) regarding the confidentiality or security of the data collected from their wearable device apps, including what was obtained and how it was transmitted or stored. The author postulates that these results reflect a wider lack of knowledge about potential data security and privacy risks throughout the general population. That these apps have received government endorsement for use in those with dementia and mental illness is of concern. Without adequate security provisions in place, health applications can be vulnerable to both active and passive attacks, resulting in data modification or theft.[85]

Insider threat

That cybersecurity mechanisms within health do not appropriately address the issue of insider threat as the 'entry point'[86] for ransomware was the final sub-theme identified (n = 7). Most data breaches involve some level of insider cooperation, either intentional or not.[87] Not recognising or responding to phishing emails remains a substantial problem[88] with email the most common vector through which healthcare organizations are attacked.[89] Most insider issues are due to ignorance rather than malice, but accidental error is equally damaging, making the lack of health information technology and cyber-hygiene knowledge an important threat. Studies indicate that respondents use weak or insecure passwords and are unaware of data security violation procedure.[90] Malicious intent as it relates to cyber-attacks is poorly understood and requires the integration of human factors into cybersecurity risk assessment to fully understand and characterise its impact upon mitigation strategies.[91] Inadvertent information leakages will remain inevitable due to the innumerable risks associated with collaborative sharing in complex healthcare network systems.[92]

Theme 2 – cybersecurity capability, countermeasures and mitigation strategies

The mitigation of risk to and protection of sensitive health information is now a global concern. The concept of a Cybersecurity Centre for Threat Control (based on the US Centers for Disease Control or a Cyber World Health Organisation)[93] is suggested to enable global recognition of the need for international collaboration to combat cybercrime. The incorporation of data breach response into organisational disaster plans, along with proactive partnerships between governments, industry and providers to enhance and develop collective security across healthcare sectors is advocated.[94]

Cryptographic architecture or technological solutions

There is strong emphasis, both in the international and Australian records, upon technological solutions and advanced cryptology to promulgate cybersecurity solutions. The greatest number of records identified (n = 63) concerned technological cybersecurity protective architecture, often developed by the authors of the records. It is beyond the scope of this paper to compare and discuss the different cryptographic security available to address data sharing and storage of patient information across network systems, cloud environments or through remote patient monitoring systems.[95] However, two cryptographies will be briefly mentioned due to their broad applicability and potential benefit for health specific challenges. The first, homomorphic encryption (HE) ensures strong security and privacy guarantees whilst enabling analysis on encrypted data and sensitive medical information.[96] Fully homomorphic encryption is versatile but has substantial computational requirements that at present slows processing significantly.[97] HE can also be used in mobile devices to transfer and store medical data without decrypting it, preserving privacy if a node is compromised.[98]

The second is Blockchain. Blockchain is a peer-to-peer distributed ledger technology that was initially used in the financial industry.[99] Its characteristics of decentralization, verifiability and immutability enable blockchain to securely store personal medical data.[100] Immutability ensures that any data, once stored in blockchain, cannot be altered or deleted.[101] Applications in health include integration of health information,[102] aggregation of data for research.[103] In blockchain all the data, including the keywords and the patients' identity are public key encrypted with keyword search. Challenges to blockchain include scalability, security and cost.[104] Whilst blockchain itself is secure, it can be accessed through stolen credentials and root privilege exploits.[105] Blockchain technology will require more research before large-scale production implementations.

Risk assessment and governance

Healthcare data breaches continue to rise[106] with at least one data breach per day in the health industry globally.[107] The average total cost of a healthcare data breach in 2019 was 6 USD.45 million compared to the 2017–18 average of 4 USD.08 million. This is 65% higher than the average total cost of a data breach in any other industry.[108] On average, it takes the healthcare industry longer than any other to identify (mean 236 days) and rectify (93 days) a data breach.[109] The longer a breach goes unnoticed, the greater the estimated cost. The importance of comprehensive cybersecurity risk assessment therefore cannot be underestimated in order to proactively identify vulnerabilities and detect threats or system breaches.[110] This must include detailed assessment and analysis of the cybersecurity risk and vulnerability of all information technology hardware, software, MCPS and vendor or third-party partner cybersecurity agreements.[111] Healthcare cybersecurity risk assessments and strategy frameworks should be standardised across jurisdictions and should include stipulations that demand vendor cybersecurity compliance and accountability.[112] The National eHealth Security and Access Framework v4.0 (NESAF) is the Australian cybersecurity risk assessment framework developed to guide health sector data protection and eHealth security.[113] The applicability, practicality and adoption of NESAF in practice is difficult to determine. The National Institute of Standards and Technology (NIST) Framework, which was developed in the US as a healthcare specific cybersecurity assessment model, could be adopted to the Australian healthcare context,[114] and is used in HCS across the US.

'Whitehat' or 'Ethical' hackers[115] should also be utilised to regularly test and assess cyber vulnerabilities. 'Whitehats' are professional hackers who undertake penetration and infiltration exercises and attempt to breach cybersecurity defences.[116]

Regulation and/or legislation

Securing the privacy of collected information and data is a major concern of patients[117] and the reason why many withhold consent for the use of their data in research.[118] Patient privacy specifically refers to 'the right of patients to determine when, how, and to what extent their health information is shared with others.'.[119] Regulatory and policy oversight can decrease data and privacy breaches, as indicated by the HIPAA Omnibus Rules 2013[120] which restricted healthcare vendor access to patient information.[121] However comprehensive policy will not guarantee cybersecurity if not reflective of actual healthcare practice, culture or infrastructure limitations, as evinced in the NHS with WannaCry. Nor will it entirely protect against insider agents.[122]

A comparison of international privacy and security frameworks and regulations is presented in Table 2.

Holistic approach toward proactive cybersecurity culture

There is recognition within the international literature that healthcare cybersecurity is a complex socio-technical challenge[123] requiring a holistic integrated approach[124] to improve staff awareness,[125] competence,[126] and mitigation of threats across the industry. The international records also highlight the importance of developing a proactive cybersecurity culture,[127] in which compliance to protecting information is embedded.[128] Significantly, this theme is not discussed within the Australian records.

There is also recognition that merely enforcing security policies and procedures will not drive cultural change or learning.[129] Healthcare leadership must embrace cybersecurity and develop strong cultures of cyber-vigilance[130] throughout organisations and amongst all staff[131] to develop a robust, proactive incident response. Building a culture that systematically and continuously analyses the cyber context of an organisation will enable vulnerabilities and threats to be identified.[132]

Education and simulated environments

That staff cybersecurity education is the most important strategy[133] against data breaches is not addressed in the identified Australian records. The essential need for comprehensive employee training and education[134] to enable the identification and assessment of risk[135] is discussed throughout the international records. Cybersecurity simulation models[136] indicate that experienced managers make less effective cybersecurity decisions than novices, as they are more likely to seek an optimal decision utilising past experiences. The unpredictable 'zero-day' cyber-attacks and ever evolving nature of cyber threats often means optimal reactive decisions are not possible. Rather, the capability to make proactive preventative decisions is key. As employees are often the inadvertent facilitators of security breaches,[137] behavioural skills training and education to raise privacy-protection awareness and change habitual information technology habits into conscious cybersecurity decisions is required.[138] Staff will engage with cybersecurity if interventions are not costly (i.e. time consuming or onerous) and if self-efficacy is enhanced through active involvement in the training.[139] Simulation based training[140] to practice and develop cybersecurity capabilities can facilitate this.[141] The magnitude of cybersecurity organisational capability and individual employee skills required to mitigate the risk of vulnerabilities and breaches cannot be underestimated.[142]

Capability and cyber maturity

Cybersecurity capability is identified as a strategic asset that every health organization must adopt,[143] along with the concepts of building organisational resilience and the capacity to learn from mistakes.[144] Cybersecurity capability includes the skills, knowledge and competence[145] of the workforce, organisation, sector and nation to detect, mitigate and protect against threat. The Australian HCS is recognised as having low cybersecurity capability maturity.[146] The lack of an Australian healthcare cybersecurity capability model is recognised as a significant security risk in a country that has adopted an opt-out digitalised health record with MHR.[147]

Cyber-hygiene practices

Organisational cyber-hygiene practices are recognised as mandatory safeguards that include email data encryption of patient information, antivirus software, software updates, and at least two-factor authentication patient data stored or shared on cloud platforms.[148] Cyber-hygiene can be practised at employee level, such as in recognition and escalation of suspicious emails, or through enforcement of organisational policy regarding information sharing and protection.[149]

Theme 3 – current cybersecurity issues within Australia

> "In Australian cybersecurity, there are only two types of healthcare organisations – those that know they've been hacked and those that don't know they've been hacked".[150]

The average cost of a data breach in Australia in 2018 was estimated to be 2 USD.5 million.[151] It takes Australia a mean of 200 days (compared to 185 in 2017) to identify a data breach and 81 days to contain the breach incidents.[152] A cross-sector survey of 1894 senior executives and senior IT managers found that almost 70% of data breaches reported in Australia during 2018 were directly attributed to human error.[153] The number of documented data breaches involving the My Health Record (MHR) system in 2017–18 was 42, an increase from 35 the preceding year.[154]

At present the Office of the Australian Information Commissioner (OAIC) Notifiable Data Breaches only cover private providers and not public institutions or healthcare systems. This makes it extremely difficult to gauge an accurate picture of the cybersecurity landscape within Australia. An independent cybersecurity report of 4067 cyber incidents, many of which were not included in the quarterly Notifiable Data Breach reports, was undertaken during 2018.[155] The report analysis estimated that there were 445 healthcare cyber incidents in Australia in 2018 which equated to almost 24% of the Australian cyber breach total. Crucially, the report found that the healthcare industry had the lowest cybersecurity capability maturity of any Australian industry to identify and manage risks and to protect against or contain attacks. Specifically, the health sector lacks the capability to anticipate and respond to vulnerabilities and has a very high risk of experiencing a cyber incident within 12 months.[156] In 2018, no community healthcare providers had a dedicated budget for cybersecurity, and only 16% of public hospitals allocate funds specifically to cybersecurity.[157] Over

40% of clinical, specialist non-clinical, and administrative health staff believe they have no responsibility for cybersecurity, and 6.2% of Australian health organisations are unable to undertake operating system updates or patches due to legacy and end of life systems.[158]

MHR is the Australian digital health record that supports clinical care and is accessible to authorised health care providers wherever and whenever health services are initiated. The accuracy and relevance of the MHR is a joint responsibility of the individual and health care provider/s.[159] MHR is intended as an integrated eHealth Record 'to provide a consolidated record of an individual's health information for consumers to access and as a mechanism for improving care co-ordination between care provider teams'.[160] However, this probably remains an ambitious ideal given the unique challenges and complexities of the Australian federated funding model combined with the ambiguous responsibilities of the commonwealth and states in relation to different aspects of healthcare delivery.[161] As of 28 July 2019, MHR has a 90.1% participation rate across Australia, with 16,400 healthcare providers registered to the system.[162] The legislative framework underpinning the My Health Record system include My Health Records Act 2012,[163] My Health Records Rule 2016 and My Health Records Regulation 2012.

The Australian Digital Health Agency (ADHA) is the System Operator of MHR. Healthcare organisations and providers are required to report potential or confirmed data 'breaches' involving MHR to the System Operator (the ADHA). MHR data breaches must also be reported to the OAIC, except where the healthcare provider organisation is a state or territory authority.[164] The Digital Health Cyber Security Centre (DHCSC) provides operational security support for the MHR on behalf of the ADHA. During a national healthcare sector cyber crisis, the DHCSC is responsible for coordinating responses across the health sector in liaison with other Government organisations such as the Australian Cyber Security Centre and CERT (Computer Emergency Response Team) Australia.[165] In other words, the ADHA coordinates the cybersecurity response for major for cybersecurity breaches potentially caused by its own system vulnerabilities.

There is a paucity of research within Australia to measure or gauge Government, public-private sector or users' cybersecurity capacity to adopt or engage with an electronic health system such as MHR,[166] or to measure public understanding or perceptions of the potential use of their data in research.[167] A 2016 study[168] of the Personally Controlled Electronic Health Record (PCEHR) which essentially incarnated into MHR in July 2018, identified a multitude of security weaknesses. PCEHR consisted of a distributed network of interconnected systems with multiple interfaces required to enable a variety of providers, services and applications have access. The potential security weaknesses included system misconfiguration and implementation flaws, inconsistent authorisation policies and authorisation errors, and insecure transfer of privileges between healthcare providers in the PCEHR system.

An analysis of the timeline of Australian electronic health record development and an examination of the failed 'HealthConnect' project which preceded it (and which subsequently has been removed from Department of Health websites)[169] concludes that enduring tensions exist between those seeking to enhance the widespread availability of individual health information reform, and those who view it as a threat to privacy. There appears to be an inability to seek compromise or learn from divergent viewpoints and values. This has been particularly evident since the transition of MHR to an opt out system[170] which commenced on 16 July 2018 and was extended to 31 January 2019.

An important note of interest and consideration in the Australian cybersecurity context is that the healthcare industry is not included as critical infrastructure in the Australian Security of Critical Infrastructure Act 2018. In contrast, healthcare is recognised as critical infrastructure internationally.[171] The cybersecurity challenges created by digital health transformation requires universal cross-sectoral governance and coordination that emphasises 'healthcare as Critical National Infrastructure'.[172] This concept must be identified and protected. Creating cybersecurity silos in which healthcare is separate from other critical infrastructure could potentially weaken healthcare cybersecurity defence and capability.

Health security breaches in Australia

The following section draws on current open access media reports to ascertain the extent of health related 'breaches' or 'incidents' occurring within Australia. It is not intended to be exhaustive, but rather indicative of public awareness around the issues of cybersecurity as it relates to health generally and MHR specifically. As this is an emerging topic there are limited scholarly studies published.

Medicare has been plagued with security and privacy issues. Medicare details have been found available for sale on the dark web,[173] though any 'breach' of MHR was denied by ADHA: '*there has not been a cyber security breach of our systems as such, but rather it is more likely to have been a traditional criminal activity*' (involving a likely insider).[174] In 2016 the Australian government published a deidentified data set comprising the health details of 10% of the Australian population with information collected since 1984.[175] A week later a group of University of Melbourne academics privately informed the government that it had been able to re-identify the entire data set. The government immediately withdrew the data set from the website, however access logs indicated the data set had been downloaded 1,500 times but could not indicate who had accessed it.

The Australian Bureau of Statistics (ABS) was 'attacked' by Macquarie University academics to illustrate weaknesses in the TableBuilder tool used by ABS to enable low dataset counts to be retrieved. TableBuilder creates tables, graphs and maps of Australian census data. As the tool could be manipulated through unlimited query counts to include cell counts of 1, it was theoretically possible to re-identify individuals from census data.[176] The ABS were made aware of the vulnerability and have consequently changed the ToolBuilder interface.

HealthEngine was the government endorsed health appointment and scheduling app recommended by the ADHA. HealthEngine was exposed for editing negative reviews of GP practices, revealing the identifying details of 75 users via a website flaw and sharing hundreds of patient's data to personal injury legal firms.[177] HealthEngine provided access to MHR information such as Medicare records, test results, scans and prescriptions, for their app users to view on mobile phones.[178]

The difficulty of estimating the extent of cybersecurity breaches at state level is also raised. The state of NSW does not currently have a mandatory notifiable data breach reporting requirement, with the NSW Privacy Commissioner recommending a voluntary reporting scheme only.[179] As the National Data Breach scheme covers only federal government agencies and private sector organisations regulated by the Australian Privacy Principles, it virtually impossible to determine at a national level how many data breaches have occurred in the patient record systems of state-based health services.[180]

In a politically interesting and provocative act, the Victorian Auditor General hacked into his own health databases to expose sensitive patient information.[181] 'Patient data in Victoria's public health system could be easily hacked in a system riddled with weaknesses. The sector is highly vulnerable to cyber-attacks but staff awareness of data security is low, with issues around physical security, password management and other access controls'.[182] The official Auditor General report of Victorian security vulnerabilities states: 'There are key weaknesses in health services' physical and logical security covering password management and other user access controls. Staff awareness of data security is low, which increases the likelihood of success of social engineering techniques such as phishing or tailgating into corporate areas where ICT infrastructure and servers may be located'.[183] Also in Victoria, Cabrini Hospital based Melbourne Heart Group was unable to access approximately 15,000 files in February 2019 due to a server ransomware attack which corrupted and encrypted data. The ransom was reportedly paid: 'The My Health Record database will be an enormously tempting target for cybercriminals, not just now but for years, if not decades, to come.'[184]

These cybersecurity breaches whether notifiable or not, highlight the need for expertly trained cybersecurity professionals within the healthcare system. At present however, across NSW and Australia, there is a significant shortfall in sufficiently skilled and experienced cybersecurity experts required to develop products and services to meet ever evolving cybersecurity threats.[185] A new Certificate IV in cyber security was accredited nationally and is being implemented in NSW. One of the key aspects of the NSW Cybersecurity Strategy is the alignment of streamlined cybersecurity training with industry. The report does not specifically mention the healthcare sector as an area of need.

The idea of informed consent is contentious within MHR, in that implied consent is taken to have been granted if there has been no active opt-out of the MHR system. Several authors question the notion of ongoing consent inherent within systems such as MHR.[186] 'The MHR Act does not specify the types of applicants that may access MHR system data for secondary use'.[187] Ongoing consent for secondary use of health information and data through MHR is condoned by the ADHA. Section 66(2) of the Framework[188] specifically enables 'secondary use of identified MHR data, noting that the System Operator (ADHA) is authorised to collect, use and disclose an individual's health care information (i.e. identifiable information) with the consent of the individual'.[189] How and when this consent is obtained, and by whom is not elucidated. The concept of ongoing consent as a breach of trust was raised when the Department of Human Services (DHS) acted on behalf of a third-party research organisation to access Medicare prescription data and contact (via letter) 50, 000 Australians who had been prescribed Lithium.[190] DHS claims that researchers had no access to private patient information disregards the point that an open access letter did contain private and potentially damaging information, as well as avoiding the issue that consent to share private prescription data had not been sought from any of the people contacted. How was consent obtained for secondary use in this case?

Health management training in Australia

Health management courses in Australia (such as Masters in Health Management) are a prerequisite for health manager jobs, yet these do not usually cover cybersecurity in their curricula. We did not identify any Masters level degree in health or hospital management which teaches cybersecurity. The Australasian College of Health Service Management (ACHSM) Guideline for Universities (2017) lists the five core competencies required of health service managers including the requisite knowledge, skills and behaviours expected of graduates. Cybersecurity (risk awareness, assessment, mitigation or management) is not listed. Nor is it mentioned by RACMA, the other peak body for health management.

Discussion

The healthcare sector is a complex system of interconnected organisations, providers, staff and patients, of which MHR is an important component. As highlighted throughout, human factors play a crucial role in cybersecurity with employees often the weakest link in organizational cybersecurity.[191] However, lack of mandatory reporting of breaches, lack of health management training in cybersecurity, lack of investment in cybersecurity infrastructure in health systems and use of old, legacy computing systems by hospitals, leaves Australia vulnerable to cyber-attacks. The potential advantages of a centralised and accessible patient health record are clear, but the cybersecurity issues inherent in collating, transferring and storing electronic patient records and health information must be comprehensively addressed. The Privacy Act 1988 protects the personal information of Australians in federal agencies or private organisations but does not cover state and territory public hospitals or health services. The OAIC Notifiable Data Breach Scheme (NDBS) has the legislative power under the Privacy Act IIIC to enforce penalties for data breaches. As of February 2018, no fines have been issued despite 967 reported breaches that have affected tens of thousands of Australians. This is in stark contrast to HIPAA in the US which accredits health care organisations to enforce cybersecurity and data protection compliance, and which issues penalties of between 50,000 USD to 1.5 USD million US for noncompliance. HIPAA was amended in 2005 to protect the electronic protected health information stored, collected or transferred by any healthcare provider. Even with the protections of HIPAA, the US has suffered ransomware attacks on hospitals and other health data breaches. Without any such protection, Australia would be even more vulnerable, and should consider adopting a data protection scheme and framework that includes a critical analysis of the capability of multiple health providers and organisations with disparate operating systems to ensure health data security, confidentiality and integrity. Mandatory reporting of breaches should also be adopted. Cybersecurity capability must integrate all aspects of information security measures to protect health information from malicious access or breach.[192] Currently this provision does not exist within Australia. Health budgets should include resources to upgrade computer systems and hire cybersecurity personnel.

Data breaches adversely affect patient and community faith in healthcare to protect privacy and can lead to health information being withheld from healthcare providers due to confidentiality concerns.[193] Non-disclosure of information could lead to inaccurate or delayed diagnoses and compromised patient safety. However, it is essential that allaying security and privacy concerns and protecting provider reputation not become motivation to withhold cybersecurity breach reporting. Mandatory reporting and open discussion of cybersecurity incidents and breaches can facilitate real world learning and become the basis for education and training programmes. Cybersecurity capability is the capacity to manage previously unknown and seen situations and is best developed through multiple experiences of dealing with new situations.[194]

There are significant concerns regarding the ethics and consent in MHR. The rights of the patient regarding information collected about them, especially when considering 'ongoing consent' for secondary research sharing and use are paramount.[195] It could be argued that the least influential and most vulnerable people are being co-opted into MHR by an opt-out system, without their informed consent, further cementing health inequity and disparity. The Government has not fully addressed access and consent issues relating to many vulnerable communities including adolescents, abuse victims, sex workers, people with HIV and those with mental illnesses.[196] MHR raises the concept of a social licence not only for the open disclosure of potential cybersecurity risks, but also regarding the secondary use of health record data for research.[197] Consumers are entitled to control how their data are used, but this must be balanced to ensure that informed consent can be obtained to enable high quality primary and public health research.

It is impossible to completely mitigate cyber threats: 'Today it has become a question of "when", and "at what level"'[198] systems such as MHR will be breached. This does not invalidate the need for comprehensive, integrated and accessible electronic health records such as MHR. Instead it indicates the need for open disclosure of and proactive dialogue about cyber-attacks, innovate and holistic strategies and policies to reduce cyber threat, and cyber education and training for all health staff in order to develop cybersecurity awareness and capability. A healthcare culture that shares risk and threat information[199] is as essential as infrastructure management such as replacing legacy software and hardware, patching and updates and undertaking comprehensive risk assessments of connected devices.[200]

The overall cybersecurity maturity of healthcare organisations should be assessed to ensure a secure healthcare environment of interconnected systems.[201] The multiple health providers, organisations and agencies combining information into a comprehensive electronic health record provide innumerable potential attack interfaces. Cybersecurity threats are emerging from new vectors. Healthcare is also vulnerable from rapidly evolving technologies including wireless sensor networked medical devices, healthcare applications, and implantable medical devices. 'Enhancing the security and privacy in MCPS remains a serious challenge demanding careful considerations and joint efforts by the industry, the health systems, and the research community'.[202]

Limitations

There are three main limitations to this systematic review. The first is that the cybersecurity landscape is evolving at such an exponential rate, that new information is emerging regularly. The second is that as this is such an emerging field, the number of scholarly research articles published on this topic is sparse. Third, the scope of this review was broad and some themes were not able to be considered in detail.

Conclusion

This review investigates the body of literature on global cyberattacks against the healthcare sector, in order to categorise the cyber threats to health, and present mitigating countermeasures or protective strategies in relation to a universal electronic health record in Australia. Cyberattacks against healthcare are rising due to the lucrative patient data available in digitalised health systems, and because healthcare has poor cybersecurity defences and awareness. Australia lacks some of the protections that other countries such as the US has, such as the HIPAA law and mandatory reporting of breaches. Outdated health computing systems and lack of investment by the hospital sector in cybersecurity is an additional problem. Health management training lacks cybersecurity content, and until this is addressed, the health system will remain vulnerable. If healthcare mangers are not taught essential cybersecurity skills, it is unlikely they will lead change in the development of healthcare cybersecurity capability and resilience in the workplace. There is no way to completely mitigate the risk of a cybersecurity incident or breach within the healthcare system, globally or within Australia. However, building a proactive healthcare culture of cybersecurity maturity can help to reduce cybersecurity risk.

Notes

1. Abd-alrazaqa et al., "Factors that affect the use of electronic personal health records among patients: A systematic review."
2. Zeb et al., U-prove based security framework for mobile device authentication in eHealth networks.
3. Abouzakhar and Angelopoulou. Internet of Things Security: A Review of Risks and Threats to Healthcare Sector.
4. Global Digital Health Partnership, Securing Digital Health 2018.
5. BDO USA Healthcare, Brace for the Breach – Cyberthreat Insights 2019.
6. Institute for Critical Infrastructure Technology (ICIT). Industry Brief: Hacking Healthcare.
7. MacIntyre et al., "Converging and emerging threats to health security."
8. Ibid.
9. IT News, "Hack linked to attack on US insurer Anthem".
10. Forcepoint Whitepaper. Life Support: Eliminating Data Breaches in the Healthcare Sector.
11. Gordon, Fairhall and Landman, "Threats to Information Security – Public Health Implications."
12. Jalali & Kaiser, "Cybersecurity in Hospitals: A Systematic, Organizational Perspective."
13. Argaw et al., "The state of research on cyberattacks against hospitals and available best practice recommendations: a scoping review."
14. See note 12 above.
15. Sittig & Singh. "A Socio-technical Approach to Preventing, Mitigating, and Recovering from Ransomware Attacks."; Small et al., "Patient Perceptions About Data Sharing & Privacy: Insights from Action."
16. Kruse et al., "Cybersecurity in healthcare: A systematic review of modern threats and trends."
17. National Audit Office Report, Investigation: WannaCry Cyber Attack and the NHS.
18. Wirth A., "Cyberinsights. Hardly Ever a Dull Moment: The Ongoing Cyberthreats of 2017."
19. See note 17 above.
20. Walker-Roberts et al., A Systematic Review of the Availability and Efficacy of Countermeasures to Internal Threats in Healthcare Critical Infrastructure.
21. O"Sullivan
22. Schwartz et al., "The evolving state of medical device cybersecurity."
23. See note 17 above.
24. Pratt, "How cyberattacks can impact physicians."; Connory, 2019 Annual Report. State of cyber security.
25. See note 20 above.
26. Farringer, "Cybersecurity Report Identifies Unique Challenges to Tackling Cybersecurity in Health Care."; Sedlack, Understanding Cyber Security Perceptions Related to Information Risk in a Healthcare Setting.
27. Boddy et al., A Study into Data Analysis and Visualisation to increase the CyberResilience of Healthcare Infrastructures.
28. Akinsanya, Papadaki & Sun. Current Cybersecurity Maturity Models: How Effective in Healthcare Cloud?.
29. See note 27 above.

30. Sittig & Singh. "A Socio-technical Approach to Preventing, Mitigating, and Recovering from Ransomware Attacks."
31. Reagin & Gentry. "Enterprise Cybersecurity: Building a Successful Defense Program."
32. Safavi et al., Cyber Vulnerabilities on Smart Healthcare, Review and Solutions.
33. Carlton, Development of a Cybersecurity Skills Index: A Scenarios-Based Hands on Measure of Non-IT Professionals Cybersecurity Skills 2016.; NSW Dept of Industry. NSW-cyber-security-industry-development-strategy 2018.
34. Chen et al., "Blockchain-Based Medical Records Secure Storage and Medical Service Framework."
35. Wilson & Khansa. "Migrating to electronic health record systems: A comparative study between the United States and the United Kingdom."
36. Zaidan et al., "A Security Framework for Nationwide Health Information Exchange based on Telehealth Strategy."
37. Nippon Telegraph and Telephone (NTT) Security. Global Threat Intelligence Report 2019.
38. Dogaru & Dumitrache, Cyber Security in Healthcare Networks. Conference Proceedings of the 6th IEEE International Conference on E-Health and Bioengineering – EHB 2017.
39. Chaudhry et al., POStCODE Middleware for Post-market Surveillance of Medical Devices for Cyber Security in Medical and Healthcare Sector in Australia.
40. See note 5 above.
41. Zhou et al., "The Effect of IoT New Features on Security and Privacy: New Threats, Existing Solutions, and Challenges Yet to Be Solved."
42. Raber, McCarthy & Yeh. "Health Insurance and Mobile Health Devices: Opportunities and Concerns. JAMA."
43. Almohri et al., On Threat Modeling and Mitigation of Medical Cyber-Physical Systems.
44. See note 27 above.
45. Zheng et al., From WannaCry to WannaDie: Security trade-offs and design for implantable medical devices.
46. Camara, Peris-Lopez & Tapiador, "Security and privacy issues in implantable medical devices: A comprehensive survey."
47. Stern, "A life cycle approach to medical device cybersecurity."
48. Rubenfire, "The nightmare scenario: dialing devices to deadly."
49. See note 22 above.
50. See note 39 above.
51. See note 47 above.
52. Smigielski, "Hardening Infusion Pump Communication Software for Medical Device Cybersecurity."
53. See note 39 above.
54. O"Dowd, "NHS patient data security is to be tightened after cyberattack."
55. Jayaratne et al., "A data integration platform for patient-centered e-healthcare and clinical decision support."
56. See note 35 above.
57. See note 43 above.
58. Holdsworth, Glisson & Choo. "Medical device vulnerability mitigation effort gap analysis taxonomy."
59. Siddique et al., A survey of big data security solutions in healthcare.
60. Shenoy & Appel, "Safeguarding Confidentiality in Electronic Health Records."
61. Wirth, "Cyberinsights. The Times They Are a-Changin": Part One."
62. Baranchuk et al., "Cybersecurity for Cardiac Implantable Electronic Devices: What Should You Know?".
63. Blanke & McGrady. "When it comes to securing patient health information from breaches, your best medicine is a dose of prevention: A cybersecurity risk assessment checklist."
64. Coventry & Branley. "Cybersecurity in healthcare: A narrative review of trends, threats and ways forward."
65. Martin et al., "Cybersecurity and healthcare: How safe are we?".
66. See note 16 above.
67. Beeksow, "Reducing Security Risk using data loss prevention technology."
68. Kruse, Smith & Vanderlinden and A. Nealand. Security Techniques for the Electronic Health Records.
69. See note 11 above.
70. Lee, Moon & Park. CloudRPS: a cloud analysis based enhanced ransomware prevention system.; Abrar et al., "Risk Analysis of Cloud Sourcing in Healthcare and Public Health Industry."
71. Sahi, Lai & Li. "Security and privacy preserving approaches in the eHealth clouds with disaster recovery plan."
72. Sajid & Abbas. "Data Privacy in Cloud-assisted Healthcare Systems: State of the Art and Future Challenges."
73. See note 71 above.
74. Rosenfeld, Torous & Vahia. "Data Security and Privacy in Apps for Dementia: An Analysis of Existing Privacy Policies."
75. Kamel Boulos, Giustini & Wheeler. "Instagram and WhatsApp in Health and Healthcare: An Overview."
76. Scott, "WhatsApp in Clinical Practice: A Literature Review."
77. Chan & Leung. "Use of Social Network Sites for Communication Among Health Professionals: Systematic Review."
78. Morris, Scott & Mars. "Security and Other Ethical Concerns of Instant Messaging in Healthcare."

79. Parker et al., "How private is your mental health app data? An empirical study of mental health app privacy policies and practices."
80. Ibid.
81. Huckvale et al., "Unaddressed privacy risks in accredited health and wellness apps: a cross-sectional systematic assessment."; Mense et al., "Analyzing Privacy Risks of mHealth Applications."
82. Thamilarasu & Lakin. "A Security Framework for Mobile Health Applications. Proceedings –5th International Conference on Future Internet of Things and Cloud Workshops (FiCloudW)".
83. Grundy et al., Finding Peace of Mind: Navigating the Marketplace of Mental Health Apps, Australian Communications Consumer Action Network, Sydney.
84. Cilliers, "Wearable devices in healthcare: Privacy and information security issues."
85. Al-Muhtadi et al., "Cybersecurity and privacy issues for socially integrated mobile healthcare applications operating in a multi-cloud environment."
86. Spence et al., "Ransomware in Healthcare Facilities: A Harbinger of the future?".
87. Yasnoff, Breach Risk Magnitude: A Quantitative Measure of Database Security.
88. Gordon et al., "Evaluation of a mandatory phishing training program for high-risk employees at a US healthcare system."
89. Klas-CHIME, Whitepaper: How Aligned Are Provider Organizations with the Health Industry Cybersecurity Practices (HICP) Guidelines?.
90. Fernandez-Aleman
91. King et al., "Characterizing and Measuring Maliciousness for Cybersecurity Risk Assessment."
92. See note 88 above.
93. Smith, "Malware and Disease: Lessons from Cyber Intelligence for Public Health Surveillance."
94. Magnus, Public Report of the Committee of Inquiry (COI) into the Cyber Attack on SingHealth 10 January 2019.
95. Coventry & Branley. "Cybersecurity in healthcare: A narrative review of trends, threats and ways forward."; Wang, Gao & Zhang. Searchable and revocable multi-data owner attribute-based encryption scheme with hidden policy in cloud storage.; Zhang, Xue & Liu. "Searchable Encryption for Healthcare Clouds: A Survey."; Gardiyawasam Pussewalage & Oleshchuk. "Privacy preserving mechanisms for enforcing security and privacy requirements in E-health solutions."
96. Raisaro et al., "Are privacy-enhancing technologies for genomic data ready for the clinic? A survey of medical experts of the Swiss HIV Cohort Study."
97. Saleem et al., Survey on cybersecurity issues in wireless mesh networks based eHealthcare.
98. Wang & Zhang. Data Division Scheme Based on Homomorphic Encryption in WSNs for Health Care Wireless sensor networks.
99. Dubovitskaya et al., Secure and Trustable Electronic Medical Records Sharing using Blockchain.
100. Akinsanya, Papadaki & Sun. Current Cybersecurity Maturity Models: How Effective in Healthcare Cloud?; Carlton, Development of a Cybersecurity Skills Index: A Scenarios-Based Hands on Measure of Non-IT Professionals Cybersecurity Skills 2016.
101. Esposito et al., "Blockchain: A Panacea for Healthcare Cloud-Based Data Security and Privacy?".
102. Park et al., "Is Blockchain Technology Suitable for Managing Personal Health Records? Mixed-Methods Study to Test Feasibility."
103. See note 99 above.
104. Alonso et al., "Proposing New Blockchain Challenges in eHealth."; Angraal, Krumholz & Schulz. "Blockchain Technology: Applications in Health Care."
105. Firdaus et al., "Root Exploit Detection and Features Optimization: Mobile Device and Blockchain Based Medical Data Management."
106. See note 35 above.
107. See note 10 above.
108. Ponemon Institute, Cost of a Data Breach Report 2019.
109. Verizon, 2019 Data Breach Investigations Report.
110. Connory, 2019 Annual Report. State of cyber security.; Ponemon Institute. Cost of a Data Breach Report 2019.
111. Holdsworth, Glisson & Choo. "Medical device vulnerability mitigation effort gap analysis taxonomy."; Upendra et al., "Operationalizing Medical Device Cybersecurity at a Tertiary Care Medical Center."
112. Terry, "HIPAA BREACH. Secure data & prevent fines."
113. Australian Digital Health Agency, National health security and access framework – NESAF.
114. Akinsanya et al., Current Cybersecurity Maturity Models: How Effective in Healthcare Cloud? Online Proceedings of the 5th Collaborative European Research Conference.
115. Taylor, "An SOS on Cybersecurity: To protect patient data, hospitals beef up risk management programs. Hello, chief security officers and "white hat hackers".
116. Perakslis & Califf. "Employ Cybersecurity Techniques Against the Threat of Medical Misinformation."
117. Papoutsi et al., "Patient and public views about the security and privacy of Electronic Health Records (EHRs) in the UK: results from a mixed methods study."

118. Carter, "Considerations for Genomic Data Privacy and Security when Working in the Cloud."
119. Andriole, "Security of electronic medical information and patient privacy: what you need to know."
120. HIPAA Omnibus Rule 2013 Summary.
121. Yaraghi & Gopal, "The Role of HIPAA Omnibus Rules in Reducing the Frequency of Medical Data Breaches: Insights from an Empirical Study."
122. See note 20 above.
123. See note 30 above.
124. Natsiavas et al., "Comprehensive user requirements engineering methodology for secure and interoperable health data exchange."
125. Pullin, "Cybersecurity: Positive Changes Through Processes and Team Culture."
126. Rajamäki et al. Cybersecurity education and training in hospitals: Proactive resilience educational framework (Prosilience EF).
127. Coventry & Branley. "Cybersecurity in healthcare: A narrative review of trends, threats and ways forward."; Verizon, 2019 Data Breach Investigations Report.; Nippon Telegraph and Telephone (NTT) Security. Global Threat Intelligence Report 2019.
128. Raths, "What to Do If a Breach Happens to You."
129. Ropp & Quammen. "Protecting health data in a troubling time. Understand who and what you're up against."
130. Dameff et al., "Clinical Cybersecurity Training Through Novel High-Fidelity Simulations."
131. See note 5 above.
132. Wickham, M. H. Exploring Data Breaches and Means to Mitigate Future Occurrences in Healthcare Institutions: A Content Analysis.
133. See note 16 above.
134. Gordon, Fairhall and Landman, "Threats to Information Security – Public Health Implications."; Dameff et al., "Clinical Cybersecurity Training Through Novel High-Fidelity Simulations."
135. Sedlack, Understanding Cyber Security Perceptions Related to Information Risk in a Healthcare Setting.
136. See note 12 above.
137. See note 11 above.
138. Zafar, Cybersecurity: Role of behavioral training in healthcare.; Sher et al., "Compliance with Electronic Medical Records Privacy Policy: An Empirical Investigation of Hospital Information Technology Staff."
139. Blythe & Coventry. "Costly but effective: Comparing the factors that influence employee anti-malware behaviours."
140. Gaynor, Omer & Turner. "Teaching EHRs security with simulation for non-technical healthcare managers."
141. Zafar, Cybersecurity: Role of behavioral training in healthcare.
142. Carlton, Development of a Cybersecurity Skills Index: A Scenarios-Based Hands on Measure of Non-IT Professionals Cybersecurity Skills 2016.
143. See note 31 above.
144. See note 30 above.
145. Carlton, Development of a Cybersecurity Skills Index: A Scenarios-Based Hands on Measure of Non-IT Professionals Cybersecurity Skills 2016.
146. Connory, 2019 Annual Report. State of cyber security.
147. Burke et al., Cybersecurity Indexes for eHealth.
148. Pratt, "How cyberattacks can impact physicians."
149. McSweeney, Motivating cybersecurity compliance in critical infrastructure industries: A grounded theory study.
150. Pinskier, Royal Australian College of General Practitioners.
151. Ponemon Institute. Cost of a Data Breach Report 2019.
152. Ibid.
153. See note 146 above.
154. Australian Digital Health Agency (ADHA). Annual Report 2017–18.
155. See note 146 above.
156. Ibid.
157. Health Informatics Society Australia, Healthcare-Cybersecurity-Report_June-2018.
158. Ibid.
159. Department of Health, Framework to guide the secondary use of My Health Record system data.
160. See note 154 above.
161. Garetty et al., "National electronic health record systems as wicked projects the Australian experience."
162. My Health Record Statistics (28 July 2019).
163. My Health Records Act 2012.
164. Office of the Australian Information Commissioner, My Health Record Privacy.
165. Global Digital Health Partnership, Securing Digital Health 2018.; ADHA. About the DH Cyber Security Centre, ADHA.
166. See note 147 above.
167. Canaway et al., "Gathering data for decisions: best practice use of primary care electronic records for research."

168. Zhou, Varadharajan & Gopinath. "A Secure Role-Based Cloud Storage System for Encrypted Patient-Centric Health Records."
169. See note 161 above.
170. Australian Government. 14 November 2018. My Health Records (National Application) Amendment (Extension of Opt-out Period No. 2) Rules 2018.
171. Ogunlana, Countering expansion and organization of terrorism in cyberspace.; Shah, Protecting Australian critical national infrastructure in an era of IT and OT convergence.; Walker-Roberts et al., A Systematic Review of the Availability and Efficacy of Countermeasures to Internal Threats in Healthcare Critical Infrastructure.; Boddy et al., A Study into Data Analysis and Visualisation to increase the CyberResilience of Healthcare Infrastructures.; Rajamäki et al. Cybersecurity education and training in hospitals: Proactive resilience educational framework (Prosilience EF).
172. Global Digital Health Partnership, Securing Digital Health 2018.
173. Farrell, "Medicare Machine – patient details of any Australian for sale on Darknet".
174. Minion, "Leaked ADHA document gives inside look at My Health Record challenges".
175. Phillips, Dove & Knoppers. "Criminal Prohibition of Wrongful Re-Identification: Legal Solution or Minefield for Big-Data?".
176. Asghar & Dali. Averaging Attacks on Bounded Perturbation Algorithms.
177. See note 174 above.
178. ABC News (24 July 2018).
179. Information and Privacy Commission NSW.
180. Information and Privacy Commission NSW, Voluntary Breach Notification.
181. ABC News (30 May 2019).
182. The Victorian Auditor General.
183. Ibid.
184. ABC News (22 February 2019); Houston & Colangelo. "Crime syndicate hacks 15,000 medical files at Cabrini Hospital demands ransom".
185. NSW Dept of Industry.
186. Garetty et al., "National electronic health record systems as wicked projects the Australian experience."; Mendelson, "The European Union General Data Protection Regulation (Eu 2016/679) and the Australian My Health Record Scheme – A Comparative Study of Consent to Data Processing Provisions."; Rumbold & Pierscionek. "The Effect of the General Data Protection Regulation on Medical Research."; Rocher et al., "Estimating the success of re-identifications in incomplete datasets using generative models."
187. See note 159 above.
188. Ibid.
189. Ibid.
190. Arnold & Bonython. "No, its not OK for the government to use your prescription details to recruit you for a study".
191. See note 12 above.
192. See note 119 above.
193. Khan & Latiful Hoque. "Digital Health Data: A Comprehensive Review of Privacy and Security Risks and Some Recommendations."
194. Baillie, Bowden & Meyer. "Threshold capabilities: threshold concepts and knowledge capability linked through variation theory."
195. Stahl et al., "Critical theory as an approach to the ethics of information security."
196. Woodruff, "Fixing My Health Record will take more than Hunt"s promises".
197. See note 159 above.
198. See note 12 above.
199. See note 13 above.
200. Nippon Telegraph and Telephone (NTT) Security, Global Threat Intelligence Report 2019.
201. See note 28 above.
202. See note 43 above.

Disclosure statement

No potential conflict of interest was reported by the authors.

ORCID

E. Sitnikova http://orcid.org/0000-0001-7392-0383
C. R. MacIntyre http://orcid.org/0000-0002-3060-0555

Bibliography

ABC News. (February 22, 2019). Accessed July 26, 2019. https://www.abc.net.au/news/2019-02-22/melbourne-heart-hack-cyber-criminals-my-health-record-risks/10834482/

ABC News. (July 24, 2018) https://www.abc.net.au/news/2018-07-24/digital-health-agency-changes-my-health-record-app-contracts/10026644/

ABC News. (May 30, 2019) https://www.abc.net.au/news/2019-05-30/victorian-hospitals-vulnerable-attack-auditor-general-hack-finds/11162352

Abd-alrazaqa, A., B. M. Bewicka, T. Farraghera, and P. Gardner. "Factors that Affect the Use of Electronic Personal Health Records among Patients: A Systematic Review." *International Journal of Medical Informatics* 126 (2019): 164–175. doi:10.1016/j.ijmedinf.2019.03.014.

Abouzakhar, N. S., A. Jones, and O. Angelopoulou. "Internet of Things Security: A Review of Risks and Threats to Healthcare Sector. Joint 10th IEEE International Conference on Internet of Things, iThings 2017, 13th IEEE International Conference on Green Computing and Communications, GreenCom 2017." *10th IEEE International Conference on Cyber, Physical and Social Computing, CPSCom 2017 and the 3rd IEEE International Conference on Smart Data, Smart Data*. June 21, 2017 - June 23, 2017, Exeter UK.

Abrar, H., S. J. Hussain, J. Chaudhry, K. Saleem, M. A. Orgun, J. Al-Muhtadi, and C. Valli. "Risk Analysis of Cloud Sourcing in Healthcare and Public Health Industry." *IEEE Access* 6 (2018): 9140–9150.

ACHSM university course accreditation guidelines. 2017. https://www.achsm.org.au/Portals/15/documents/education/university-accreditation/ACHSM-university-accreditation-guidelines.pdf

ADHA. "About the DH Cyber Security Centre, ADHA." https://www.digitalhealth.gov.au/about-the-agency/digital-health-cyber-security-centre/about

Ahanger, T. A., and A. Aljumah. "Internet of Things: A Comprehensive Study of Security Issues and Defense Mechanisms." *IEEE Access* 7 (2019): 11020–11028. doi:10.1109/ACCESS.2018.2876939.

Akinsanya, O., M. Papadaki, and L. Sun. "Current Cybersecurity Maturity Models: How Effective in Healthcare Cloud?" *Online Proceedings of the 5th Collaborative European Research Conference (CERC)* March 29-30, 2019. http://ceur-ws.org/Vol-2348/

Almohri, H., L. Cheng, D. Yao, and H. Alemzadeh. "On Threat Modeling and Mitigation of Medical Cyber-Physical Systems." *2017 IEEE/ACM International Conference on Connected Health: Applications, Systems and Engineering Technologies (CHASE)*. DOI 10.1109/CHASE.2017.84

Al-Muhtadi, J., B. Shahzad, K. Saleem, W. Jameel, and M. A. Orgun. "Cybersecurity and Privacy Issues for Socially Integrated Mobile Healthcare Applications Operating in a Multi-cloud Environment." *Health Informatics Journal* 25, no. 2 (2019): 315–329. doi:10.1177/1460458217706184.

Alonso, S. G., J. Arambarri, M. Lopez-Coronado, and I. de la Torre Diez. "Proposing New Blockchain Challenges in eHealth." *Journal of Medical Systems* 43, no. 64 (2019). doi:10.1007/s10916-019-1195-7.

Andriole, K. P. "Security of Electronic Medical Information and Patient Privacy: What You Need to Know." *Journal American College of Radiology* 11, no. 12 (2014): 1212–1216. doi:10.1016/j.jacr.2014.09.011.

Angraal, S., H. M. Krumholz, and W. L. Schulz. "Blockchain Technology: Applications in Health Care." *Circulatory & Cardiovasc Qual Outcomes* 10 (2017): e003800. doi:10.1161/CIRCOUTCOMES.117.003800.

Argaw, S. T., N. E. Bempong, B. Eshaya-Chauvin, and A. Flahault. *The State of Research on Cyberattacks against Hospitals and Available Best Practice Recommendations: A Scoping Review*. BMC Medical Informatics and Decision Making 19, 10 (2019). https://doi.org/10.1186/s12911-018-0724-5.

Arnold, B. B., and W. Bonython. 2019. "No, It's Not OK for the Government to Use Your Prescription Details to Recruit You for a Study". *The Conversation*, July 31

Asghar, H. J., and K. Dali. *Averaging Attacks on Bounded Perturbation Algorithms*. Australia: Macquarie University, 2019. February.

Australian Cyber Security Centre (ACSC). 2018. "Joint Report on Publicly Available Hacking Tools. Australian Government Signals Directorate." https://www.cyber.gov.au/sites/default/files/2019-03/u5-joint-product-acsc-release-final.pdf

Australian Digital Health Agency. "National Health Security and Access Framework – NESAF V.4." *Australian Government*. Accessed August 18, 2019. https://www.digitalhealth.gov.au/implementation-resources/ehealth-foundations/EP-1544-2014.

Australian Digital Health Agency (ADHA). "Annual Report 2017–18." *Australian Government*.

Australian Government. 2018. "My Health Records (National Application) Amendment (Extension of Opt-out Period No. 2) Rules 2018." *Federal Register of Legislation*, November 14.

Australian Privacy Act. 1988. https://www.legislation.gov.au/Details/C2019C00241

Baillie, C., J. A. Bowden, and J. H. Meyer. "Threshold Capabilities: Threshold Concepts and Knowledge Capability Linked through Variation Theory." *Higher Education* 65, no. 2 (2012): 227–246. doi:10.1007/s10734-012-9540-5.

Baranchuk, A., M. M. Refaat, K. K. Patton, M. K. Chung, K. Krishnan, V. Kutyifa, G. Upadhyay, J. D. Fisher, and D. R. Lakkireddy. "Cybersecurity for Cardiac Implantable Electronic Devices: What Should You Know?" *Journal of the American College of Cardiology (JACC)* 71, no. 11 (2018): 1284–1288. doi:10.1016/j.jacc.2018.01.023.

BDO USA Healthcare. 2019. "Brace for the Breach - Cyberthreat Insights." https://www.bdo.com/getattachment/630056fa-52ef-48e8-a25c-8e9fcff168a6/attachment.aspx?HC_Cyber-Threats_Insight_2-19_WEB.pdf

Beeksow, J. 2015. "Reducing Security Risk Using Data Loss Prevention Technology." *Healthcare Financial Management*, November, p.108–111.

Blanke, S. J., and E. McGrady. "When It Comes to Securing Patient Health Information from Breaches, Your Best Medicine Is A Dose of Prevention: A Cybersecurity Risk Assessment Checklist." *Journal of Healthcare Risk Management* 36, no. 1 (2016): 14–24. doi:10.1002/jhrm.21230.

Blythe, J. M., and L. Coventry. "Costly but Effective: Comparing the Factors that Influence Employee Anti-malware Behaviours." *Computers in Human Behavior* 87 (2018): 87–97. doi:10.1016/j.chb.2018.05.023.

Boddy, A., W. Hurst, M. Mackay, and A. El Rhalibi. "A Study into Data Analysis and Visualisation to Increase the CyberResilience of Healthcare Infrastructures." *Online Proceedings of the Institute of Managers and Leaders (IML) Conference 'International Conference on Internet of Things and Machine Learning'* October 17-18, 2017. http://iml-conference.org

Boddy, A., W. Hurst, M. Mackay, A. El Rhalibi, T. R. Baker, and C. A. C. Montañez. "An Investigation into Healthcare-data Patterns." *Future Internet* 11, no. 2 (2019): p1–23. doi:10.3390/fi11020030.

Burke, W., T. Oseni, A. Jolfaei, and I. Gondal. "Cybersecurity Indexes for eHealth." *Proceedings - Australasian Computer Science Week Multiconference, ACSW* January 29-31, 2019: 2019. doi:10.1145/3290688.3290721.

Camara, C., P. Peris-Lopez, and J. E. Tapiador. "Security and Privacy Issues in Implantable Medical Devices: A Comprehensive Survey." *Journal of Biomedical Informatics* 55 (2015): 272–289. doi:10.1016/j.jbi.2015.04.007.

Canaway, R., D. I. R. Boyle, J. E. Manski-Nankervis, J. Bell, J. S. Hocking, K. Clarke, M. Clark, J. Gunn, and J. Emery. "Gathering Data for Decisions: Best Practice Use of Primary Care Electronic Records for Research." *Medical Journal of Australia* 210 (2019): S12–S16. doi:10.5694/mja2.50026.

Carlton, M. 2016. *Development of A Cybersecurity Skills Index: A Scenarios-Based Hands on Measure of Non-IT Professionals Cybersecurity Skills*. Doctoral dissertation. Nova Southeastern University. NSU Works, College of Engineering and Computing. (979). https://nsuworks.nova.edu/gscis_etd/979

Carter, A. B. "Considerations for Genomic Data Privacy and Security When Working in the Cloud." *The Journal of Molecular Diagnostics* 21, no. 4 (2019): 542–552. doi:10.1016/j.jmoldx.2018.07.009.

Chan, W. S. Y., and A. Y. M. Leung. "Use of Social Network Sites for Communication among Health Professionals: Systematic Review." *Journal Medical Internet Research* 20, no. 3 (2018): e117. doi:10.2196/jmir.8382.

Chaudhry, J., M. Crowley, P. Roberts, C. Valli, and J. Haass. "POStCODE Middleware for Post-market Surveillance of Medical Devices for Cyber Security in Medical and Healthcare Sector in Australia." *Conference: 2018 12th International Symposium on Medical Information and Communication Technology (ISMICT)*. Sydney, NSW, Australia.

Chen, Y., S. Ding, Z. Xu, H. Zheng, and S. Yang. "Blockchain-Based Medical Records Secure Storage and Medical Service Framework." *Journal Medical Systems* 43, no. 5 (2019). doi:10.1007/s10916-018-1121-4.

Cilliers, L. "Wearable Devices in Healthcare: Privacy and Information Security Issues." *Health Information Management Journal* (Online Access 2019): 1–7. https://doi.org/10.1177/1833358319851684.

Connory, M. 2019 "Annual Report." State of Cyber Security. Security in Depth. https://securityindepth.com.au/

Coventry, L., and D. Branley. "Cybersecurity in Healthcare: A Narrative Review of Trends, Threats and Ways Forward." *Maturitas* 113 (2018): 48–52. doi:10.1016/j.maturitas.2018.04.008.

Dameff, C. J., J. A. Selzer, J. Fisher, J. P. Killeen, and J. L. Tully. "Clinical Cybersecurity Training Through Novel High-Fidelity Simulations." *Journal of Emergency Medicine* 56, no.2 (0736-4679 2019): 233–238. doi:10.1016/j.jemermed.2018.10.029.

Department of Health. Framework to guide the secondary use of My Health Record system data. 2018. "Australian Government." May. https://www1.health.gov.au/internet/main/publishing.nsf/Content/F98C37D22E65A79BCA2582820006F1CF/$File/MHR_2nd_Use_Framework_2018_ACC_AW3.pdf

Department of Industry. "NSW Cyber Security Industry Development Strategy 2018." NSW Government.

Dogaru, D. I., and I. Dumitrache. "Cyber Security in Healthcare Networks." *Conference Proceedings of the 6th IEEE International Conference on E-Health and Bioengineering - EHB* 2017, June 22-24. 978-1-5386-0358-1/17/

Dubovitskaya, A., Z. Xu, S. Ryu, M. Schumacher, and F. Wang. "Secure and Trustable Electronic Medical Records Sharing Using Blockchain." *Proceedings - Annual Symposium proceedings. AMIA Symposium*. 2017, p.650–659. New York, United States.

Esposito, C., A. De Santis, G. Tortora, H. Chang, and -K.-K. R. Choo. "Blockchain: A Panacea for Healthcare Cloud-Based Data Security and Privacy?" *IEEE Cloud Computing* 5, Jan/Feb (2018): 31–37. doi:10.1109/MCC.2018.011791712.

Farrell, P. 2017. "Medicare Machine – Patient Details of Any Australian for Sale on Darknet". *The Guardian*, July 04. https://www.theguardian.com/australia-news/2017/jul/04/the-medicare-machine-patient-details-of-any-australian-for-sale-on-darknet/

Farringer, D. "Cybersecurity Report Identifies Unique Challenges to Tackling Cybersecurity in Health Care." *J. Health & Life Sci. L* 11, no. 1 (2017): 117.

Fernandez-Aleman, J. L., A. Sanchez-Henarejos, A. Toval, A. B. Sanchez-Garcia, I. Hernandez-Hernandez, and L. Fernandez-Luque. Analysis of health professional security behaviors in a real clinical setting: An empirical study. *International Journal of Medical Informatics*. 84 (2015): 454–467.

Firdaus, A., N. B. Anuar, M. F. A. Razak, I. A. B. Hashem, S. Bachok, and A. K. Sangaiah. "Root Exploit Detection and Features Optimization: Mobile Device and Blockchain Based Medical Data Management." *Journal of Medical Systems* 42 (2018): 112. doi:10.1007/s10916-018-0966-x.

Flaumenhaft, Y., and O. Ben-Assuli. "Personal Health Records, Global Policy and Regulation Review." *Health Policy* 122, no. 8 (2018): 815–826. doi:10.1016/j.healthpol.2018.05.002.

Food and Drug Administration (FDA). https://www.fda.gov/medical-devices

Forcepoint Whitepaper. 2018. "Life Support: Eliminating Data Breaches in the Healthcare Sector." https://www.forcepoint.com//whitepapers/

Gardiyawasam Pussewalage, H. S., and V. A. Oleshchuk. "Privacy Preserving Mechanisms for Enforcing Security and Privacy Requirements in E-health Solutions." *International Journal of Information Management* 36 (2016): 1161–1173. doi:10.1016/j.ijinfomgt.2016.07.006.

Garetty, K., I. McLoughlin, A. Dalley, R. Wilson, and P. Yue. "National Electronic Health Record Systems as Wicked Projects the Australian Experience." *Information Polity* 21 (2016): 367–381. doi:10.3233/IP-160389.

Gaynor, M., G. Omer, and J. S. Turner. "Teaching EHRs Security with Simulation for Non-technical Healthcare Managers." *Journal of Healthcare Protection Management* 32, no. 1 (2016): 84–97.

General Data Protection Rule. 2018. https://gdpr-info.eu/

Global Digital Health Partnership. 2018. "Securing Digital Health." https://www.gdhp.org/media-hub/news_feed/gdhp-reports

Gordon, W. J., A. Fairhall, and A. Landman. "Threats to Information Security — Public Health Implications." *The New England Journal of Medicine* 377, no. 8 (2017): 707–709. doi:10.1056/NEJMp1707212.

Gordon, W. J., A. Wright, R. J. Glynn, J. Kadakia, C. Mazzone, E. Leinbach, and A. Landman. "Evaluation of a Mandatory Phishing Training Program for High-risk Employees at a US Healthcare System." *Journal of the American Medical Informatics Association* 26, no. 6 (2019): 547–552. doi:10.1093/jamia/ocz005.

Grundy, Q., L. Parker, M. Raven, D. Gillies, B. Mintzes, J. Jureidini, and L. Bero. *Finding Peace of Mind: Navigating the Marketplace of Mental Health Apps*. Sydney: Australian Communications Consumer Action Network, 2017.

"Health Informatics Society Australia." *Healthcare-Cybersecurity-Report*, June-2018.

HIPAA Omnibus Rule. 2013. "Summary." http://www.hipaasurvivalguide.com/hipaa-omnibus-rule.php

HIPAA Privacy Rule 1996.

Holdsworth, J., W. B. Glisson, and K. K. Choo. "Medical Device Vulnerability Mitigation Effort Gap Analysis Taxonomy." *Smart Health* 12 (2017): 82–98. doi:10.1016/j.smhl.2017.12.001.

Houston, C., and A. Colangelo. 2019. "Crime Syndicate Hacks 15,000 Medical Files at Cabrini Hospital Demands Ransom". *The Age*, February 22. Accessed July 30, 2019. https://www.theage.com.au/national/victoria/crime-syndicate-hacks-15-000-medical-files-at-cabrini-hospital-demands-ransom-20190220-p50z3c.html

Huckvale, K., J. T. Prieto, M. Tilney, P.-J. Benghozi, and J. Car. "Unaddressed Privacy Risks in Accredited Health and Wellness Apps: A Cross-sectional Systematic Assessment." *BMC Medicine* (2015) 13:214. doi:10.1186/s12916-015-0444-y.

Information and Privacy Commission NSW. https://www.ipc.nsw.gov.au/data-breach-guidance

Information and Privacy Commission NSW. Accessed July 27, 2019. https://www.ipc.nsw.gov.au/privacy/voluntary-data-breach-notification/

Institute for Critical Infrastructure Technology (ICIT). 2016. Industry Brief: Hacking Healthcare. https://icitech.org/wp-content/uploads/2016/01/ICIT-Brief-Hacking-Healthcare-IT-in-2016.pdf

IT News. 2015. "Hack linked to attack on US insurer Anthem." June 22. https://www.itnews.com.au/news/opm-hack-linked-to-attack-on-us-insurer-anthem-405514

Jalali, M. S., and J. P. Kaiser. "Cybersecurity in Hospitals: A Systematic, Organizational Perspective." *J Med Internet Res* 20, no. 5, May (2018): e10059. doi:10.2196/10059.

Jalali, M. S., M. Siegel, and S. Madnick. "Decision-making and Biases in Cybersecurity Capability Development: Evidence from a Simulation Game Experiment." *Journal of Strategic Information Systems* 28 (2019): 66–82. doi:10.1016/j.jsis.2018.09.003.

Jayaratne, M., D. Nallaperuma, D. De Silva, D. Alahakoon, B. Devitt, K. E. Webster, and N. Chilamkurti. "A Data Integration Platform for Patient-centered E-healthcare and Clinical Decision Support." *Future Generation Computer Systems* 92 (2019): 996–1008. doi:10.1016/j.future.2018.07.061.

Kamel Boulos, M., D. Giustini, and S. Wheeler. "Instagram and WhatsApp in Health and Healthcare: An Overview." *Future Internet* 8, no. 37 (2016): 37. doi:10.3390/fi8030037.

Khan, S. I., and A. S. L. Hoque. "Digital Health Data: A Comprehensive Review of Privacy and Security Risks and Some Recommendations." *Computer Science Journal of Moldova* 24, no. 71 (2016): 2.

King, Z. M., D. S. Henshel, L. Flora, M. G. Cains, B. Hoffman, Blaine, and C. Sample. "Characterizing and Measuring Maliciousness for Cybersecurity Risk Assessment." *Frontiers in Psychology* 9, no. 39 (2018): p1–19.

Klas-CHIME. 2019. "Whitepaper: How Aligned are Provider Organizations with the Health Industry Cybersecurity Practices (HICP) Guidelines?" *KLAS Research and College of Healthcare Information Management Executives (CHIME)*. www.klasresearch.com/reports

Kruse, C. S., B. Frederick, T. Jacobson, and D. K. Monticone. "Cybersecurity in Healthcare: A Systematic Review of Modern Threats and Trends." *Technology and Health Care* 25 (2017): 1–10. doi:10.3233/THC-161263.

Kruse, C. S., B. Smith, H. Vanderlinden, and A. Nealand. "Security Techniques for the Electronic Health Records." *J Med Syst* 41 (2017): 127. doi:10.1007/s10916-017-0778-4.

Lee, J. K., S. Y. Moon, and J. H. Park. "CloudRPS: A Cloud Analysis Based Enhanced Ransomware Prevention System." *The Journal of Supercomputing* 73, no. 7 (2016): 3065–3084. doi:10.1007/s11227-016-1825-5.

MacIntyre, C. R., T. E. Engells, M. Scotch, D. J. Heslop, A. B. Gumel, G. Poste, X. Chen, et al. "Converging and Emerging Threats to Health Security." *Environment and System Decisions* 38, no. 2 (2018): 198–207. doi:10.1007/s10669-017-9667-0.

Magnus, R. 2019. "Public Report of the Committee of Inquiry (COI) into the Cyber Attack on SingHealth." January 10. https://www.mci.gov.sg/coireport

Martin, G., P. Martin, C. Hankin, A. Darzi, and J. Kinross. "Cybersecurity and Healthcare: How Safe are We?" *BMJ (Online)* 358 (2017): j3179. doi:10.1136/bmj.3179.

McSweeney, K. "Motivating Cybersecurity Compliance in Critical Infrastructure Industries: A Grounded Theory Study." Dissertation Abstracts International Section A: Humanities and Social Sciences, 79. Dissertation Thesis. Capella University, January 2018

Mendelson, D. "The European Union General Data Protection Regulation (Eu 2016/679) and the Australian My Health Record Scheme – A Comparative Study of Consent to Data Processing Provisions." *Journal of Law and Medicine* 26 (2018): 23–38.

Mense, A., A. Steger, M. Sulek, D. Jukic-Sunaric, and A. Meszaros. "Analyzing Privacy Risks of mHealth Applications." *Studies in Health Technology & Informatics* 221 (2016): 41–45.

Minion, L. "MHR Security Concerns Persist - ADHA Issues Amended Contracts for Third Party Apps". Healthcare IT News. Accessed July 26 2019. https://www.healthcareit.com.au/article/my-health-record-security-concerns-persist-adha-issues-amended-contracts-third-party-apps

Minion, L. 2018. "Leaked ADHA Document Gives inside Look at My Health Record Challenges". *Healthcare IT News*, August. https://www.healthcareit.com.au/article/exclusive-leaked-adha-document-gives-inside-look-my-health-record-challenges

Morris, C., R. E. Scott, and M. Mars. "Security and Other Ethical Concerns of Instant Messaging in Healthcare." *Studies in Health Technology & Informatics* 254 (2018): 77–85. doi:10.3233/978-1-61499-914-0-77.

My Health Record Statistics. 2019, July 28. Accessed August 12, 2019. www.myhealthrecord.gov.au

My Health Records Act 2012, No. 63. https://www.legislation.gov.au/Details/C2017C00313

National Audit Office Report. *Investigation: WannaCry Cyber Attack and the NHS*. https://www.nao.org.uk/wp-content/uploads/2017/10/Investigation-WannaCry-cyber-attack-and-the-NHS.pdf (2017).

National Institute of Standards and Technology (NIST) Framework. https://www.nist.gov/cyberframework

Natsiavas, P., J. Rasmussen, M. Voss-Knude, K. Votis, L. Coppolino, P. Campegiani, I. Cano, et al. "Comprehensive User Requirements Engineering Methodology for Secure and Interoperable Health Data Exchange." *BMC Medical Informatics & Decision Making* 18, no. 85 (2018). doi:10.1186/s12911-018-0664-0.

Nippon Telegraph and Telephone (NTT) Security. 2019. "Global Threat Intelligence Report." https://www.nttsecurity.com/landing-pages/2019-gtir

NSW Dept of Industry. 2018. "NSW-cyber-security-industry-development-strategy."

O'Dowd, and A. O'Dowd. "NHS Patient Data Security Is to Be Tightened after Cyberattack." *BMJ* 358 (2017): j3412. doi:10.1136/bmj.j3412.

O'Sullivan, D. M., E. O'Sullivan, M. O'Connor, D. Lyons, and J. McManus. "WhatsApp Doc?" *BMJ Innovations* 3 (2017): 238–239. doi:10.1136/bmjinnov-2017-000239.

Office of the Australian Information Commissioner. My Health Record Privacy. (July 19, 2019). https://www.oaic.gov.au/privacy/other-legislation/my-health-record/

Ogunlana, S. O. "Countering Expansion and Organization of Terrorism in Cyberspace." *Dissertation Abstracts International: Section B: The Sciences and Engineering* 80 (2019): 3-B(E).

Papoutsi, C., J. E. Reed, C. Marston, R. Lewis, A. Majeed, and D. Bell. "Patient and Public Views about the Security and Privacy of Electronic Health Records (Ehrs) in the UK: Results from a Mixed Methods Study." *BMC Medical Informatics & Decision Making* 15, no. 86 (2015). doi:10.1186/s12911-015-0202-2.

Park, Y. R., E. Lee, W. Na, S. Park, Y. Lee, and J.-H. Lee. "Is Blockchain Technology Suitable for Managing Personal Health Records? Mixed-Methods Study to Test Feasibility." *Journal Med Internet Research* 21, no. 2 (2019): e12533. doi:10.2196/12533.

Parker, L., V. Halter, T. Karliychuk, and Q. Grundy. "How Private Is Your Mental Health App Data? an Empirical Study of Mental Health App Privacy Policies and Practices." *International Journal of Law & Psychiatry* 64 (2019): 198–204. doi:10.1016/j.ijlp.2019.04.002.

Perakslis, E., and R. M. Califf. "Employ Cybersecurity Techniques against the Threat of Medical Misinformation." *JAMA*. 322: 207. Published online June 14, 2019. https://jamanetwork.com/

Phillips, M., E. S. Dove, and B. M. Knoppers. "Criminal Prohibition of Wrongful Re-Identification: Legal Solution or Minefield for Big-Data?" *Bioethical Inquiry* 14 (2017): 527–539. doi:10.1007/s11673-017-9806-9.

PHIPA http://www.health.gov.on.ca/english/providers/project/priv_legislation/phipa_pipeda_qa.html

Pinskier, N. "Royal Australian College of General Practitioners; Cited by Whigham, N." https://www.news.com.au/technology/online/hacking/health-sector-tops-the-list-as-australians-hit-by-300-data-breaches-since-february/news-story/5e95c47694418ad072bf34d872e22124

PIPEDA http://www.health.gov.on.ca/english/providers/project/priv_legislation/phipa_pipeda_qa.html

Ponemon Institute. Cost of a Data Breach Report. 2019. *IBM Security*. https://www.ibm.com/security/data-breach/2019

Pratt, M. "How Cyberattacks Can Impact Physicians." *Medical Economics* 93, no. 12 (June, 2016): 43–47.

Privacy Amendment (Notifiable Data Breaches) Act 2017, No. 12. https://www.legislation.gov.au/Details/C2017A00012

Pullin, D. W. "Cybersecurity: Positive Changes through Processes and Team Culture." *Frontiers of Health Services Management* 35, no. 1 (2018): 3–12. doi:10.1097/HAP.0000000000000038.

Raber, I., C. P. McCarthy, and R. W. Yeh. "Health Insurance and Mobile Health Devices: Opportunities and Concerns." *Journal of the American Medical Association* 321, no. 18 (2019): 1767–1768. doi:10.1001/jama.2019.3353.

Raisaro, J. L., P. J. McLaren, J. Fellay, M. Cavassini, C. Klersy, and J.-P. Hubaux. "Are Privacy-enhancing Technologies for Genomic Data Ready for the Clinic? A Survey of Medical Experts of the Swiss HIV Cohort Study." *Journal of Biomedical Informatics* 79 (2018): 1–6. doi:10.1016/j.jbi.2017.12.013.

Rajamäki, J., J. Nevmerzhitskaya, and C. Virág. "Cybersecurity Education and Training in Hospitals: Proactive Resilience Educational Framework (Prosilience EF)." *Proceedings - IEEE Global Engineering Education Conference (EDUCON)*, 17-20 April 2018, p.2042–2046. doi:10.1109/EDUCON.2018.8363488

Raths, D. "What to Do if a Breach Happens to You." *Behavioral Healthcare* V0l.36, no. 2 (2016): 45–46.

Reagin, M. J., and M. V. Gentry. "Enterprise Cybersecurity: Building a Successful Defense Program." *American College of Healthcare Executives Journal* 35, no. 1 (2018): 13–22.

Rocher, L., . L., J. M. Hendrickx, and Y. de Montjoye. "Estimating the Success of Re-identifications in Incomplete Datasets Using Generative Models." *Nature Communications* 10, no. 1 (2019). doi:10.1038/s41467-019-10933-3.

Ropp, R., and B. Quammen. "Protecting Health Data in a Troubling Time. Understand Who and What You're up Against." *Health Management Technology* 36, no. 7 (2015): 14–15.

Rosenfeld, L., J. Torous, and I. V. Vahia. "Data Security and Privacy in Apps for Dementia: An Analysis of Existing Privacy Policies." *American Journal Geriatric Psychiatry* 25, no. 8 (2017): 873–877. doi:10.1016/j.jagp.2017.04.009.

Rubenfire, A. "The Nightmare Scenario: Dialing Devices to Deadly." *Modern Healthcare* 47 (2017): 4.

Rumbold, J. M. M., and B. Pierscionek. "The Effect of the General Data Protection Regulation on Medical Research." *Journal of Medical Internet Research* 19, no. 2 (2017): e47. doi:10.2196/jmir.7108.

Safavi, S., A. M. Meer, E. K. J. Melanie, and Z. Shakur. "Cyber Vulnerabilities on Smart Healthcare, Review and Solutions." *Online Proceedings Cyber Resilience Conference (CRC)*. 2018 November 15- 18. doi:10.1109/CR.2018.8626826

Sahi, A., D. Lai, and Y. Li. "Security and Privacy Preserving Approaches in the eHealth Clouds with Disaster Recovery Plan." *Computers in Biology and Medicine* 78 (2016): 1–8. doi:10.1016/j.compbiomed.2016.09.003.

Sajid, A., and H. Abbas. "Data Privacy in Cloud-assisted Healthcare Systems: State of the Art and Future Challenges." *Journal of Medical Systems* 40, no. 155 (2016). doi:10.1007/s10916-016-0509-2.

Saleem, K., K. Zeb, A. Derhab, H. Abbas, J. Al-Muhtadi, M. A. Orgun, and Gawanmeh. "Survey on Cybersecurity Issues in Wireless Mesh Networks Based eHealthcare." *Proceedings - 18th IEEE International Conference on e-Health Networking, Applications and Services, Healthcom*, September 14-16, 2016. DOI: 10.1109/HealthCom.2016.7749423

Schwartz, S., A. Ross, S. Carmody, P. Chase, S. C. Coley, J. Connolly, C. Petrozzino, and M. Zuk. "The Evolving State of Medical Device Cybersecurity." *Biomedical Instrumentation and Technology* 52, no. 2 (2018): 103–110. doi:10.2345/0899-8205-52.2.103.

Scott, R. E. "WhatsApp in Clinical Practice: A Literature Review." *Studies in Health Technology and Informatics* 231 (2016): p 82–90. http://ovidsp.ovid.com/ovidweb.cgi?T=JS&CSC=Y&NEWS=N&PAGE=fulltext&D=emexa&AN=621263287.

Sedlack, D. J. "Understanding Cyber Security Perceptions Related to Information Risk in a Healthcare Setting." *Conference Proceedings: Cyber Security Strategy in Healthcare*. Twenty-second Americas Conference on Information Systems, San Diego, California, USA, 2016.

Shah, R. "Protecting Australian Critical National Infrastructure in an Era of IT and OT Convergence." Policy Brief Report No. 18/2019.

Shenoy, A., and J. M. Appel. "Safeguarding Confidentiality in Electronic Health Records." *Cambridge Quarterly of Healthcare Ethics* 26, no. 2 (2017): 337–341. doi:10.1017/S0963180116000931.

Sher, M. L., P. C. Talley, C.-W. Yang, and K.-M. Kuo. "Compliance with Electronic Medical Records Privacy Policy: An Empirical Investigation of Hospital Information Technology Staff." *INQUIRY: The Journal of Health Care Organization, Provision, and Financing* 54 (2017): 1–12.

Siddique, M., M. A. Mirza, M. Ahmad, J. Chaudhry, and R. Islam. "A Survey of Big Data Security Solutions in Healthcare." *14th International EAI Conference on Security and Privacy in Communication Networks, (SecureComm)* August 8-10, 2018. Lecture Notes of the Institute for Computer Sciences, Social-Informatics and Telecommunications Engineering, LNICST, 255, p.391–406. Doi: 10.1007/978-3-030-01704-0_21

Sittig, D. F., and H. Singh. "A Socio-technical Approach to Preventing, Mitigating, and Recovering from Ransomware Attacks." *Appl Clin Inform* 7 (2016): 624–632. doi:10.4338/ACI-2016-04-SOA-0064.

Small, S., D. Peddie, C. Ackerley, C. M. Hohl, and E. Balka. "Patient Perceptions about Data Sharing & Privacy: Insights from Action." In *Context Sensitive Health Informatics: Redesigning Healthcare Work*, C. Nøhr, C.E. Kuziemsky, Z.S.-Y. Wong edited by. 2017, p.109–116. IOS Press: Amsterdam, Netherlands.

Smigielski, R. "Hardening Infusion Pump Communication Software for Medical Device Cybersecurity." *Biomedical Instrumentation & Technology* (2017): 46–50. https://search.proquest.com/docview/1967813395?accountid=12763.

Smith, F. L. "Malware and Disease: Lessons from Cyber Intelligence for Public Health Surveillance." *Health Security* 14, no. 5 (2016): 305–314. doi:10.1089/hs.2015.0077.

Spence, N., N. Niharika Bhardwaj, D. P. Paul III, and A. Coustasse. "Ransomware in Healthcare Facilities: A Harbinger of the Future?" *Perspectives in Health Information Management, Summer* (2018): 1–22.

Stahl, B. C., N. F. Doherty, M. Shaw, and H. Janicke. "Critical Theory as an Approach to the Ethics of Information Security." *Science and Engineering Ethics* 20, no. 3 (2014): 675–699. doi:10.1007/s11948-013-9496-6.

Stern, G. "A Life Cycle Approach to Medical Device Cybersecurity." *Biomedical Instrumentation and Technology* 52, no. 6 (2018): 464–466. doi:10.2345/0899-8205-52.6.464.

Taylor, M. "An SOS on Cybersecurity: To Protect Patient Data, Hospitals Beef up Risk Management Programs. Hello, Chief Security Officers and 'White Hat Hackers'." *Hospitals & Health Networks* 89, no. 2 (2015): 36–38.

Terry, K. "HIPAA BREACH. Secure Data & Prevent Fines." *Medical Economics* 92, no. 14 (2015): 26–32.

Thakkar, V., and K. Gordon. "Privacy and Policy Implications for Big Data and Health Information Technology for Patients: A Historical and Legal Analysis." *Studies in Health Technology & Informatics* 257 (2019): 413–417. doi:10.3233/978-1-61499-951-5-413.

Thamilarasu, G., and C. Lakin. "A Security Framework for Mobile Health Applications. *Proceedings –5th International Conference on Future Internet of Things and Cloud Workshops (FiCloudW)*". 2017, p.221–226. DOI 10.1109/W-FiCloud.2017.35

UK Data Protection Act 2018 ico.org.uk. 2018-07-20
Upendra, P., P. Prasad, G. Jones, and H. Fortune. "Operationalizing Medical Device Cybersecurity at a Tertiary Care Medical Center." *Biomedical Instrumentation & Technology* 49, no. 4 (2019): 251–258. doi:10.2345/0899-8205-49.4.251.
"Verizon 2019 Data Breach Investigations Report." Verizon Enterprise Solutions. https://enterprise.verizon.com/resources/reports/dbir/
The Victorian Auditor General, Andrew Greaves. https://www.theguardian.com/australia-news/2019/may/29/victorias-patient-data-vulnerable-to-cyber-attacks-says-audit/.
Victorian Auditor General's Office. 2019. "Independent Assurance Report to Parliament 2018–19." May 23.
Walker-Roberts, S., M. Hammoudeh, and A. Dehghantanha. "A Systematic Review of the Availability and Efficacy of Countermeasures to Internal Threats in Healthcare Critical Infrastructure, 2018." *IEEE Access.* doi:10.1109/ACCESS.2018.2817560i.
Wang, S., R. Gao, and Y. Zhang. "Searchable and Revocable Multi-data Owner Attribute-based Encryption Scheme with Hidden Policy in Cloud Storage." *PLoS ONE [Electronic Resource]* 13, no.11 (pone 2018): 0206126. doi:10.1371/journal.
Wang, X., and Z. Zhang. "Data Division Scheme Based on Homomorphic Encryption in WSNs for Health Care Wireless Sensor Networks." *Journal of Medical Systems* 39, no. 12 (2015): 1–7. doi:10.1007/s10916-015-0340-1.
Wickham, M. H. "Exploring Data Breaches and Means to Mitigate Future Occurrences in Healthcare Institutions: A Content Analysis." *Dissertation Northcentral University, San Diego*, School of Business and Technology Management, April 2019.
Wilson, K., and L. Khansa. "Migrating to Electronic Health Record Systems: A Comparative Study between the United States and the United Kingdom." *Health Policy* 122, no. 11 (2018): 1232–1239. doi:10.1016/j.healthpol.2018.08.013.
Wirth, A. "Cyberinsights. Hardly Ever a Dull Moment: The Ongoing Cyberthreats of 2017." *Biomedical Instrumentation & Technology* 51, no. 5 (2017): 431–443. doi:10.2345/0899-8205-51.5.431.
Wirth, A. "Cyberinsights. The Times They are a-Changin': Part One." *Biomedical Instrumentation & Technology* 52, no. 2 (2018): 148–152.
Woodruff, T. 2018. "Fixing My Health Record Will Take More than Hunt's Promises". Crikey INQ, August 02. https://www.crikey.com.au/2018/08/02/fixing-my-health-record-will-take-more-than-hunts-promises/
Wright, A., S. Aaron, and D. W. Bates. "The Big Phish: Cyberattacks Against U.S. Healthcare Systems." *Journal of General Internal Medicine* 31, no. 10 (2016): 1115–1118. doi:10.1007/s11606-016-3741-z.
Yaraghi, N. I., and R. A. Gopal. "The Role of HIPAA Omnibus Rules in Reducing the Frequency of Medical Data Breaches: Insights from an Empirical Study." *Milbank Quarterly* 96 (2018): 144–166. doi:10.1111/1468-0009.12314.
Yasnoff, W. A. "Breach Risk Magnitude: A Quantitative Measure of Database Security." *AMIA 2016 Annual Symposium Proceedings/AMIA Symposium*, 2017, (2016): p. 1258–1263.
Zafar, H. "Cybersecurity: Role of Behavioral Training in Healthcare." *Proceedings - 22nd Americas Conference on Information Systems: Surfing the IT Innovation Wave*, AMCIS 2016, August 11-14. San Diego, California, USA.
Zaidan, B. B., A. Haiqi, A. A. Zaidan, M. Abdulnabi, M. L. Kiah, and H. Muzamel. "A Security Framework for Nationwide Health Information Exchange Based on Telehealth Strategy." *Journal of Medical Systems* 39 (2015): 5. doi:10.1007/s10916-015-0235-1.
Zeb, K., K. Saleem, J. Al Muhtadi, and C. Theummeler. "U-prove Based Security Framework for Mobile Device Authentication in eHealth Networks." *2016 IEEE 18th International Conference on e-Health Networking, Applications and Services (Healthcom)*. DOI: 10.1109/HealthCom.2016.7749518
Zhang, R., R. Xue, and L. Liu. "Searchable Encryption for Healthcare Clouds: A Survey." *IEEE Transactions on Services Computing* 11, no. 6 (2018): 978–996. doi:10.1109/TSC.2017.2762296.
Zheng, G., G. Zhang, W. Yang, C. Valli, R. Shankaran, and M. A. OrguA. "From WannaCry to WannaDie: Security Trade-offs and Design for Implantable Medical Devices." *Proceedings - 17th International Symposium on Communications and Information Technologies (ISCIT)*, September 25-27, 2017. DOI: 10.1109/ISCIT.2017.8261228
Zhou, L., V. Varadharajan, and K. Gopinath. "A Secure Role-Based Cloud Storage System for Encrypted Patient-Centric Health Records." *Computer Society Journal* 59, no. 11 (2016): 1159–1611.
Zhou, W., Y. Jia, A. Peng, Y. Zhang, and P. Liu. "The Effect of IoT New Features on Security and Privacy: New Threats, Existing Solutions, and Challenges yet to Be Solved." *IEEE Internet of Things Journal* 6, no. 2 (2019): 1606–1616. doi:10.1109/JIOT.2018.2847733.

Improving 'Five Eyes' Health Security Intelligence capabilities: leadership and governance challenges

Patrick F. Walsh

ABSTRACT

This article explores common organizational pressure points for 'Five Eyes' intelligence communities in their ability to understand, prevent and disrupt potential emerging bio-threats and risks. The acceleration in the development of synthetic biology and biotechnology for legitimate markets (e.g. pharmaceuticals, food production and energy) is moving faster than current intelligence communities' ability to identify and understand potential bio-threats and risks.

The article surveys several political leadership and intelligence governance challenges responsible for the current sub-optimal development of health security intelligence capabilities and identifies possible policy suggestions to ameliorate challenges.

Introduction

For some practitioners across 'Five Eyes' Intelligence Communities (IC) the mention of 'health security' and 'intelligence' together still seem a strange combination of words. For others in the IC even if 'health security threats and risks' are seen as legitimate collection and analytical priorities akin to others such as counter-terrorism and cyber–there is a reticence to invest in them. This somewhat disengaged perspective is explainable partly because there is yet no clear trajectory for bio-threats and risks. Disengagement is also arguably due–in part because historically ICs have not had a good understanding of bio-threats and risks from the Cold War up to and after the Coalition invasion of Iraq in 2003.

Based on recent research, this article investigates how 'Five Eyes' partner countries can improve their health security intelligence capabilities to gain a deeper understanding of emerging bio-threats and risks. It concludes that sustained and coordinated capability improvements are largely a function of two aspects of intelligence governance: political leadership/external governance and internal IC governance issues. The article explores the significance of both factors before assessing the future outlook of health security intelligence capability over the next five years (2020-2025). Before addressing the central question of how to improve health security intelligence capability, however, it is important first to define how 'health security intelligence' is used in this article.

Health security intelligence

There are multiple interpretations on what constitutes 'health security intelligence' based largely on the diverse disciplinary backgrounds of scholars who seek to define it. In particular, the literature highlights this diversity between how public health specialists, clinicians, epidemiologists use the term compared to intelligence and security specialists. Aldis provides a useful discussion on the lack of agreement and understanding, particularly between developed and developing countries, on the concept of health security. He stated that the term 'health security,' like 'biosecurity,'

> 'sits at the intersection of several disciplines which do not share a common methodology (e.g., practitioners from security studies, foreign policy, IR [international relations], development theory and practice of UN agencies).'[1]

As in biosecurity, inconsistencies arise in how health security is defined. Bernard has referred to a 'tribalism' between the public health and security sectors, which has prevented both from understanding each other and perceiving common priorities.[2] Historically, this has led to different disciplines talking past each other and not seeing how their perspectives can provide potentially a more accurate and inclusive definition of health security intelligence. As a former intelligence analyst and intelligence studies scholar, my own perspectives of health security intelligence has evolved over time. In my most recent work in this area – *Intelligence, Biosecurity and Bioterrorism* the focus is largely on biosecurity and the intentional weaponising of biology.[3] However, I concluded that biosecurity should be seen as one aspect of a broader health security community–the other being public health. The human security agenda, which emerged from the international relations and security studies literature in the 1990s provides a unifying concept for understanding health security intelligence. Human security scholars sought to broaden traditional notions of security–beyond being solely about war and peace between states. Human security also emphasised the security of individuals within and between states, and included security against pandemics, poverty, access to education, and safe water amongst other basic human rights.[4]

In the context of a growing human security agenda, several scholars working in public health, particularly clinicians and sociologists begun to argue increasingly the response to global pandemics (HIV, SARs, H1N1, Zika and Ebola) as not just regional/global health emergencies, but also grave health security events.[5] Such events not only had the potential to make many sick, but their implications globally – particularly for developing countries with fragile public sector infrastructure – had security implications for states involved. The 2014–16 Ebola outbreak in Western Africa, which killed 10,000 people illustrates how a major public health emergency not only has catastrophic health outcomes, but can also destabilise the capacities of nation-states to respond to such crises.[6] Similarly, since 2018 another Ebola outbreak has occurred in the Democratic Republic of Congo's North Kivu and Ituri provinces. Further at the time of writing, there has been an outbreak of corona virus (COVID-19) first reported from Wuhan, China on 31 December 2019, which also underscores the fragility of even economically wealthy states' ability to respond to regional and global health security crises.

In the case of the recent Ebola outbreak, there have been over 1900 deaths and although over 80,000 people have been immunized with a new Ebola vaccine, public health responders have been attacked by rebel militia and prevented from tracing and treating population in surrounding areas. This situation provides another example of the critical link between public health and security.[7] In summary, if naturally occurring public health incidents and security are linked then it follows that intentional public health (biosecurity incidents involving bio-crimes and bio-terrorism) need to be seen not only as intelligence and security priorities, but also clearly as public health incidents. For example, the release of anthrax into a metropolitan transport hub, will require both intelligence and public health personnel coming together to assess whether the threat/risk is primarily a biosecurity or public health emergency. 'Health security' thus becomes a useful over-arching terminology to capture *both* biosecurity and public health dimensions of health incidents in order to assess the security implications of both. Clearly not all health security incidents as they unfold will rely on a similar composition of public health, intelligence and security personnel. However, both dimensions will remain co-dependent on each other as discussed in greater detail below.

With health security defined, the last aspect of 'health security intelligence' requiring clarification is 'intelligence.' Again depending on the context (e.g. national security, policing, military, private sector), there are many diverse perspectives on what 'intelligence' *is and does*. Leaving aside these debates, and for the objectives of this article, I argue that intelligence has at least three unique defining attributes: *secrecy, surveillance* and the *security environment*.[8] All these terms are relative in the sense that in certain contexts (e.g. the Central Intelligence Agency, CIA) some intelligence collected would be considered highly secret with profound impacts on a given nation's interests if it was shared widely – perhaps even in that nation's intelligence community. Whereas a local policing agency could possess material on file classified as 'secret' or 'protected' (or more accurately privileged information), but the consequences of its release may be less deleterious. The point is secrecy is a relative term, but in its broadest sense most intelligence practice regardless of context cannot operate without a relative level of secrecy. The second term *surveillance* underscores another primary objective of all intelligence practice regardless of context. Intelligence activities can include an array of activities including research and information management. However, intelligence would not be intelligence without an ability to warn decision-makers about impending risks and threats. This requires active and sometimes passive surveillance of threat actors and risks in the security environment, which is the third defining characteristic of intelligence. The *security environment* again depending on the context in which intelligence is practiced is large, diverse and ever changing. It includes an open-ended list of threats such as state based military threats, terrorism, cyber, failed states and bio-threats and risks–the subject of this article.

With health security intelligence now defined, I now turn to a brief assessment of emerging bio-threats and risk across 'Five Eyes' countries. Given limited space, the focus here is squarely on post 9/11 emerging bio-threats and risks because it is the capability of 'Five Eyes' countries in managing both *contemporary and emerging threats and risks* that is most germane to our discussion. This is not to suggest that understanding the evolution of bio-threat and risk trajectories pre-9/11 is not relevant to situating current or emerging threats. Indeed the rapid development of modern micro-biology and the industrialisation of various biological weapons in state based programs (e.g. Soviet Union, USA, UK and Canada) since 1945 – and the attempt by rogue states (particularly Iraq but also Iran, North Korea and Syria) to do the same – provides a foundation upon which more recent bio-threat and risk typologies can be understood. Additionally, the rapid development of synthetic biology and biotechnology from the 1990s to the present and the potential weaponisation of aspects of these technological advancements should also be examined against the broader historical context of bio-threats and risk from 1945, throughout the Cold War and the immediate pre 9/11 period. But these developments are chronicled in detail elsewhere for readers seeking this background material.[9]

Discussion here of contemporary and emerging bio-threats and risks starts with the *Amerithrax* incident of 2001. I argue *Amerithrax* represented a water shed moment in helping ICs and policy-makers recalibrate their understanding about future bio-threats trajectories. In September and October 2001, seven envelopes containing a dried powder form of anthrax spores were posted to several media outlets and to the US Senate offices of Senators Thomas Daschle and Patrick Leahy. The letters resulted in 22 cases of anthrax–five of which led to fatal inhalational anthrax. The anthrax letters also resulted in the contamination and closure of several major US postal offices.[10] The *Amerithrax* attack came only a week after 9/11 so the United States was already unsettled about the possibility of more terrorist attacks. The incident resulted in a 7 year long investigation, where the US Department of Justice (DOJ) determined a single spore batch created by anthrax specialist Dr Bruce E Ivins at the US Army Medical Research Institute of Infectious Diseases (USAMRID) was the parent material for the letter spores. In July 2008 Ivins committed suicide before being indicted. However, since the FBI officially closed the investigation in 2010 several biologists and chemists disagree on whether the Bureau got the right perpetrator based on the presence of silicon and tin coating on the anthrax spores. In the opinion of some experts this suggest a greater complexity of manufacturing beyond the scope of what Ivins could do in his lab. Additionally, earlier in the investigation another army research scientist Steven Hatfield was targeted, but later exonerated with the DOJ paying a 4.6 million dollar legal settlement to the scientist.[11] The DOJ has not changed its position that Ivins was responsible and complex investigations such as *Amerithrax* underscore the difficulties in attribution of individuals involved in bio-attacks.

Amerithrax while not a major casualty attack was significant for a number of reasons. First it influenced IC assessments about how easy it would be for non-state actors such as Al Qaeda to produce and disseminate biological agents as weapons. *Amerithrax* showed the difficulties an anthrax scientist had in producing the spores in ideal laboratory conditions. Al Qaeda and other jihadist groups may have held an interest in developing bio-weapons, yet for the most part had limited access to similar scientific expertise or a safe laboratory setting for their development. In summary, the incident injected more subtlety and complexity into policy discussions given that during the late 1990 s and early 2000 s a dominant strand in the political discourse was that it would be relatively easily for terrorist groups to develop bio-weapons. Second, and more importantly, *Amerithrax* demonstrated that the terrorist may be 'an insider' – for example a scientist going rogue. *Amerithrax* therefore, ignited another arc of the debate about the most likely profile of bio-threat actors that continues to the present.

Despite the lessons contained in *Amerithrax*, a comprehensive understanding of contemporary bio-threats and risks remains unclear across the 'Five Eyes' countries and the broader scientific community. However, there are two broad threat/risk typologies: *stolen biological agents and dual use research and synthetic biology*, which illustrate where concerns exist for the potential malicious use of biology into the future. I will focus more on the latter as this area is currently of greatest concern by ICs and the scientific community.

Stolen biological agents

Stealing a controlled biological agent appears rare due to increased bio-safety regulations and control of physical space (BSL 3 and 4 labs) that has developed since the *Amerithrax* incident in all 'Five Eyes' countries.[12] Legislation and bio-safety regulations, which also include more stringent security background checks for employees working with select biological agents (such as anthrax, tularaemia, the plague) has provided greater protection. However, despite enhanced security measures in the US and to some extent the UK, there have been a number of handling and transportation safety episodes (particularly in the 2014 USD–2015), which demonstrate vulnerabilities in safety practices remain. Such episodes involved the US Department of Defense and the Centers for Disease Control and Prevention (CDC) and included safety protocols not being followed fully in transporting select biological agents across the United States and internationally as well as the shipping of bio-culture equipment from BSL 3 and 4 labs to lower safety rated labs without being sufficiently decontaminated. In July 2019, safety concerns have again been highlighted when the US Army Medical Research Institute of Infectious Diseases (USAMRID) – a key centre for the development of biological countermeasures against bioterrorism suspended operations under the authority of the Federal Select Agent Program for failing to meet federal biosafety requirements.[13]

Despite bio-safety lapses and given more stringent physical and personnel safety measures, it seems that this bio threat/risk typology (stolen biological agents) is likely to remain very low across 'Five Eyes' countries. While it is unclear if there is a criminal market for the theft of controlled bio-agents from secure labs, it would seem that organised criminal groups would have other comparatively less risky and more immediately profitable markets to pursue such as drug trafficking. In particular, given the attribution of many controlled biological agents in BSL 3 to 4 labs can be assessed forensically, criminal interest in stealing such substances is likely to be further dissuaded.[14] The other main threat scenario of a terrorist group breaking in and stealing a controlled bio-agent also seems less likely.

While 9/11 represented a sophisticated and impactful attack modality, most lethal attacks since (at least in Western countries) have been simpler using readily available materials and weapons such as improvised explosive devices, vehicles and knives. None of these require the same expertise as stealing, handling or using controlled biological substances. Nonetheless, there are two areas of potential concern in this bio-threat/risk typology (stolen biological agents), which 'Five Eyes' countries still need to collect and assess against: *intellectual property theft by an 'insider' and the potential for theft from some BSL 3 to 4 labs* in fragile or vulnerable states.

Given the exponential rise in synthetic biology, biotechnology research and commercialisation both in the public and private sector – state and non-state sponsored theft of intellectual property will likely increase. Such theft will be linked in many instances to broader cyber security and information security threats that are currently impacting on 'Five Eyes' economies. Again, the IC's ability to manage the rising complexity in the broader cyber threat space remains a challenge. It is likely then that ICs will continue to confront expertise and knowledge gaps in how the bio-economy is being attacked and IP stolen by cyber-threat actors.[15]

The second area of concern (theft of controlled biological substances) in fragile or vulnerable states, particularly those in the Middle East and Africa (e.g. Iraq, Syria, Pakistan) is also another area where greater focus by 'Five Eyes' ICs is warranted. Such locations intersect hotspots for jihadist inspired instability. It is possible that bio-safety lapses in research facilities near unstable locations or radicalised individuals working within biological institutions could steal bio-agents for terrorist attacks. Legitimate biological research facilities in vulnerable states require ongoing multi-lateral global security efforts to promote bio-safety. 'Five Eyes' defence and foreign ministries have funded bio-safety initiatives in vulnerable states in the past, but there is scope for a better coordinated approach to bilateral and multilateral programs into the future.[16]

Dual use research and synthetic biology

Dual use research is defined here as research of dangerous biological agents that might be weaponised, and the publication of that research, which theoretically could be disseminated to bio-criminals or terrorists for their own nefarious objectives.[17] There are a growing number of perspectives of whether criminals and terrorists will exploit biotechnology and synthetic biology research developed for legitimate purposes (e.g. health care, energy and food supply) for harm or profit.[18] The debates are complex and care should be exercised in not over-simplifying them, however it is possible to discern two main intellectual strands from them. These are: technological (determinism) and socio-technological perspectives. The technological determinists argue the upsurge in biotechnological advancements will make the access, use and exploitation of relevant knowledge and skills easier and cheaper for those with malevolent intentions.[19] Some of the consequences of the industrialisation of biology adds weight to their arguments about easier access and use of biotechnology. For example, the entire human genome sequenced by 2013 took a team of scientists 13 years and 500 USD million to identify 20,500 genes. Today, the human genome can be sequenced in a day using bench top equipment costing around 1000 USD. [20]

In contrast, the socio-technologists while not discounting that criminals and terrorists may exploit advances in synthetic biology and technology – argue that access to knowledge and skill is not the same as being able to adeptly exploit these in order to produce a bio-weapon. Accessing, developing, manipulating or exploiting knowledge and skills still requires significant training – often in more than one of the biological sciences (e.g. microbiology, molecular biology, genetics, and medicine). Training requires not just being able to read and replicate the latest experiments but is also dependent on applying skills intuitively in a social and collaborative sense frequently working with a team of scientists. In summary, the ability of a threat actor to weaponise any dual use and synthetic biology is dependent also on the inter-play of other social, economic and psychological variables.[21] Both intellectual perspectives are not sterile academic debates. They matter because they inform how policy makers, scientists and the intelligence community conceptualise how dual use research and synthetic biology might be exploited by threat actors.

Shortly, the focus will turn to a brief summary of examples of bio-threats that may arise with the exploitation of dual use research and synthetic biology. First however, in order to understand how bio-threats may manifest, it is useful to distinguish between two broad threat trajectories for dual use research and synthetic biology. The first ('insiders') refers to skilled scientists, researchers and technicians, who use knowledge and skills to create dangerous bio-agents under the veil of legitimate research. The second ('outsiders') refers to the exploitation of legitimate advances in biology, synthetic biology and biotechnology for dangerous and criminal ends. In the second case, it could be one or more of the recent 'gain of function' (GOF) experiments, where genetic material has been manipulated to encourage the development of dangerous pathogens thought to be rare, absent or dormant in the general population (e.g. small pox, reconstruction of 1918 influenza virus) – or experiments that make biological agents more virulent (e.g. mouse pox, horse pox, H5N1 avian influenza transmissible between human surrogates such as ferrets).[22] Such experiments are often promoted as benefiting medicine by identifying vaccines or better ones against hard to treat viruses and bacteria. The November 2018 announcement by Chinese scientist He Jiankui that he had allegedly created the word's first genetically edited babies that could be resistant to HIV is another recent example of many scientific, ethical and security concerns raised about both GOF and gene editing experiments.[23]

Given both the insider and outsider threat trajectories, the critical question remains what types of specific bio-threats are evolving? There is no satisfactory answer to this question, and debates continue amongst scholars, scientists and to some extent within the ICs about where bio-threats are likely to emerge within dual use research and synthetic biology. I argue in this article and elsewhere that assessing bio-threats and risks will rely on a more strategic and comprehensive assembling of scientific evidence on how developments in biotechnology and synthetic capabilities could be exploited by threat actors. Additionally, identifying threats and risks will also rely on ICs gaining a greater understanding of the intentions of particular actors to select capabilities as weapons or for profit over other more conventional sources. Assessing intention and capability to misuse dual use research and synthetic biology remains difficult because the science is moving rapidly – which in turn makes it difficult to get a 'fix' on where vulnerabilities for malevolent exploitation are located. Such difficulties are also a product of some of the ongoing capability issues across 'Five Eyes' countries in adapting to technologically enabled threats more broadly (e.g. cyber).

Leaving aside the ongoing difficulties in assessing emerging bio-threats and risks, I summarise here three threat cluster areas where 'Five Eyes' countries might consider developing better knowledge of bio-threats and risks. These are: *bio-unabombers, identify theft and bio-piracy*. As noted earlier, biotechnology is big business particularly in the United States and other 'Five Eyes' countries.[24] Given the massive acceleration in biotechnology and synthetic biological sciences – probability alone suggests that there will be more individuals (some mentally unstable) with a range of grievances (e.g. personal, psychological, political and religious) working in the biological sciences and some may escalate these to acts of violence. Disgruntled insiders (scientists), who can make a synthetic organism and sidestep theft of natural organisms under lock and key in highly regulated high containment labs are uniquely placed under the disguise of a bigger legitimate scientific project to become bio-unabombers. As discussed earlier, the alleged involvement of scientist Bruce Ivins in the *Amerithrax* case is illustrative here.[25] Secondly, 'identify theft' – long an enabler of crime and terrorism in other contexts is also likely to be a developing concern. The increase in DNA holdings in various government departments and the private sector provide greater opportunities to steal or manipulate DNA. For example, it is possible that individuals could assume someone's identity by stealing their DNA, or leaving someone else's blood and saliva at a crime scene by genetic cloning to frustrate national security (terrorist) and law enforcement investigations.[26] Thirdly, bio-piracy could become a greater bio-threat and risk in 'Five Eyes' countries. Recent developments in drugs, vaccines and medicines can be manipulated. Moreover, in the last few years the development of gene editing techniques like CRISPR, Finger Nuclease and Talen could be exploited criminally.[27] Though currently there is an increasing 'hype' over the threat significance of CRISPR–further fueled by a national assessment by the US IC during the Obama Administration, which declared that it could be a national security threat.[28] But it remains difficult to know what if any threat actors, for example jihadists, ultra-nationalists, anarchists, bio-hackers, environmentally motivated individuals will exploit gene editing techniques like CRISPR.

Capability gaps

As noted earlier, there remain both gaps in scientific evidence and intelligence on what may constitute emerging bio-threats and risks, particularly those arising from dual use research and synthetic biology. The acceleration of scientific discovery in biotechnology and synthetic biology make assessing threats and risks in any comprehensive way difficult and this is unlikely to change in the future. However, it is possible that some threats and risks might be 'knowable' – at least sufficiently to provide decision-makers with warning. However, this will rely on each 'Five Eyes' country's ability to reflect on current capabilities to assess bio-threats and risks in order to identify capability gaps. With the above outline on potential bio-threat and risk trajectories in mind, this section explores what are the principle capability gaps across the 'Five Eyes' countries. The final section (outlook) will assess how, or indeed whether the gaps identified can be closed in the near future.

Before describing the key capability gaps within and across 'Five Eyes' intelligence communities, it is useful to clarify first how I will be using the term 'capability.' Based on previous research on intelligence reform issues, I argue that capability is the sum of two inter-related factors. The first I refer to as *core intelligence processes* and the second *key enabling activities*. Both factors are critical to effective intelligence capabilities at the agency and community levels.[29] In simple terms, core intelligence processes include the key stages in the production process of intelligence products that hopefully will influence and support decision-maker's policy deliberations. These stages are: tasking and coordination, collection, analysis, production and evaluation. The core intelligence processes can be thought of as the functional aspects of intelligence production. In contrast, the key enabling activities provide the structural foundation under which the core intelligence processes can operate effectively. Intelligence product is not developed in a vacuum and it is the agency and community key enabling activities (governance, ICT, human resources, legislation and research) that support the 'intelligence production line.'[30] In this section, I argue that health intelligence capability gaps include a range of issues across core intelligence processes and key enabling activities. In the remaining space, I will summarise some of the key capability gaps in both the core intelligence processes and key enabling activities.

Core intelligence processes

There are capability gap issues in three core intelligence processes: tasking and coordination, collection and analysis. The gaps in each area impact upon one another and as will be demonstrated shortly also influence how capability gaps arise in the key enabling activities. Tasking and coordination include a range of activities by decision-makers and internally within ICs about how intelligence assets particularly collection and analytical resources are to be applied against various threats and risks. Given intelligence is a decision-maker's support tool, priorities about the tasking and coordination of intelligence resources are formally determined at heads of government and cabinet level in 'Five Eyes' countries. The identification of other collection and assessment priorities not currently tasked by senior cabinet ministers obviously are also made by 'Five Eyes' intelligence communities on a regular basis. However, some recent (albeit tentative) research on tasking and coordination against emerging bio-threats and risks suggest that both decision-makers and the intelligence communities themselves remain relatively disengaged from these threats.[31] This is not to suggest some bio-threat and risk issues are not getting tasking and coordination attention both by governments and as part of the routine internal mechanisms of 'Five Eyes' communities. There still seems to be some interest in state sponsored WMD (as it relates to bio) and bioterrorism, however this interest is limited compared to earlier periods such as *Amerithrax* and the faulty WMD assessments that preluded the coalition invasion of Iraq in 2003. There are any number of comparatively more 'urgent' threats and risks vying for the attention of 'Five Eyes' leaders such as conventional terrorism, cyber, the resurgence of Russia, the rise of China and North Korea's nuclear proliferation. In comparison, emerging bio-threats and risks are akin to cyber threats – they are deeply technical, which compounds the difficulty by IC and decision-makers understanding them. Many are also currently assessed (rightly or wrongly) as low probability/high impact threats, which influences the amount of tasking such issues receive by both political decision-makers and from within the 'Five Eyes' intelligence machinery. Low levels of tasking have a knock on effect in the other two stages of the core intelligence processes: collection and analysis.

From the perspective of collection, the first capability issue is that low or *ad hoc* levels of tasking impact on 'Five Eyes' countries' ability to develop better risk and threat methodologies that would allow more accurate assessment of emerging bio-threats and risks. Poor ability to assess bio-threats and risks circuitously results in even lower and *ad hoc* levels of tasking and therefore collection against these issues by both decision-makers and within ICs. This latter point also raises a broader question of whether current collection capabilities are suited ideally for gaining better calibration against emerging bio-threats and risks. As noted earlier, emerging bio-threats and risks may well arise from dual use research and synthetic biology, but given these areas are predominantly focused on legitimate research and commercial development, will traditional and more covert IC collection platforms (e.g. SIGINT, HUMINT and Geo-spatial intelligence) be best placed to 'discover' the illicit weaponisation of biology in these sectors? The answer to this question is not clear. Clearly threat and risk context will be important. Much will depend on the nature of the bio-threat and risk. Is it local, national or transnational and is it at the planning, operational or attack stage? Given the emerging nature of some bio-threats and risks, traditional collection platforms may be less helpful (at least initially) compared to other open source intelligence such as scientific peer reviewed sources, social media, epidemiology and microbial forensics in improving assessments of such threats and risks.[32]

However, current research suggests that while progress has been made in 'Five Eyes' countries to link into and learn from these open sources, a more systematic and strategic approach needs to be adopted to accessing bio-threat and risk related open source intelligence.[33] Additionally, capability improvements are needed in many open source intelligence areas derived from the scientific community such as microbial forensics. Collection capabilities in the bio-threat and risk context are also limited by other issues impacting on broader collection efforts across all 'Five Eyes' communities. Of particular importance is the post Snowden impact of threat actors 'going dark' due to them becoming aware of how to reduce their exposure to traditional IC collection platforms. The increased encryption of communications via Apps and the use of the dark web present ongoing collection capability challenges – not just in the bio-threat and risk area but across the entire security environment.[34]

The third core intelligence process area where there are capability gaps is analysis. Similar to the collection capability issues discussed some of the gaps in analysis on bio-threats and risks are not unique to assessing these issues. They are symptomatic of broader concerns and debates across 'Five Eyes' countries about how one improves analytical capabilities.[35]

The way ICs build analytical capability is influenced by external and internal factors. As noted earlier in the discussion on tasking and coordination if political leaders do not demonstrate an appetite for reading intelligence assessments on specialised or less 'bread and butter' issues then the capability investment in these areas becomes depleted. While the exact headcount of analysts working on bio-threat and risk issues across all 'Five Eyes' countries is unclear, discussions with people with more intimate knowledge of the ICs work flows suggest that numbers within agencies can be counted with the fingers on one or two hands.[36] It seems that many analysts working on bio-threat and risk issues are likely working on other accounts, including the broader suite of WMD issues (e.g. chemical and nuclear). There are pockets of excellence and specialisation for example, in the United States the FBI WMD Directorate Outreach program and in recent years within the Defense Intelligence Agency (DIA). However, analytical expertise in emerging bio-threats and risks generally remains shallow and fragmented within and across agencies. In summary, if decision-makers are not calling for product on bio-threats and risks, then the internal leadership within ICs are less compelled to increase the depth and breadth of analytical expertise in these areas. This in turn further reduces both the skills and repository of knowledge in bio-threat and risk areas. This phenomenon of intelligence leaders reducing the depth and breadth of analytical coverage in some areas has played out in different agencies across 'Five Eyes' countries. For example, CIA agency leaders have in recent years focused on getting more analysts to work flexibly across a range of areas to meet the ever increasing demand of current intelligence rather than necessarily cultivate subject matter expertise.[37] Flexibility has some merits, though it can prevent a deeper more sustained investment in analysts with expertise in one specialised area, who arguably can write better current and strategic products based on a deeper knowledge of the subject matter.[38]

Leadership decisions about where to invest in building analytical capability leads us to the main key enabling activity related capability issue – governance. As discussed earlier, governance is only one of five key enabling activities (governance, ICT, human resources, legislation and research). In recent research, I found that there were also capability gaps in the other four key enabling activities, including in human resources and legislation.[39] However, given space limitations the focus here is on governance issues as they are the most consequential for understanding capability gaps arising in other key enabling activity areas. For example, poor governance can lead to poor human resource planning as well as inadequate or not fit for purpose legislation in which to manage more effectively bio-threats and risks.

Governance

Intelligence governance is a term I have used in research on IC capability issues since 2011. From research resulting in the book *Intelligence and Intelligence Analysis*, I developed an effective intelligence framework. The framework showed that sound and adaptable IC capability relied on how well both core intelligence processes and key enabling activities worked together to produce intelligence outcomes decision-makers needed.[40] In this research governance was defined as 'attributes and rules pertaining to strong sustainable leadership, doctrine design, evaluation, and effective coordination, cooperation and integration of intelligence processes.'[41] In simple terms, governance is about effective leadership and it has an external dimension ('the political leadership') and an internal one (heads of IC agencies and communities). It's logical that sound governance (in both its external and internal dimensions) should result in better intelligence capabilities. It is also follows that effective capabilities allow the creation of a working environment where higher standard products inform decision-making.

Research into the governance capability issues as they relate to bio-threats and risks is ongoing so the observations here are generalised, incomplete and require further validation across each 'Five Eyes' country. However, based on discussions with some IC personnel and secondary literature there is evidence that there are both external and internal governance capability issues. These have a knock-on effect on how bio-threats and risks are coordinated and prioritised across each 'Five Eyes' country. At this stage, the evidence is strongest in the US IC, where both public health stakeholders and current and former members of IC and the broader security community have been calling in recent years for better leadership both at the political and IC agency level over managing bio-threats and risks. The United States Blue Ribbon Panel Report of 2015 is one example of concerns raised about the lack of consistent leadership of broader health security issues including the role of the IC.[42] In the United States, several executive policy declarations on health security and bioterrorism have been produced by successive administrations from George W Bush to the current Trump administrations. However, what seems to be missing is a clear articulation of how any national health security strategy will be operationalised generally and how political and IC leadership will coordinate effectively the limited resources to collect and assess against bio-threats and risks. Additionally, and less clear, is how do ICs reach out more explicitly and strategically to important stakeholders (e.g. scientists, public health specialists, clinicians) in order to improve the quality of collection and analytical efforts? In the final section below, the paper revisits the capability gaps discussed here to determine if they can be closed. It also provides an assessment of where 'Five Eyes' ICs capabilities might be on managing bio-threats and risks in five years' time.

Outlook

Turning first to improving tasking and coordination processes, in the next five years this will continue to be a difficult *ad hoc* process across 'Five Eyes' countries. Care needs to be exercised in generalising across each 'Five Eyes' country. Further detailed research is also required to assess how each 'Five Eyes' IC arranges tasking and coordination of bio-threats and risks. However, as noted earlier, research to date suggest in all five countries while cross IC and broader government coordination has improved, decision makers and therefore the IC leadership do not appear to routinely task on emerging bio-threat and risk issues. The recent Trump Administrations' national biodefense strategy and the UK's Biological Security Strategy both include rhetoric about the need of greater coordination of IC, public health and other stakeholders.[43] However in each case, there is little detail about how these strategic documents will be operationalised. In the UK case, at the time of writing (August 2019) the Joint Committee on the National Security Strategy has commenced an inquiry into the how the strategy is addressing biosecurity and human health. The launch of the inquiry does suggest that further work is required to fully implement it across the UK government. In particular, the US and UK policy documents, do not identify a leadership position within the ICs, who could be responsible for ensuring there is regular tasking and effective coordination of efforts in the collection and assessment of bio-threats and risks. As discussed earlier, the core intelligence process of tasking and coordination is closely linked to the key enabling activity of governance. Governance is crucially about effective political and internal leadership of ICs. Hence tasking and coordination on bio-threats and risks is intricately linked to whether improvements can be made in governance over the next five years.

On the other two core intelligence processes (collection and analysis) and leaving aside the stultifying effect of a relatively low engagement in bio-threats and risks by the political leadership of 'Five Eyes' countries–there are opportunities to build on existing collection platforms in ways that would improve information feeds on these issues. It may not be that ICs need to build additional expensive collection platforms just for bio-threats and risks. In some cases, using existing covert and open source intelligence that are already being applied against comparatively more conventional threats and risks (terrorism and organised crime) will likely provide opportunities to collect incidentally against bio-threats and risks.

Governance

Whether tasking and coordination can be improved depends first on whether a renewed interest in bio-threats and risks can be garnered from the political leadership in 'Five Eyes' countries in the absence of an actual bio-attack. In the United States, the Trump Administration has developed an adversarial and mistrusting attitude to the US IC – making it difficult for IC leaders to discern which intelligence priorities the President is interested on a day to day basis let alone emerging bio-threat and risk issues. Additionally, effective tasking and coordination is further compounded by President Trump's focus mainly on border security and political matters including the US Congress impeachment inquiry and earlier the Mueller special investigation into whether he and members of his campaign team colluded with Russia in ways that influenced the outcome of the 2016 presidential election. Combined these factors demonstrate a lack of a sustained political commitment and interest in improving tasking and coordination, collection and assessments on emerging bio-threats and risks.

Similarly in the UK, at the time of writing the government continues to be pre-occupied with securing a Brexit deal from the EU, and it remains to be seen how cabinet ministers will focus on implementing both the Biological Security Strategy and how the strategy might improve the way the UK IC tasks, coordinates, collects and assesses emerging bio-threats and risks. Australia, Canada and New Zealand all have the necessary IC and public health bureaucratic institutions in place to theoretically respond to emerging bio-threats and risks. However, there is no evidence that these governments have developed national health security strategic plans, which clearly articulate how their ICs will improve their understanding of emerging bio-threats; or better integrate their resources with important stakeholders such as scientists and the public health sector.

At the time of writing, there are major reform changes underway in the Australian Intelligence Community (AIC) – including the establishment in 2018 of a new Office of National Intelligence to better coordinate the Community. Other reforms include the establishment of a capability fund to help the AIC identify where future investment needs to take place.[44] Though given the amount of other work ONI has to address across the Australian intelligence enterprise, it is unlikely the current reform agenda in the near term will produce a national health security strategic plan that includes reflection on how the AIC can play a role in understanding emerging bio-threats and risks.

Further, given the short electoral cycles in 'Five Eyes' countries and the perceived low probability and high impact nature of bio-threats and risks by many policy makers – it seems unlikely political leaders of each 'Five Eyes' country will address in any significant way current governance issues relating to emerging bio-threats and risks. But the rapidly changing nature of all threats and risks particularly those technologically enabled ones such as cyber, underscore the need for stronger governance that can identify and remedy IC capability gaps in understanding bio-threats and risks. As a start, better governance at the political level could be facilitated by formalised high-level coordination. For example, the establishment of a Health Security Coordination Council led preferably by head of government (or the very least a senior cabinet minister) would provide a more coherent 'whole of government' approach to tasking and coordination of bio-threats and risks as well as identifying other capability gaps discussed in the paper. Current US and UK strategic plans outlined earlier seem to place senior bureaucrats largely in charge of national level biosecurity, biodefense committees. A senior cabinet minister (from either a health or security portfolio) is a more appropriate choice to chair such a council. The council should also contain in addition to heads of IC, other senior stakeholders including public and animal health specialists, and scientific advisors. A broad and diverse council membership is critical to ensure national health security strategies articulate a whole of government (including ICs) approach. The next ideal step in improving governance arrangements would be for each stakeholder to develop operational plans to implement government tasking priorities as well as ensuring effective coordination of resources.

For each 'Five Eyes' country a senior sub-cabinet level national health security intelligence officer should also be established. This appointee would have authority to identify and implement tasking and coordination, collection and analytical priorities across the entire IC. The national health security intelligence officer would liaise with other important stakeholders that are part of the health security coordination council; including public/animal health, scientists and their counter parts in other 'Five Eyes' countries to gain a national and international understanding of emerging bio-threats and risk as well as identifying IC capability gaps.

Closing collection capability gaps

A national health security intelligence officer sitting across the entire IC enterprise should be able to implement coherent and coordinated national collection plans for bio-threats and risks that help both collection and assessment agencies identify what role they can play in overall collection efforts. A national health security intelligence officer can consider for example, how traditional collection platforms (SIGINT, HUMINT, Geospatial Intelligence) are best applied to retrieve information about both current and emerging bio-threats. Threat and risk evolution will also be an important consideration in what collection capabilities need to be deployed. In other words, at what developmental stage is the threat? Can it be prevented, disrupted or only treated after the event? It is quite possible as noted earlier, that traditional collection platforms might be initially applied against more 'here and now' threats such as terrorism or organised crime – yet may also reveal in some circumstances an interest by these threat actors or their associates in bio-threats and risks. This in turn would allow a more focused application of other specialised, scientific collection tools such as microbial forensics.

Arguably though with many bio-threats and risks, there are likely to be an even larger volume of relevant information accessible to the IC from non-security stakeholders on the prevention, disruption and treatment of bio-threats and risks. While 'Five Eyes' ICs have in the past reached out to some stakeholders, a more strategic and explicit approach to building trusted external expert networks would improve collection efforts, particularly in areas such as dual use research of concern and synthetic biology. The potential lists of relevant stakeholders is almost endless. They can be found at the multi-lateral, bilateral, national, regional and local levels.[45] At a multi-lateral level, historically important security measures such as the Biological and Toxin Weapons Convention (BTWC) will continue to provide ICs with information, albeit not always reliable about states' adherence to the Convention. Other recent multilateral biosafety and biosecurity initiatives such as the Global Health Security Agenda established by the Obama Administration could provide opportunities for 'Five Eyes' ICs to increase awareness of potential bio-threats and risks in addition of course to their public health capacity-building effects.[46]

In each 'Five Eyes' country, albeit some with more capacity (e.g. US and UK) defence departments or their allied defence research divisions there are biodefence research capabilities which the ICs could tap into more regularly. In the case of the United States, other government research bodies such as the Intelligence Advanced Research Projects Activity (IARPA) also sponsor biodefense research that is directly relevant to how ICs may participate in the future in the identification and prevention of weaponised dual use research and synthetic biology. For example, in July 2017, IARPA commissioned the Project Felix program to fund research that can detect signals of bio-engineering including types of changes, location and possibly in the future where changes were made. Such work could be used in cases where suspicious circumstances suggest the malicious exploitation of bio-engineered material is occurring.[47] Leaving aside what the defence, security and intelligence research groups offer the IC in this area, it's clear that the medical community (epidemiology and public health) are also naturally indispensable partners for the ICs. Medical, public health and epidemiological knowledge provides the ICs with a common understanding of how to identify natural and intentional disease outbreaks and in some cases can inform attribution about what threat actors may be responsible. Finally, first responders have critical knowledge about the physical environment(s), where an attack occurs as well as forensic evidence, which can help inform tactical and operational intelligence collection and analysis.

Analysis

In any intelligence agency, an effective operation of all core intelligence processes requires an almost symbiotic relationship between collection and analysis. Uncoordinated and insufficient strategic and operational collection planning will reduce the ability of analysts to improve the reliability and validity of their products. There are no 'off the shelf' solutions to current analytical capability gaps discussed earlier. Evaluating whether the analytical workforce is 'fit for purpose' as far as assessing bio-threats and risks is really a sub-set of a bigger issue about whether 'Five Eyes' ICs have the right mix of subject matter expert vs generalist analysts – against a whole range of current and emerging threats. Significant investment has gone into training and education of analysts across 'Five Eyes' countries in the military, national security and to lesser degree the law enforcement community.[48] But debates continue within ICs and amongst teachers and scholars what skills, knowledge and competencies entry level analysts need to deal with the fast paced changes in the security environment. Less consideration is currently given to how to deploy subject matter experts in specialised areas such as bio-threats and risks. Do 'Five Eyes' ICs try to develop specialised expertise in this subject internally or should this work be out-sourced to trusted, security cleared outsiders who might be scientists?

I argue that it shouldn't be an either/or decision given that all 'Five Eyes' ICs need to maintain corporate repositories of knowledge in specialised areas – yet at the same time it would be impossible for those few individuals responsible for interpreting bio-threats and risks across the entire IC to be experts in all bio-threat matters. Given resources are limited, another aspect of workforce analytical training of staff on bio-threat and risk issues is that heads of agencies and ICs need to also think carefully about what role subject matter experts may play. Logically some should be deployed in prevention roles that can provide strategic early warning of potential bio-threat and risk trajectories. Others would need to focus on disruption of evolving bio-threats and risk in operational settings; whilst others would be useful in assessing the treatment of threats and risks.

Further evidence is required, but IC leaders currently do not appear to be planning in any systematic way the future bio-threat and risk analytical workforce. As part of work force planning, it is unclear whether IC leaders are considering in any strategic way what analytical capability gaps are best met by external stakeholders (scientists, clinicians, and public health officials)–and how to integrate more seamlessly this knowledge into the closed working environment within ICs. Finally, with respect to sub-optimal analytical capabilities, further reflection by IC leaders needs to be given on how potentially a diverse and voluminous amount of information collected across health security sector (clinicians, epidemiologists, scientists, military, national security, law enforcement, animal and agricultural health) can best be interrogated rapidly by analysts. Again the ability to quickly makes sense of large data sets and intelligence is obviously a problem writ large for ICs not just an issue to be resolved in the bio-threat and risk context.

In summary, this article argues it is unlikely that each 'Five Eyes' country will improve dramatically their IC capabilities for managing bio-threats and risks in the next five years (2020–25). Barring a catastrophic bio-attack by a terrorist group or other health security crisis resulting in high mortality rates, bio-threats and risks will continue to be seen as low probability-high impact threats for political decision-makers. This translates within the ICs as at best a watching brief of bio-threats and risks and at worse them being largely ignored. At this time, bio-threats and risks only get ad-hoc attention by the 'Five Eyes' ICs. For example, ICs may focus periodically on them as part of broader WMD threat assessments ahead of hosting a major international event.

In addition to low levels of political tasking and coordination, systematic and proactive approaches to managing bio-threats and risks at the IC level are not likely without stronger IC governance by its leaders. This includes a national health security intelligence officer, who can champion the threat and risk area and help agencies close capability gaps. In some 'Five Eyes' countries there has been some capability improvements since 9/11, however, based on available evidence, I assess no substantial move towards a greater strategic approach to health security intelligence across 'the Five Eyes' countries during the next five years. There is no available public knowledge that there are any impending substantive bio-threats and risks, particularly emanating from dual use research and synthetic biology. Nonetheless the rise in the cyber threat trajectory and the struggle by ICs to understand it provides a good lesson that building capability takes time. It is now time to invest in capability to better manage potential and emerging bio-threats and risks. Hopefully the COVID-19 pandemic might provide a catalyst to build the kinds of capabilities in ICs discussed throughout the article.

Notes

1. Aldis, "Health Security as a Public Health Concept," 370.
2. Bernard, "Health and National Security," 157.
3. Walsh, *Intelligence Biosecurity and Bioterrorism*.
4. The Human Security Centre, *The Human Security Centre*.
5. See for example, Elbe, "Pandemic Security," 163–173.
6. Heymann, "Global Health Security: the Wider Lessons from the West WHO." "Ebola Virus Disease in West Africa – The First Nine Months of the Epidemic and Forward Projections," 1481–1495; "Global Health Security: the Wider Lessons from the West African Ebola Virus Disease Epidemic," 1884–1901; Marston, "Ebola Response Impact on Public Health Programs, West Africa 2014–2017"; WHO, "Ebola Virus Disease in West Africa – The First Nine Months of the Epidemic and Forward Projections," 1481–1495.
7. Soucheray, "With New Cases, Katwa Remains Epicenter of Ebola Outbreak."
8. Walsh, *Intelligence and Intelligence Analysis*, 29–32.

9. Alibek, Biohazard: *The Chilling True Story of the Largest Covert Biological Weapons Program in the World*; Balmer, Britain *and Biological Warfare. Expert Advice and Science Policy*; Christopher, et al., "Biological Warfare: A Historical Perspective," 412–417; Geissler, & Ellis van Courtland Moon, (Eds.). *Biological and Toxin Weapons: Research, Development and Use from the Middle Ages to 1945*; Koblentz, *Living Weapons*; and Walsh, *Intelligence, Biosecurity and Bioterrorism*.
10. Walsh, Intelligence, Biosecurity and Bioterrorism, 30–31.
11. Broad and Shane, "Scientist's Analysis Disputes FBI Closing of Anthrax Case."
12. In BSL-3 to 4 rated labs, scientists work on pathogens that can cause serious or potentially lethal disease. Generally, the most lethal agents, where there is no vaccine or an unknown risk of transmission are worked on in BSL-4 labs.
13. Lizotte, "Research Halted at USAMRID Over Biosecurity Issues," CDC, *Report on the Potential Exposure to Anthrax*; CDC, *90 Day Internal Review of the Division of Select Agents and Toxins*; Dennis Brady and Lena Sun, 'FDA Found More than Smallpox Vials in Storage Room.' *Washington Post*. 16 July 2014, https://www.washingtonpost.com/national/health-science/fda-found-more-than-smallpox-vials-in-storage-room/2014/07/16/850d4b12-0d22-11e4-8341-b8072b1e7348_story.html?utm_term=.978241b9d1f8.
14. Walsh, "Managing Intelligence and Responding to Emerging Threats," 837–57; Walsh, "Managing Emerging Health Security Threats Since 9/11: The Role of Intelligence," 341–67.
15. Koblentz and Mazanec, "Viral Warfare: The Security Implications of Cyber and Biological Weapons," 418–34; and Murch, "Emerging New Discipline to Help Safeguard the Bioeconomy."
16. For a brief discussion on some of the bilateral and multi-lateral biosafety programs that 'Five Eyes' countries have been active in see, Walsh, *Intelligence, Biosecurity and Bioterrorism*, 179–231.
17. Ibid., 179–231.
18. Tucker, *Innovation, Dual Use and Security*; Suk et al., "Dual Use Research and Technological Diffusion. Reconsidering the Bioterrorism Threat Spectrum," 1–3; Gerstein, Bioterror *in the 21st Century: Emerging Threats in a New Global Environment*; National Academy of Sciences, *Human Genome Editing. Science Ethics and Governance*; Arnason, "Synthetic Biology between Self-Regulation and Public Discourse," 246–56.
19. Chyba, "Biotechnology and the Challenge to Arms Control," 11–17; Carlson, "The Pace and Proliferation of Biological Technologies," 203–14; Petro and Carus, "Biological Threat Characterisation Research," 295–308.
20. Walsh, *Intelligence, Biosecurity and Bioterrorism*, 44.
21. Kathleen Vogel's work on the non-technical aspects of bio-threats provide a good background to all the non-technical variables that should be considered in assessing bio-threats and risks. See, Vogel, "Biodefense," 227–55; "Intelligent Assessment: Putting Emerging Biotechnology Threats in Context," 45–54; "Necessary Interventions. Expertise and Experiments in Bioweapons Intelligence Assessments," 61–88; and, *Phantom Menace or Looming Danger?*.
22. Walsh, Intelligence, Biosecurity and Bioterrorism, 41–51.
23. Kolata, "Chinese Scientist Claims to Use Crispr to Make First Edited Babies".
24. In the US, easily over 2 million people are employed with over 73,000 businesses working across range of biosciences (medicine, agriculture, pharmaceuticals, research). Similarly in Australia, around 48,000 Australians are employed in the biotechnology sector with the sector estimated to obtain a 4.4% annual growth reaching 8.67 billion AUD in revenues by 2021. See, Battelle. *Battelle/Bio State Bioscience, Jobs, Investments and Innovation*; Ausbiotech, Australia's Biotechnology Organisation (website), 2018. https://www.ausbiotech.org/biotechnology-industry/fast-facts.
25. Walsh, Intelligence, Biosecurity and Bioterrorism, 51.
26. Ibid., 41.
27. Willingham, "A Fresh Threat: Will CAS9 Lead to CRISPR Bioweapons?"; National Academy of Sciences. *Human Genome Editing. Science Ethics and Governance*; Revill, "Could Gene Editing Tools Such as CRISPR be Used as a Biological Weapon."
28. Willingham, "A Fresh Threat"; Clapper, *Statement for the Record. Worldwide Threat Assessment of the US Intelligence Community*.
29. A more detailed discussion of these factors and how they relate to theorising about effective intelligence frameworks can be found in Walsh, *Intelligence and Intelligence Analysis*, 131–147; Walsh, "Building Better Intelligence Frameworks Through Effective Governance," 123–42.
30. Ibid.
31. Walsh, *Intelligence, Biosecurity and Bioterrorism*, 59–89.
32. Ibid., 89–121.
33. Ibid.
34. Walsh and "Rethinking "Five Eyes" Security Intelligence Collection Policies and Practice Post Snowden," 345–68; Chertoff, "A public policy perspective of the Dark Web," 26–38; and Chen, Bioterrorism *and Knowledge Mapping Dark Web Exploring and Data Mining the Dark Side of the Web*, 335–67.
35. Walsh, & Ratcliffe, "Strategic Criminal Intelligence Education: A Collaborative Approach," 152–66. Walsh, "Teaching intelligence in the twenty-first century: towards an evidence-based approach for curriculum design,"

1005–1021; Harrison, & Et al., "Tradecraft to Standards – Moving Criminal Intelligence Practice to a Profession through the Development of Criminal Intelligence Training and Development Continuum," 1–13.
36. Walsh, Intelligence, *Biosecurity and Bioterrorism*, 127–128.
37. Gentry and Gordon, *Strategic Warning Intelligence*, 223.
38. Ibid., 218.
39. Walsh, *Intelligence, Biosecurity and Bioterrorism*.
40. Walsh, *Intelligence and Intelligence Analysis*, 31–152.
41. Ibid., 149.
42. Blue Ribbon Study Panel, *Blue Ribbon Study Panel on Biodefense. A National Blueprint for Biodefense: Leadership and Major Reform Needed to Optimise Efforts*; Blue Ribbon Study Panel, *Biodefense Indicators One Year Later. Events Outpacing Federal Efforts to Defend the Nation*.
43. White House, *National Biodefense Strategy*; HMG. *UK Biological Security Strategy*.
44. For a discussion of the main aspects of the reform agenda currently underway in the AIC, see my ISA Paper: "Transforming the Australian Intelligence Community: Mapping Change, Impact and Governance Challenges," paper given at the 60th International Studies Association Conference, 27 August 2019.
45. For a detailed discussion of what non-security stakeholders can bring to the IC see: Walsh, *Intelligence, Biosecurity and Bioterrorism*, 179–231.
46. Ibid., 192–3.
47. Ibid., 183.
48. Walsh, "Teaching intelligence in the twenty-first century," 1005–21.

Disclosure statement

No potential conflict of interest was reported by the author.

Bibliography

Aldis, W. "Health Security as A Public Health Concept: A Critical Analysis." *Health Policy and Planning* 23, no. 6 (2008): 369–375. doi:10.1093/heapol/czn030.

Alibek, K. *Biohazard: The Chilling True Story of the Largest Covert Biological Weapons Program in the World- Told from the inside by the Man Who Ran It*. New York: Random House, 1999.

Arnason, G. "Synthetic Biology between Self-Regulation and Public Discourse: Ethical Issues and the Many Roles of the Ethicist." *Cambridge Quarterly of Healthcare Ethics* 26, no. 2 (2017): 246–256. doi:10.1017/S0963180116000840.

Ausbiotech. 2018. *Australia's Biotechnology Organisation (Website)*. https://www.ausbiotech.org/biotechnology-industry/fast-facts.

Balmer, B. B., and B. Warfare. *Expert Advice and Science Policy, 1930-65*. Basingstoke, UK: Palgrave Macmillan, 2001.

Battelle. *Battelle/Bio State Bioscience, Jobs, Investments and Innovation*. Columbus, OH: Battelle, 2014.

Bernard, K. "Health and National Security: A Contemporary Collision of Cultures." *Biosecurity and Bioterrorism: Biodefense Strategy, Practice, and Science* 11, no. 2 (2013): 157–162. doi:10.1089/bsp.2013.8522.

Blue Ribbon Study Panel. *Blue Ribbon Study Panel on Biodefense. A National Blueprint for Biodefense: Leadership and Major Reform Needed to Optimise Efforts*. Washington, D.C: Hudson Institute for Policy Studies, 2015.

Blue Ribbon Study Panel. *Biodefense Indicators One Year Later. Events Outpacing Federal Efforts to Defend the Nation*. Arlington, VA.: Potomac Institute for Policy Studies, 2016.

Brady, D., and L. Sun. 2014. "FDA Found More than Smallpox Vials in Storage Room." *Washington Post*, July 16. https://www.washingtonpost.com/national/health-science/fda-found-more-than-smallpox-vials-in-storage-room/2014/07/16/850d4b12-0d22-11e4-8341-b8072b1e7348_story.html?utm_term=.978241b9d1f8.

Broad, W., and S. Shane. 2011. "Scientist's Analysis Disputes FBI Closing of Anthrax Case." *The New York Times*, October 9. https://www.nytimes.com/2011/10/10/science/10anthrax.html?_r=1&hp.

Carlson, R. "The Pace and Proliferation of Biological Technologies." *Biosecurity and Bioterrorism: Biodefense Strategy, Practice, and Science* 1, no. 3 (2004): 203–214. doi:10.1089/153871303769201851.
CDC. *Report on the Potential Exposure to Anthrax*. Atlanta, GA: CDC, 2014.
CDC. *90 Day Internal Review of the Division of Select Agents and Toxins*. Atlanta, GA: CDC, 2015.
Chen, H. *Bioterrorism and Knowledge Mapping Dark Web Exploring and Data Mining the Dark Side of the Web*. New York, N.Y.: Springer, 2011.
Chertoff, M. "A Public Policy Perspective of the Dark Web." *Journal of Cyber Policy* 2, no. 1 (2017): 26–38. doi:10.1080/23738871.2017.1298643.
Christopher, G. W., T. J. Cieslak, and E. M. Eitzen Jr. "Biological Warfare: A Historical Perspective." *Journal of the American Medical Association* 278, no. 5 (1997): 412–417. doi:10.1001/jama.1997.03550050074036.
Chyba, C. "Biotechnology and the Challenge to Arms Control." *Arms Control Today* 36 (2016): 11–17.
Clapper, J. *Statement for the Record. Worldwide Threat Assessment of the US Intelligence Community*. Armed Services Committee, 2016. Washington,DC.
Elbe, S. "Pandemic Security." In *The Routledge Handbook of New Security Studies*, edited by J. Peter Burgess, 163–173. Abingdon, UK: Routledge, 2010.
Elbe, S. "Pandemic Security." In *The Routledge Handbook of New Security Studies*, edited by J. Peter Burgess, 163–173. Abingdon, UK: Routledge, 2010.
Geissler, E., and J. E. van Courtland Moon, eds. *Biological and Toxin Weapons: Research, Development and Use from the Middle Ages to 1945*. New York: Oxford University Press, 1999.
Gentry, J., and J. Gordon. *Strategic Warning Intelligence*. Washington DC: Georgetown University Press, 2019.
Gerstein, D. *Bioterror in the 21st Century: Emerging Threats in a New Global Environment*. New York: Naval Institute Press, 2010.
Harrison, M., P. F. Walsh, S. Lysons-Smith, D. Truong, C. Horan, and R. Jabbour. "Tradecraft to Standards– Moving Criminal Intelligence Practice to a Profession through the Development of Criminal Intelligence Training and Development Continuum." *Policing* (2018): 1–13.
Heymann, D. et al. Global Health Security: The Wider Lessons from the West WHO." "Ebola Virus Disease in West Africa - the First Nine Months of the Epidemic and Forward Projections. *The New England Journal of Medicine* 371 (2015): 1481–1495.
Heymann, D., L. Chen, K. Takemi, D. P. Fidler, J. W. Tappero, M. J. Thomas, T. A. Kenyon. "Global Health Security: the Wider Lessons from the West African Ebola Virus Disease Epidemic." *The Lancet*, no. 9980 (2015): 1884–1901. doi:10.1016/S0140-6736(15)60858-3
HMG. *UK Biological Security Strategy*. London: HMG, 2018.
The Human Security Centre. *The Human Security Centre: Human Security Report*. Oxford, UK: Oxford University Press, 2005.
Koblentz, G. *Living Weapons*. New York: Cornell University Press, 2009.
Koblentz, G., and B. Mazanec. "Viral Warfare: The Security Implications of Cyber and Biological Weapons." *Comparative Strategy* 32, no. 5 (2013): 418–434. doi:10.1080/01495933.2013.821845.
Kolata, G., S. Wee, P. Belluck. 2018. "Chinese Scientist Claims to Use Crispr to Make First Edited Babies." *The New York Times*, November 26. https://www.nytimes.com/2018/11/26/health/gene-editing-babies-china.html.
Lizotte, S. 2019. "Research Halted at USAMRID over Biosecurity Issues." *Global Biodefense*, August 5. https://globalbiodefense.com/2019/08/05/research-halted-at-usamriid-over-biosafety-issues/CDC, Report on the Potential Exposure to Anthrax.
Marston, B., E. Kainne Dokubo, A. van Steelandt, L. Martel, D. Williams, S. Hersey, A. Jambai, S. Keita, T. G. Nyenswah, J. Redd. "Ebola Response Impact on Public Health Programs, West Africa 2014-2017" *Emerging Infectious Diseases Journal* 28, no. Supplement (2017): 25–31.
Murch, R., W. So, W. Buchholz, S. Raman, J. Peccoud. "Emerging New Discipline to Help Safeguard the Bioeconomy." *Frontiers in Bioengineering and Biotechnology* 6, no. 39 (2018): 1–6. doi:10.3389/fbioe.2018.00039.
National Academy of Sciences. *Human Genome Editing. Science Ethics and Governance*. Washington, D.C: National Academies Press, 2017.
Petro, J., and S. Carus. "Biological Threat Characterisation Research: A Critical Component of National Biodefense, Biosecurity, and Bioterrorism." *Biodefense Strategy, Practice and Science* 3 (2005): 295–308.
Revill, J. 2017. "Could Gene Editing Tools Such as CRISPR Be Used as a Biological Weapon." *The Conversation*, August 31. https://theconversation.com/could-gene-editing-tools-such-as-crispr-be-used-as-a-biological-weapon-82187?utm_source=twitter&utm_medium=twitterbutton.
Soucheray, S. 2019. "With New Cases, Katwa Remains Epicenter of Ebola Outbreak." *CIDRAP News*, February 18. http://www.cidrap.umn.edu/news-perspective/2019/02/new-cases-katwa-remains-epicenter-ebola-outbreak
Suk, J., A. Zmorzynska, I. Hunger, W. Biederbick, J. Sasse, H. Maidhof, and J. Semenza. "Dual Use Research and Technological Diffusion. Reconsidering the Bioterrorism Threat Spectrum." *PLOS Pathogens* 7, no. 1 (2011): 1–3. doi:10.1371/journal.ppat.1001253.
Tucker, J., Ed. *Innovation, Dual Use and Security*. Cambridge, MA: The MIT Press, 2012.
Vogel, K. "Biodefense." In *Biosecurity Interventions*, edited by A. Lakoff and S. Collier, 227–255. New York: Columbia University, 2008.

Vogel, K. "Intelligent Assessment: Putting Emerging Biotechnology Threats in Context." *Bulletin of the Atomic Scientists* 35, no. 1 (2013): 45–54.

Vogel, K. "Necessary Interventions. Expertise and Experiments in Bioweapons Intelligence Assessments." *Science, Technology and Innovation Studies* 9, no. 2 (2013): 61–88.

Vogel, K. *Phantom Menace or Looming Danger?* Baltimore, MD: The Johns Hopkins University Press, 2013.

Walsh, P. F. *Intelligence and Intelligence Analysis*. Abingdon, UK: Routledge, 2011.

Walsh, P. F. "Managing Intelligence and Responding to Emerging Threats: The Case of Biosecurity." In *The Handbook of Security*, edited by M. Gill, 837–857. Basingstoke: Palgrave Macmillan, 2014.

Walsh, P. F. "Building Better Intelligence Frameworks Through Effective Governance." *International Journal of Intelligence and Counterintelligence* 28, no. 1 (2015): 123–142. doi:10.1080/08850607.2014.924816.

Walsh, P. F. "Managing Emerging Health Security Threats since 9/11: The Role of Intelligence." *International Journal of Intelligence and Counterintelligence* 29, no. 2 (2016): 341–367. doi:10.1080/08850607.2016.1121048.

Walsh, P. F. "Teaching Intelligence in the Twenty-first Century: Towards an Evidence-based Approach for Curriculum Design." *Intelligence and National Security* 32, no. 7 (2017): 1005–1021.

Walsh, P. F. *Intelligence Biosecurity and Bioterrorism*. London: Palgrave Macmillan, 2018.

Walsh, P. F. 2019. "Transforming the Australian Intelligence Community: Mapping Change, Impact and Governance Challenges." *Paper given at the 60th International Studies Association Conference*, August 27. Toronto, Canada.

Walsh, P. F., and S. Miller. "Rethinking 'Five Eyes' Security Intelligence Collection Policies and Practice Post Snowden." *Intelligence and National Security* 31, no. 3 (2016): 345–368. doi:10.1080/02684527.2014.998436.

Walsh, P. F., and J. Ratcliffe. "Strategic Criminal Intelligence Education: A Collaborative Approach." *IALEIA Journal* 16 (2005): 152–166.

White House. *National Biodefense Strategy*. Washington DC: White House, 2018.

WHO. "Ebola Virus Disease in West Africa - the First Nine Months of the Epidemic and Forward Projections." *The New England Journal of Medicine* 371 (2015): 1481–1495.

Willingham, D. "A Fresh Threat: Will CAS9 Lead to CRISPR Bioweapons?" *Journal of Biosecurity, Biosafety, and Biodefense Law* 9, no. 1 (2018). doi:10.1515/jbbbl-2018-0010.

Index

Note: Figures are indicated by *italics*. Tables are indicated by **bold**. Endnotes are indicated by the page number followed by 'n' and the endnote number e.g., 20n1 refers to endnote 1 on page 20.